PRAISE FOR *E-COMMERCE GR*

T0292804

'Kunle Campbell expertly unravels the complexities of scaling an online business. His unique perspectives and practical advice make this book an essential resource for e-commerce entrepreneurs and teams.'
Nir Eyal, *Wall Street Journal* bestselling author of *Hooked* and *Indistractable*

'As a lifelong CX and e-commerce leader, I'm delighted to see Kunle Campbell write *the* book to lead the e-commerce direction for the future. No longer do businesses desire to simply exist in the e-commerce channel – they want to thrive. Kunle's guidance marries strategy and profitability expectations with business potential, providing a clear roadmap for exceptional e-commerce leadership.'
Jen Bailin, Chief Commercial Officer, Nintex

'This book is like having a savvy mentor by your side, showing you the ropes of building a successful business online. If you wish you could have been a fly on the wall in the rooms where Kunle Campbell interviewed business leaders, this is the book for you.'
Jason Wong, Founder, Doe Lashes

'A solidly researched guide by an industry veteran to avoiding the landmines of e-commerce. Get it before your competitors do!'
Tim Ash, International keynote, bestselling author and executive adviser

'A must-read, packed with innovative ideas and crucial insights for navigating the e-commerce world.'
Chase Dimond, Partner, Structured

'If you want to sell online, buy this book NOW. As an industry veteran who has made all possible mistakes (and even invented new ones!), I can attest that *E-Commerce Growth Strategy* is genuinely transformative. I found myself wishing I could turn back time and gift this to my younger self. Kunle Campbell has meticulously crafted the most comprehensive and accurate guide for launching and sustaining e-commerce success.'
Moshe Saraf, CEO, Pareto.Solutions

'Essential reading for anyone who wants to grow their online business. Kunle Campbell provides clear and concise advice on how to reach your target market, acquire new customers and retain existing ones. This book is packed with valuable insights and strategies that will help you take your e-commerce business to the next level.'
Gary Ingram, Co-Founder and Chief Revenue Officer, The Diamond Store

'E-commerce is both a blessing and a curse, the blessing being that anyone can now set up a business and launch a new brand or product direct to consumer. The curse is exactly the same. D2C will be the most competitive and essential industry over the coming decades, so arming yourself with a resource to equip you to compete on a level playing field with any other brand or in any product or service category is key, and in *E-Commerce Growth Strategy* you have just that. Kunle Campbell has expressed his passion for this space into an incredible read that dives deep into the key functions and elements any e-comm business needs to survive and thrive.'
Thomas 'Hal' Robson-Kanu, Founder, The Turmeric Co.

'A masterful guide that navigates the intricate and rapidly evolving landscape of digital commerce. Being in a digital-first era, this book provides businesses with a competitive edge, making it a must-read for anyone serious about e-commerce success.'
Josh Snow, Founder, Snow Teeth Whitening

'This book is a gold mine. It takes you from 0 to 100 really fast. Master the e-commerce world and build a rockstar brand. My advice? Dive in and soak it all up.'
Jake Karls, Co-Founder, Mid-Day Squares

'*The* playbook every DTC professional should read if they want to take their business to the next level. It is an incredibly detailed guide to everything a brand or operator needs to know (and more). I promise, if you read this book, you will gain e-commerce superpowers!'
Ben Parr, Co-Founder and President, Octane AI

E-Commerce Growth Strategy

*A brand-driven approach to attract shoppers,
build community and retain customers*

Kunle Campbell

KoganPage

First published in Great Britain and the United States in 2023 by Kogan Page Limited

2nd Floor, 45 Gee Street	8 W 38th Street, Suite 902	4737/23 Ansari Road
London	New York, NY 10018	Daryaganj
EC1V 3RS	USA	New Delhi 110002
United Kingdom		India
www.koganpage.com		

Kogan Page books are printed on paper from sustainable forests.

ISBNs

Hardback	978 1 3986 0800 9
Paperback	978 1 3986 0798 9
Ebook	978 1 3986 0799 6

British Library Cataloguing-in-Publication Data
A CIP record for this book is available from the British Library.

Library of Congress Cataloging-in-Publication Data
Names: Campbell, Kunle, author.
Title: E-commerce growth strategy : a brand-driven approach to attract
  shoppers, build community and retain customers / Kunle Campbell.
Description: London ; New York, NY : Kogan Page Inc, [2023] | Includes
  bibliographical references and index.
Identifiers: LCCN 2023021654 (print) | LCCN 2023021655 (ebook) | ISBN
  9781398607989 (paperback) | ISBN 9781398608009 (hardback) | ISBN
  9781398607996 (ebook)
Subjects: LCSH: Electronic commerce. | Internet marketing. | Customer
  relations.
Classification: LCC HF5548.32 .C3556 2023 (print) | LCC HF5548.32 (ebook)
  | DDC 658.8/72–dc23/eng/20230504
LC record available at https://lccn.loc.gov/2023021654
LC ebook record available at https://lccn.loc.gov/2023021655

Typeset by Integra Software Services, Pondicherry
Print production managed by Jellyfish
Printed and bound by CPI Group (UK) Ltd, Croydon, CR0 4YY

Thank you, Gbemi, Dad, Mum and my children, for making my life so rich and meaningful. This book is dedicated to you with all my heart.

CONTENTS

16 Finance: what you should know and an overview for growth 278

17 Tracking success: team makeup and key metrics 288

18 Develop your growth roadmap 301

ABOUT THE AUTHOR

Kunle Campbell is an internationally acclaimed e-commerce opinion leader. He is best known for his roles as a fractional e-commerce CMO/adviser, speaker and co-founder of Octillion, a forward-thinking, digital-first, CPG brand house. Based in Oxford, he offers strategic growth advice to a wide array of online and omnichannel retailers while operating numerous consumer brands. With his extensive expertise, he has established himself as an influential figure in the e-commerce world.

His profound influence extends to the audio realm as the creator and host of the premier 2X eCommerce podcast. The podcast has amassed over 2 million downloads and counting, having spotlighted the insights of more than 400 e-commerce leaders and experts from various verticals.

Specializing in e-commerce strategy, customer acquisition, on-site user experience and customer retention, Kunle is a frequently invited speaker at esteemed international conferences and workshops. His insightful talks have graced platforms organized by industry heavyweights including Meta (Facebook), SAP Commerce and Barclays.

He has also garnered international media attention, with features in prominent news outlets including the BBC, *The New York Times* and *International Herald Tribune*, as well as accolades from industry titans such as BigCommerce, Crazy Egg, Practical Ecommerce, VWO and Econsultancy. His blend of industry knowledge, operational expertise and innovative thinking continually shapes the e-commerce landscape, marking him as a pivotal thought leader in the sector.

In *E-Commerce Growth Strategy*, Kunle leverages his e-commerce expertise to present an indispensable guide to understanding the strategies utilized by disruptive, digital-native consumer brands that have successfully gained market share in numerous retail verticals by selling directly to their customers through e-commerce channels. The book provides essential insights and strategies for thriving in the fast-paced e-commerce landscape, covering topics such as customer-centricity, cross-functional collaboration, customer acquisition and lifecycle marketing strategies.

Kunle's pragmatic and competent approach ensures that this book will serve as an essential guide for a broad audience, including retail executives, e-commerce marketers, ambitious entrepreneurs, students, aspiring consumer brand founders and practitioners. It offers comprehensive insights into building a meaningful, hyper-growth e-commerce brand, thus making it a must-read for anyone keen to navigate and succeed in the dynamic e-commerce landscape.

Introduction

Why I wrote this book

To set the scene for what has gone into creating this book, and the trials, tribulations and hard-won insights of mine that you are about to benefit from reading, I have a folder on my Google Drive named 'Book Project', and in that folder there are four sub-folders titled '2017', '2020', '2021' and '2022 Kogan Page'. From the folder-naming convention, you would be right if you picked up that I had three failed attempts at writing this book about e-commerce. In hindsight, I am grateful for the sequence of failures because, at each of these timestamps, my fundamental first-principle thinking that underpins e-commerce growth strategy had been evolving, and doing so rapidly.

By 2017, I had interviewed over 120 e-commerce founders, operators and experts on my podcast, the 2X eCommerce podcast. Additionally, I had over 11 years of experience in demand-capture marketing, where I was considered an expert in search engine marketing. I had also been involved in some complex e-commerce web development projects, supporting information architecture, UX (user experience) and user journey development. Furthermore, I had some experience in CRO (conversion rate optimization). As a side hustle, I also gained invaluable experience in affiliate marketing, promoting products for a range of e-commerce brands. However, even with this experience, 2017 was not the time to write this book.

By 2020 and 2021, I'd published over 300 episodes of the 2X eCommerce podcast and had first-hand demand-generation experience spanning all the way from 2018. For me, the ability to sell a brand's product through social media, emails, video, sales copy, community and targeting was pure alchemy and really excited me. This passion has led me to study and apply consumer behaviour, customer data and lifecycle marketing principles to e-commerce growth. By this time, not only was I an established expert in my field, I had spent hours downloading the insights of the best in the business, hundreds of hours, through my 2X eCommerce podcast interviews and bringing them to our listeners weekly. But I was missing one final piece of the puzzle before I could truly feel like it was time to write this book. The only thing was, I didn't know what that puzzle piece looked like, or where it would come from.

I didn't have to wait long for it to appear in front of me, however. In 2022 it was clear the timing was perfect. As I co-founded Octillion, an acquisition platform company and consolidator of 'clean' digital-first CPG brands, I finally had the sense that my words were ready for the printing press and for your consumption. Octillion was founded on the premise that the foods we put into our bodies and the products we apply to our bodies should be clean. It was my first truly mission-driven venture, as I'd had health setbacks a decade earlier as a result of the dietary decisions I had made. Our focus has been growing and scaling good-for-you consumer brands with a healthy, low-sugar and 'clean' profile.

Today, as an e-commerce operator with a marketing background, it is clear that adopting a cross-functional approach is the underlining first principle to delivering sustained, long-term e-commerce growth. I have adopted and applied this holistic approach to growth and will be sharing it with you in this book. So, in addition to the principles I have mentioned above, other tools in my e-commerce growth strategy toolkit now include brand strategy, channel marketing, product development, mergers and acquisitions and finance (to name just a few).

As you read this book, be aware that you are not just getting insights from me; I have also drawn subject-matter expertise from 30 of my (and our listeners') favourite guests that have appeared on the 2X eCommerce podcast. I started the podcast in 2014 as a way to share insights and learnings from experts at the forefront of technology and innovation in digital retail. Over 400 episodes later, the podcast has become an invaluable resource for those looking to grow their consumer brand businesses. This book only adds to that value by combining many hundreds of hours of insights from the world's best brand builders and highest-paid e-commerce and marketing professionals, and countless hard-won lessons of my own, into the ultimate cross-functional growth playbook for e-commerce brands. If you want to learn more about strategies employed by high-growth digital-native product brands, subscribe to the 2X eCommerce podcast today at https://2xecommerce.com/podcast and join the tens of thousands of other listeners turning actionable insights into revenue growth for their brands.

This book aims to help you

If you are curious about how to grow a consumer e-commerce brand, this book is for you. Whether you are a founder that has just raised funds for your consumer brand or bootstrapping, a student, a starting executive or a senior-level executive trying to understand how to use e-commerce as a major growth channel, this book provides fundamental first principles to grow an e-commerce brand, and aims to help you:

- Build a foundational understanding of what cross-functional e-commerce truly means.
- Discover the importance of understanding consumer psychology and learn tips and psychological hacks for optimizing each stage of the e-commerce funnel.
- Learn how to use customer data to create unique, personalized experiences that optimize the customer journey.
- Uncover the top automated messaging essentials such as welcome series, abandoned cart emails and win-back flows.
- Discover how to build a loyal audience and community for your e-commerce brand and learn about the benefits of using influencer marketing for testing messaging and creative.
- Explore how to develop a growth roadmap that will guide your e-commerce business through all stages of its journey.
- Learn the specific metrics that e-commerce businesses need to be tracking in order to optimize their operations, finances, marketing and customer success.
- Know how to use paid social and influencer marketing to engage potential customers, optimize ad campaigns and drive awareness, traffic and sales.
- Discover the importance of building an omnichannel brand and learn how you can do that using real-world examples from companies that have successfully implemented an effective omnichannel growth strategy.
- Understand the importance of product innovation and development for competitive advantage.

- Learn how to create a culture that not only accepts failure but facilitates it in ways that make your e-commerce brand more creative, productive and resilient.

- Gain insights into alternative routes to growth for e-commerce brands, including building a culture of inclusivity, sustainable commerce, joint ventures and mergers and acquisitions and the role of public relations in brand building.

- Discover how to take your e-commerce brand from $0 to $1 million, to $50 million to $100 million and beyond.

This book is strategic rather than tactical and will help you develop your e-commerce growth roadmap wherever you are in your journey. For deeper guidance on the specifics of each framework, tactic or growth lever mentioned in each chapter, you can visit http://2xecommerce.com/book, where each of the 18 chapters is complemented by an extensive repository of additional resources, recommended further readings, links to subject matter experts and technology recommendations. If you'd like more direct guidance, you can apply for e-commerce growth group coaching or 1-to-1 e-commerce coaching via http://2xecommerce.com/coaching.

How the book is structured

Chapter 1. This chapter covers several key principles for achieving growth in e-commerce. The chapter begins by exploring the concept of habitual buying and how brands can strive to convert customers into habitual buyers. It also discusses the importance of establishing a purchasing frequency and repeat purchase rate and offers advice on how to accomplish this. It then delves into the principles of experimentation and continuous improvement, as well as channel agnosticism, which involves embracing channel marketing to grow. Other topics covered include the importance of developing a strong brand and storytelling, and the role of cross-functional planning in achieving e-commerce growth. The chapter offers practical advice and insights for anyone looking to build and grow a successful e-commerce business.

Chapter 2. We'll cover key elements for building a successful e-commerce business, including branding, product development, customer experience, logistics and analytics. This chapter serves as a primer to introduce you to all that will come throughout the book and build your foundational understanding of what cross-functional e-commerce truly means.

Chapter 3. This chapter explains the importance of brand building for e-commerce growth. It covers the foundation of a brand, including values, story, positioning, voice and tone, visual identity and culture. It also discusses the concept of brand persona and building trust and credibility with customers through strong brand values. We will cover the five components of brand equity and the three essential pillars of brand building: consistency, frequency and anchoring.

Chapter 4. In this chapter we discuss consumer psychology and its relevance to e-commerce. It provides tips and psychological hacks for optimizing each stage of the e-commerce funnel, including the attention and awareness stage, the consideration stage, and the decision and action stage. The chapter emphasizes the importance of understanding consumer psychology for meeting informational needs, building trust and authority, and creating a brand persona that resonates with the target audience. By utilizing these concepts and the tools and tactics outlined in the chapter, e-commerce marketers can establish strong, long-lasting brands that attract and retain loyal customers.

Chapter 5. This chapter focuses on advanced strategies for data segmentation and personalization, which are essential for acquiring and retaining customers. In this chapter, we will explore how to use customer data to create unique, personalized experiences that optimize the customer journey. We will also discuss various tactics and technologies that can help e-commerce businesses segment and personalize their marketing strategies, including machine learning models, data enrichment services and customer data platforms (CDPs). We will draw on insights from experts in the field, including Ben Parr, co-founder of Octane AI and Ivan Mazour, co-founder of Ometria. The changing landscape of data gathering is also an important topic in this chapter, as regulations like the GDPR and changes in technology impact how e-commerce businesses collect and use customer data. Whether you are just starting out or looking to take your customer data strategy to the next level, Chapter 5 will provide valuable insights and practical advice to help you get the most out of your customer data.

Chapter 6. Chapter 6 of this book covers strategies to generate demand for your product. We'll discuss the importance of community and influencer marketing. You'll learn about the principles of influence and persuasion, referral marketing and tools like ratings, reviews, demand capture and retargeting.

We feature insights from the best in marketing, such as Robert Cialdini and from top direct-to-consumer brands such as Glossier and Gymshark, to unlock the secrets of demand generation and capture.

Chapter 7. Learn how to build a loyal audience and community for your e-commerce brand. By focusing on audience and community building, you can foster customer loyalty, leading to increased retention and sales. Discover how to leverage social media, content marketing and influencer partnerships, and create a unique brand experience to engage and retain customers. Featuring insights and advice from industry experts, including Nir Eyal, author of *Hooked: How to build habit-forming products* and Joe Vancena, product marketing manager at Loop Returns.

Chapter 8. In this chapter, we dive into the importance of building an audience and community for your e-commerce brand. By creating a loyal community, you can gain valuable insights into your customers' needs and behaviours, which can inform your decision making and drive long-term growth. This chapter discusses the key aspects of community building, including identifying your target audience, leading the tribe and creating a powerful narrative. You will learn from the actions of experts in the field, including Kelley Higney, founder of Bug Bite Thing and Nick Devlin, group CEO at Naked Wines, and learn practical tips for how to build a successful community, engage with your customers and create a tribe that is loyal and invested in your brand.

Chapter 9. Here we will discuss channels and strategies to engage customers during the customer journey, including email, SMS, push notifications and direct mail. The chapter covers capturing customer information, messaging funnels, segmentation, RFM analysis, targeted campaigns and automation. You will uncover the top automated messaging essentials such as welcome series, abandoned cart emails and win-back flows. Industry leaders Alex Beller and Josh Wetzel are featured throughout the chapter, and we learn from their experiences, insights and advice as well.

Chapter 10. This chapter covers the importance of search engine marketing (SEO and SEM) for e-commerce brands. Topics include creating an XML sitemap to help search engines index your site, and using markup schemas and breadcrumbs to improve search listings. The chapter offers actionable tips on optimizing your search engine presence for success. Finally, the chapter provides guidance on hiring an agency or building an internal team to manage SEM efforts. By implementing the lessons learned in this chapter, readers can expect to increase their brand's visibility in search engine results pages with a clear and simple-to-follow roadmap to SERP success.

Chapter 11. Discover how paid social and influencer marketing can help grow your e-commerce business. We'll cover different types of video content, such as user-generated, product/explainer and shoppable videos. You'll also learn about the benefits of using influencer marketing for testing messaging and creative. Throughout the chapter, industry experts like Moshe Saraf of Pareto Solutions share their hard-won and valuable insights. Saraf, who has been a guest on the 2X eCommerce podcast, runs highly effective ad campaigns for unicorn brands. By the end of the chapter, you'll know how to use paid social and influencer marketing to engage potential customers, optimize ad campaigns and drive awareness, traffic and sales.

Chapter 12. In today's digital age, businesses are constantly looking for ways to reach their customers through various channels. Omnichannel marketing offers a seamless and integrated experience across all channels, providing a strong brand presence and increasing customer loyalty. Providing us with insights in this chapter are thought leaders such as Rory Sutherland and Josh Elizetxe. The key takeaway from this chapter is that to truly scale, you need to be an omnichannel brand, and I show you exactly how you can do that using real-world examples from companies like Hero Cosmetics, Tony's Chocolonely and Warby Parker, who have successfully implemented effective omnichannel marketing in varied, unique and effective ways.

Chapter 13. This chapter is all about product development cycles for growth. The chapter starts by showing you how a great product can either make or break a brand and goes on to discuss the pitfalls of penny-pinching on product development. You will be introduced to the concept of product-led growth and how it can be applied in the e-commerce industry. Throughout the chapter, we'll cover examples from various brands such as e-commerce giant Shein to illustrate the importance of product innovation and development for competitive advantage. You'll learn what it means to build offers, not just products, and drive development with data.

Chapter 14. Failure is a prerequisite to invention, and creating a culture that not only accepts that but facilitates it in ways that make your e-commerce brand more creative and more productive is crucial for a thriving business. The fact is, in today's rapidly changing commerce and technological landscape, companies need strong cultures and processes around experimentation and failure to stay afloat. This chapter features insights from thought leaders like Nassim Taleb, Steve Jobs and Charles F Kettering. These insights, translated into an e-commerce growth framework, provide tips and tricks for running successful experiments, building transparency and communication into the process and involving leadership in experimentation. By implementing the lessons learned in this chapter, readers can expect to create a thriving business that is well-equipped to handle the constant changes and challenges of the e-commerce industry, whatever they may be.

Chapter 15. Here we cover alternative routes to growth for e-commerce brands. The chapter begins by discussing the importance of building a culture of inclusivity to attract top talent and increase profitability. It then delves into sustainable commerce and the dangers of greenwashing, before exploring joint ventures and mergers and acquisitions as potential growth strategies. It also covers the role of public relations in brand building, highlighting the importance of a strong brand culture and messaging system. Finally, we discuss the effectiveness of guerrilla marketing as a PR tactic. This chapter is designed to broaden your perspectives about how to generate growth in the e-commerce world, and start you thinking not just like a brand owner or marketer, but also as a c-suite executive with the ability to build, operate and grow stable unicorn brands.

Chapter 16. In this chapter, we'll explore how to develop a growth roadmap that will guide your e-commerce business through all stages of its journey. Industry experts like Sean De Clercq of Kickfurther and Nathan Hirsch of AccountsBalance will share their insights and tips for creating a successful e-commerce business from a finance and accounting perspective. Believe me, this is not a chapter you want to skip or skim – absorb everything written on these pages or learn the lessons the hard (and very painful) way. You'll learn the best financing options available to accelerate your growth depending on your brand's maturity and needs, as well as the best way to structure your accounting and optimize your financial reporting.

Chapter 17. In this penultimate chapter, we cover everything you need to know about tracking success in e-commerce, including the key metrics and KPIs you can use to keep your finger on the pulse of your brand's cross-functional growth levers. You'll learn the specific metrics that e-commerce businesses need to be tracking in order to optimize their operations, finances, marketing and customer success. Key metrics covered include inventory turnover ratio, customer effort score, first response time and self-service resolution rate – all covered in full detail.

Chapter 18. In this final chapter, we will explore the strategies necessary to take your e-commerce brand from start up to $100 million and beyond. We break down the growth strategy into specific stages and phases of growth that your company will go through, laying out a clear roadmap and showing you exactly which levers you need to be pulling at each stage. From getting started and achieving your first sales to scaling up to $1 million, $10 million, $50 million and beyond, we provide practical advice and actionable steps that will give you clarity and confidence while scaling your brand.

1

How to think about and approach e-commerce growth

Commerce has been the bridge that has connected the world's far-flung regions for millennia. It has been the binding language that has improved lives, restored territories and expanded cultures. It's how we've made our daily bread and spread innovation, propelling forward the world that which we know, love and continue to improve today. We simply wouldn't be here without the Silk Road, the Spice Route or the Salt Route – all key global arteries for commerce since antiquity. Today, the digital revolution has turned 'trade' routes digital and flung us into a new era of commerce, change, progress and innovation.

The very first recorded instance of e-commerce was in 1948–49 during the Berlin airlift, when goods were purchased over telex (Zwass, 2022). But like me, most of you would probably have to Google what a telex actually is. E-commerce as we know it today, selling and purchasing goods, wares and services over the internet, is a much more recent, and powerful, evolution of e-commerce. The artefacts of its inception grew to become one of the largest e-commerce operations of our time; you've probably even used the platform to sell, or purchased something from it yourself. Modern e-commerce began with Jeff Bezos founding Amazon in 1994 (Walker, 1998). The company went public in 1997, and by 1998 it was selling books, music and videos online (Amazon, 1997). So in comparison to the ages-old commerce as we knew it that relied on established trade routes like the Spice Route, e-commerce, which has been a part of our lives for less than 30 years at the time of writing in 2022, is still green and evolving rapidly. In fact, it's taken the whole world by storm, so much so that it's impossible to imagine our lives without it. This rapid and continuing development means that it's hard for the e-commerce professional to keep up. We're up against developments and innovations occurring around the world, at huge scale, and with the potential to upend our best-laid marketing plans in the blink of an eye – much like we saw with the innovation that is TikTok bursting onto the scene and capturing a huge share of consumers' attention, and correspondingly of our marketing mix in a matter of months (Tidy and Galer, 2020). Frankly, it can be hard to keep up – that's why I've written this book, to ground brands and marketers in the core first principles of e-commerce marketing and engineering growth, that bring you out of the hair-pulling game of pinball where no sooner than you are thrown in one direction, you're bounced back where you came from, or to some other corner of the space, struggling to make sense of an ever-changing topography.

When you are grounded in the first principles of e-commerce marketing, you are able to guide innovation, not simply react to it. You're equipped with the tools you need to build clear, understandable and proven roadmaps to your goals no matter how the topography is changing around you. This book, for the e-commerce marketer, is the much-needed calm in the storm. The beacon and guiding light that will smooth and add clarity to all your discussions around marketing mix, product development, lifetime marketing, financial strategy and more. The truth is, e-commerce growth is complex, yet paradoxically simple. But I didn't always see it that way; in fact, at times after some crushing failures, I thought it was anything but simple.

I have been involved in digital marketing since 2004; at the time, I was an eager MSc student at Warwick University, keen to work on any dissertation related to helping an organization solve a problem. It plunged me into the world of analytics, performance marketing and organic traffic generation. Ten years later, I decided to focus exclusively on e-commerce. My initial thesis on e-commerce was all about traffic generation. My thinking at the time was that if I kept driving relevant traffic to an e-commerce storefront, it would continue to grow proportionally in sales. This theory came to a crushing halt when I helped a top 20 pure-play UK e-commerce brand double their traffic in a period of just 12 months, yet the commercial benefit of my team's efforts was just a 30 per cent revenue uplift. Before that, I had agreed with the founder of this business that if we doubled traffic, we would more than likely double revenue growth. I walked away from that experience with a fire in my belly, determined to figure out where I had gone wrong, why we didn't get the results we were expecting, and exactly how I could ensure the kind of results that e-commerce brands need. Through this journey, I absorbed everything I could about e-commerce, marketing, consumer psychology, business, you name it. I left no stone unturned. I came to the realization that e-commerce, and indeed commerce itself, is more than just traffic or 'footfall'. There are a tremendous number of moving parts involved in orchestrating growth. E-commerce growth, I found, is wonderfully and beautifully cross-functional. When you're zoomed in on a niche like I was – traffic – you miss the forest. It's like looking at a Van Gogh through a magnifying glass fixed on one square inch of the painting. You miss the synchronicities, the symbiotic nature of it all, the interaction of the colours, the scratches on the canvas, that make a Van Gogh, well, a Van Gogh.

To think about growth, you need to think about the business unit and its functions as a whole first. And then you need to specifically look or zoom into its functions, mapping out how each area optimizes for a single end goal of customer experience. This will be covered in the next section.

In order to drive an e-commerce business's growth programme, each of these business functions needs to be continually optimized to improve the customer experience at the leanest of costs possible:

1 People

2 Product development (or R&D)

3 Logistics

   a. Sourcing

   b. Manufacturing

   c. Inbound logistics

   d. Warehousing

   e. Outbound logistics or last mile delivery

   f. Finance

4 Marketing and brand

   a. Lifecycle marketing

   b. Performance marketing

   c. Influencer marketing

5 Storytelling

   a. PR

   b. Social commerce

6 Outbound

7 Customer services

8 Technology

9 Capital raising

   a. The capital markets

   b. Banks, RBFs (revenue-based finance)

   c. M&A

   d. Legal

In this book, I will explain how all of the above business functions can be orchestrated to drive significant growth to e-commerce companies with a consumer focus. We will discuss the core first principles as a guide for growing any e-commerce business that I have uncovered and decoded during my almost two decades in the industry, as well as my over 400 podcast interviews with leading marketers, founders and unicorn, billion-dollar plus, brand builders. You will learn the very same e-commerce growth marketing methodology that I use with my many clients as a consultant, in my own businesses, and as part of Octillion Capital Partners, which you may utilize in your business or organization. First, let's cover where many go wrong…

Why most people fail

You can save yourself the crushing embarrassment of plans gone wrong, KPIs missed by a mile, and having your peers and colleagues wondering whether you really know what you're doing by just getting this part right. Having a clear set of choices that define what you will and won't do is what constitutes a real strategy (Vermeulen, 2017). Many strategies that fail, despite the ample efforts of hard-working people, do so because they do not represent a set of clear choices. Many so-called 'strategies' are in fact goals.

For an example of a strategy that is a goal in disguise by name only, see exhibit A as follows: 'We want to be the number one or number two in all the markets in which we operate.'

So what is wrong with that? Well, dear reader, it does not tell you what you are going to do; all it does is tell you what you hope the outcome will be. A strategy on the other hand is a plan of action that is designed to achieve a long-term or overall aim. Leaders, marketers, brand owners and founders all too often skip the critical 'plan of action' needed to turn a goal into a strategy. Partly because formulating a real cross-functional plan of action is something that requires a strategy of its own, a strategy that if you were to set out to build it, you would find there are very few resources out there to help you do so. And so, this book was born. This book provides a foundation and roadmap for developing your very own growth strategy. The foundation lies in first principles, and the roadmap lies in each chapter and topic throughout this book, from customer data to cash flow-based finance, from multichannel strategy to mergers and acquisitions.

Starting with a first principles approach to e-commerce growth

René Descartes, who was an advocate for this type of fundamentalist logic, outlined what constitutes a first principle long ago in the preface of his 1644 book *Principles of Philosophy* (1985), in which he wrote:

> we must commence with the investigation of those first causes which are called Principles. Now, these principles must possess two conditions: in the first place, they must be so clear and evident that the human mind, when it attentively considers them, cannot doubt their truth; in the second place, the knowledge of other things must be so dependent on them as that though the principles themselves may indeed be known apart from what depends on them, the latter cannot nevertheless be known apart from the former.

Much predating Descartes, the concept of first principles was discussed by ancient Greek philosopher Aristotle more than 2,000 years ago. Aristotle stated that true understanding of a topic comes from uncovering the basic assumptions or propositions that cannot be derived from any other (Aristotle and Barnes, 1998). That form the fundamental base material of all other, that cannot be negated. It is when you have found these that you have found the fundamental truths of your domain. First principles are present in e-commerce and other businesses just as much as they are in the disciplines which uncover the very laws and fundamentals of our universe like mathematics, physics, engineering and medicine.

Other famous proponents of first principles thinking in their work that you might be familiar with, perhaps even admire, include:

- Richard Feynman, American theoretical physicist
- St Thomas Aquinas, Italian theologian and jurist
- Copernicus, Polish astronomer
- Elon Musk, South African entrepreneur

- Nikola Tesla, Serbian inventor
- Thomas Edison, American inventor
- Johannes Gutenberg, German inventor and printer
- Euclid, Greek mathematician
- John Boyd, American military and litigation strategist

According to James Clear, the *New York Times* bestselling author of *Atomic Habits*, Elon Musk has utilized first principles thinking to establish his success. Clear writes that 'First principles thinking is one of the most successful strategies for tackling complex issues and developing novel solutions' (Clear, 2017). It might also be the best approach to learning how to think for yourself. Why did Clear come to this conclusion? Well, you see, Musk hit a roadblock almost immediately after deciding to enter the space exploration and travel industry: space rockets cost $65 million. An insurmountable sum for even a very rich man, given the cost and frequency of error in the space game of even just getting off the launch pad. To address the issue, Musk took a first principles approach. He started by finding out how much the materials required to make a rocket, such as aerospace-quality aluminium alloys, titanium and carbon fibre, actually cost. What he discovered changed the fortunes of SpaceX forever: he discovered that these materials accounted for only 2 per cent of the final price (Johnson, 2015). Musk decided that the solution to his rocket problem was simple: make his own rocket with the same raw materials. And so his SpaceX division was born in 2002 (Eldridge, 2023).

When faced with a challenging situation, a first principles thinker breaks it down into its component parts as a scientist would, then breaks down those parts into smaller parts until they reach the fundamental base elements, the first principles.

But the greatest obstacle to becoming a first principles thinker and strategist is our strong desire to imitate rather than truly innovate. Rarely do we find ourselves breaking something down to its core first principles to manipulate, create and innovate our own strategies and solutions. Why do we do this? Because we're fundamentally social beings; we tend to copy each other. In fact, as the work of renowned Canadian-American psychologist Albert Bandura shows, observing, modelling and imitating the behaviours of others play key roles in how we learn as humans (Bandura, 1977; McLeod, 2016). Not to mention that our collective and individual ability to evolve and survive had been precisely because of our ability to blend in, to conform and to be sociable – to not rock the boat or be too different. We are still afraid to do so today, even though it is increasingly those who are able to that we adore, admire, praise and follow en masse on social media.

The true innovators throughout history have typically been the 'outliers' of society, the outcasts and the 'misfits'. Much for the reason that in order to innovate, and break down to first principles, you need to be equipped with fundamentally different ways of thinking. You need to be somewhat immune from the tendency to learn only the surface-level details that are possible through mimicry and modelling. That doesn't mean one has to be a social outcast or iconoclast just to innovate, of course, but understanding our innate 'socialized wiring' as humans can help you to respect that for what it is and to forge ahead nevertheless in your first principles thinking.

It does this through decoding the first principles of e-commerce for you, as well as learning from the best innovators in direct-to-consumer e-commerce, whose playbooks I have uncovered, analysed and integrated through my many hundred podcasts, interviews and events.

So, what are the fundamental first principles or established laws of e-commerce growth?

Principle 1: The customer is front and centre

It is technology that is the face of today's commerce environment. Laptops, mobile phones, internet-connected devices, all connected to digital websites and user interfaces, all connected via a network of APIs to various third-party software services and databases. Tech is propelling e-commerce forward at a rapid pace. But that's just the skeleton of e-commerce. It's consumers, people, that breathe life into this digital world. And these consumers are now armed with unprecedented access to information about products and services. All that means unprecedented choice and the information they need to make those choices. The rise of mobile, social media and online review sites has changed the game for digital-first commerce brands. Consumers are more than ever ready and able to share their experiences. And when they do, the whole world hears. Customer-centricity has never been out of fashion and will never go out of fashion, but it has been no more important at any time in history as it is today. It's never been more critical for e-commerce brands to be customer-centric.

As a segway, one of the most memorable dining experiences I have had with my family was at a restaurant in Lagos, Nigeria called SLoW. The staff at the restaurant were courteous, detail oriented and proactive to address every single need of ours whilst we sat at the table. I recall that our then-10-month-old baby kept throwing cutlery and objects on the floor, and at every single instance, a waiter was at hand to pick it up right away and another member of staff provided a replacement in the most impressive of presentations. In another instance, whenever our glasses of wine, water or drinks were nearly 80 per cent empty, a waiter was at hand to refill them with a nod of approval from us. It was extremely easy to let the members of staff know whatever we needed because they were a stone's throw away from us and at the same time respected our privacy. How were they able to pull off this feat? There were always three waiters on standby hawkishly watching two tables and addressing any of their diners' needs. Because we were a family with quite a sizable contingent, they paid extra attention to our table. They were obsessed with every one of their customers and the only way to be proactive was to gather as much information as they could about their customers in real-time and address every single one of their needs. Much in the same way that, to stand out from the competition, e-commerce brands must move beyond a product-centric business model, focusing on how to delight customers with exceptional service and value by understanding what they want, when they want it and how they want it delivered.

Drawing parallels to e-commerce, the three members of staff represent your customer data collection strategy. It is the foundation of every single customer-driven action or move you make. You need to watch your customers and gather as much information as possible with the aim of getting a 360-degree view. Today's customers expect personalized experiences and value from brands that go beyond a one-size-fits-all strategy. They demand continuous interactions and frictionless experiences across channels and devices. To meet these needs, businesses must leverage customer data to create a segmented, cohesive, end-to-end customer experience that surprises and delights throughout their organizations. Customer data is the engine that makes this customer flywheel go round.

The central idea, or first principle of the customer flywheel, is that your customers are your best salespeople. If you make them happy, they will tell their friends. If you make your customer experience attractive and optimize your sales funnel, those friends will also buy. And the process repeats, eventually becoming a self-perpetuating process. But you, as an e-commerce brand operator, are tasked with first getting the flywheel up to speed and then maintaining frictionless experiences that let the inertia of the customer flywheel continue to generate revenue for your business and add extra velocity by continuously surprising and delighting customers as they enter into your brand ecosystem.

Principle 2: Optimize experience for habitual purchase

You know that feeling when you discover a new brand and fall head over heels in love with their products? You stalk their Instagram account, join their mailing list and buy their products as soon as they're released. You become obsessed with that brand and you can't imagine your life without them. But then something happens, and eventually the obsession fizzles out. Your love for the brand is only a distant memory, and you stop buying from them. Maybe it fizzles out slowly and your purchasing frequency drops, or maybe you go cold turkey altogether, perhaps without even realizing it. Well, that brand probably didn't make buying from them habitual.

Habitual buying is the buying behaviour of customers in which they make repeat purchases of an already-known brand a number of times without the process of high involvement and decisioning. The product is perceived as a commodity and doesn't provide much difference from its rivals. The Marketing Dictionary adds that it is usually 'a low-involvement purchase and involves repeatedly buying the same brand within a given product category' (Marketing Accountability Standards Board, nd). It is an extension of what is also referred to as 'routinized choice (or routinized response) behaviour', which is when decision making has become habitual or routine and little or no cognitive effort is needed to make the choice. As Figure 1.1 demonstrates, habitual buying is the principal cog that is in turn driven by the twin cogs of repeat purchase behaviour and high customer loyalty. You cannot have habitual buyers as customers unless they make repeated purchases and, critically, they are loyal to your brand. Consumers who are not loyal will brand switch, meaning there's always cognitive effort involved in evaluating different options on the market.

FIGURE 1.1 Building retention through habitual buying

There are different ways in which brands can strive to convert customers into habitual buyers, even for 'non-essential' or luxury products. One way of achieving that is to tap into what is referred to as 'purchasing cadence'.

Stand the test of time with a purchase cadence

Brands that endure share some things in common. They are trusted, respected and loved. That sounds a lot like the kind of emotions and qualities that are fostered in marriage. Love, trust and respect. Fostering these in the brand/consumer relationship takes no less integrity and consistent, conscious effort than fostering a long, happy and healthy marriage does. Habit forming begins with forming a connection with customers that gets stronger with each purchase. The result is a lifelong relationship between the customer and the brand that leads to consistent purchases. So, before you read further, ensure this is etched into the very fibres of your being. That if you rely on tactics alone, without putting in the foundational work of being the kind of person and brand that consumers would want to commit to long term, your customers might not even make it part-way through the first date. With that being said, there are some things that you can do to give your brand the best chance of long-term success.

Establishing purchasing frequency

As you will learn in Chapter 17, 'Tracking success: team makeup and key metrics', you can't hit a target that you haven't first been able to quantify into a metric. So, the first step for you to hit a purchase frequency KPI is to calculate it, correctly. There are two ways to calculate purchase frequency. First you can calculate the number of times a client purchases a product or service from a supplier over a predetermined time period. When you divide the number of orders by the number of distinct clients over a 365-day period, purchase frequency is calculated. Typically, this is done over a 365-day period, so that all peak sales periods, including Christmas and Black Friday, as well as all other times of the year, are accounted for. You must only record unique clients, as counting duplicates would interfere with calculating purchase frequency. A second metric is the repeat purchase rate (RPR), which tells you what proportion of your total clients have purchased at least two items from you.

Now that you've defined how you will measure your progress, the hard work really begins. Establishing and then maintaining customers who are frequent purchasers is much easier said than done.

Principle 3: Hone a culture of experimentation and continuous improvement

What do all the best inventors have in common? They were also avid experimenters. Rarely do you stumble upon the best solution at first pass. For curious individuals like Isaac Newton, experimentation is simply the default mode of operation. But for most businesses, this is far from the case. As individuals come together to form a business unit, somewhere along the way, experimentation becomes more difficult. Firstly, most people are not Isaac Newton, and most do not possess the natural disposition and burning desire that he had for experimentation and uncovering the secrets, or first principles, of the universe. Most people have a natural tendency to seek the safety of familiarity and routine. They tend to stick with what they know and are afraid of venturing into the unknown. But innovation will purposefully and consciously elude such people. Not even luck will save them. Innovation, you see, likes to be pursued, earned and wanted. Innovation in your e-commerce business requires taking risks and experimenting with new ideas, processes, products, services or ways of doing things. But business environments, like any social environment, often stifle innovation to a minimum through social pressures, fear of making a mistake in front of your peers, and even fear of retribution in the form of lost opportunities or even lost jobs. The safe and well-travelled path of incremental advantages by stealing playbooks and ideas from other brands and marketers becomes all too enticing. Getting out of this rut requires a conscious effort in building a culture of experimentation.

Principle 4: Channel agnosticism – embrace channel marketing to grow

In the traditional sense, being an 'agnostic' means one doesn't have any particular religious or spiritual preference. In e-commerce, a 'channel agnostic' is a shopper that does not have a particular preference regarding what channel or channels they use to shop, be it online or offline. In fact, one could consider the 'channel agnostic' as the 'new omnichannel'. These are generally sophisticated shoppers who are able to glide (read: browse and shop) seamlessly between different channels. Retailers have recognized that not only do they have to be everywhere – with e-commerce, mobile commerce and in-store marketing strategies and sales opportunities – but they have to make it as easy as possible for customers to shop through any of those channels.

In today's retail climate, consumers expect brands to have a strong online presence. One that is integrated, connected and consistent across platforms – something we will cover in Chapter 3, 'Brand core: the foundation for growth'. However, this requires brands to develop a multichannel marketing strategy that goes beyond the usual one-off website or social media account, and towards building communities through an interconnected ecosystem of social and shopping channels. In today's fast-paced world of digital commerce, brands need omnichannel retail strategies as well as an omnichannel marketing strategy to accommodate customers wherever they are, no matter how they prefer to shop. As consumers continue to shift their spending toward online purchases, they expect brands to meet them where they are. This means that e-commerce brands need to deliver consistent and seamless experiences wherever their customers prefer to shop. This isn't limited to websites, either. Consumers' expectations extend to being able to shop via smartphone apps, voice-activated speakers, email, SMS, traditional snail mail or social media. Not only do consumers expect you to be available across multiple channels, they also expect an integrated shopping experience that allows them to move seamlessly from one channel to another.

This brings with it significant demands for customer data management and integration. In Chapter 5, 'Customer data', we cover just that – the specific data strategy that your brand needs at all stages of growth, from single channel to omnichannel. In Chapter 12, 'Channel marketing', we cover the top strategies that brands can implement today to take advantage of increased distribution via an omnichannel strategy, and exactly how you can roll yours out for maximum success depending on the nature of your brand. A multichannel strategy is not just for established brands. If you're starting from scratch, and launching a new brand or product to market, then you won't want to miss Chapter 12 and the wisdom within. We cover one play-book that led to a $600+ million acquisition in only a few short years from brand launch that you can implement yourself. The best part is that it's actu-ally also one of the least capital-intensive ways to launch a brand, and thanks to the channel characteristics we have available to us today, one of the most profitable. You will also learn the data drawbacks of third-party platforms, and how this will affect your marketing mix, segmenting and targeting capabilities. But when combined with data enrichment tactics that you will learn in Chapter 5, you will learn how many channel-specific data drawbacks can be overcome. As you are probably starting to get a feel for it now, e-commerce is complicated, with intricate cross-functional relation-ships that need to be tweaked and adjusted as your strategy develops. It is also, however, profoundly simple, based on core first principles for growth.

Advertising

Let me reiterate this one more time: single-channel advertising is dead. Marketing via a single channel, which was a shaky proposition even before the advent of digital marketing, is simply unacceptable in the digital era. There are various reasons for this:

- Multiple channels are readily available, online and offline, so why not capitalize on these multiple channel options where possible and feasible?
- The web space has become highly decentralized, which means customers have multiple avenues in which to find products. That means you need to be on as many channels as possible if you are to be found in an increas-ingly 'nebulous' online space. This is particularly relevant for new or unestablished brands.
- Customers will be frustrated with your lack of channel options, especially channel agnostics who expect multiple choices.

- Your brand will be considered 'old school', 'outdated' or even 'fuddy-duddy', none of which are a good look for any modern brand, regardless of product type or niche.

- Some channels may be slower for your product or brand than others, which is why a diversified channel presence is wise.

- The 'don't put all your eggs in one basket' analogy may be a cliché, but remains pertinent in this regard.

You need to align your advertising and marketing channels with customer journeys that are possible across as many channels, both online and offline, as feasible for your brand.

The lifecycle of a digital native brand in an omnichannel world

Digital native brands grow up to become retail brands. What this means is that the ideal end goal of any brand should be to operate both online and offline. Even if your brand was born as a digital native consumer brand, the only way it can truly grow to be formidable and sustainable is to exist both offline and online.

As stated before, the cliché of putting all your eggs in one basket in terms of marketing strategy will almost certainly be folly. The same applies as a first principle to e-commerce growth. Building breakout e-commerce brands with sustained growth is not a single-channel initiative. E-commerce brands should view themselves as retail brands in the making and not restrict their activities to a single channel. The majority of our customers' lives are spent offline, in the real world. Selling exclusively on a single channel will ultimately restrict your brand's growth potential.

Principle 5: Winning in e-commerce requires a brand-driven attitude

A winning e-commerce company is essentially a brand that gets things right. A brand is a blend of tangible and intangible elements, each of which contributes to brand value, brand loyalty and brand longevity. We cover this in detail in Chapter 3, 'Brand core: the foundation for growth'.

Brand is an essential element that underpins the foundation of your cross-functional growth stack. When you have at least a dozen competitors even in the narrowest of niches, sometimes it's all that differentiates you from the competition. Take Pepsi and Coke as an example. Pepsi wins out on taste tests (most of the time), but when it comes to who wins out on the shelves, it's Coke hands down (Yglesias, 2013). You can put it down to differences in ad budgets or whatever you like, but what it really comes down to is that brands and consumer psychology are crucial for your company's growth, and the principles you will learn about in this chapter, throughout the book, and in Chapter 3 especially, will make everything else you do easier. Much easier.

Getting to the heart of the brand matter

Much like you as a person are doomed to failure without a heart, either the organ itself or your own core values, principles and empathy – whether you want to look at it from a literal biological perspective or a more spiritual and psychological one – so is a brand. When we talk about the heart of a brand, of course we are talking about the spiritual and psychological one that is made up of its core values. Broadening out from there, we have its story and its personality or archetype. All key elements in the brand recipe that give your brand soul and the ability to be liked by consumers, who seek familiar human elements in brands, just as they do in people. A brand's core values are the essence of what makes it stand out from other brands, namely those attributes that make the brand unique, special, differentiated, valuable and, critically, successful. One could consider these core values the 'DNA' of a given brand.

In order for brand values to be effective, they must be authentic and aligned with the company's mission and vision. This means that they must be truly representative of what the brand stands for and what it believes in. For example, if a company claims to value sustainability, it must actively work to reduce its environmental impact and make eco-friendly products. No greenwashing. Importantly, these brand values need to be aligned with those of your target consumers. This, as you will learn, requires deep research and lots of customer data. In my own experience building new brands or growing existing ones, brand values are rarely solidified into a compelling story until deep customer research has been done. Time and time again it is customer data that drives brand value creation.

When starting a new e-commerce venture, or scaling an existing brand, one of the first things I do is dig deep into the brand archetype, ensuring that it is well defined and has the potential to communicate and connect with the brand's core audience. When you establish a brand archetype and personality, everything you do becomes much more powerful. Your product, be it a hot sauce or a mobile phone case, a skincare cream or a pair of sneakers, becomes something so much more. It represents something real in the minds of consumers, because it's connected with the archetypes they know, understand and love. Your logo becomes more than just a pretty mark that sits on your website and packaging; it begins to represent ideas and values. Take the three-pointed star of Mercedes Benz as an example, or the large bending golden arches of McDonald's. Ask anyone what the logos represent and the answers you receive will be much deeper than 'it looks a little like a star, or a bicycle wheel' or 'it looks like a large M or the trajectory of a ball bouncing on the ground after someone has dropped it'.

The principles of branding and consumer psychology covered in this book are valuable tools that will make other growth efforts more effective. In a world with many choices and competitors, your brand is a key differentiator. Building a strong brand involves leveraging psychology to create value in the minds of consumers and establish a unique and consistent brand voice. Without a well-defined brand, you only have a product.

Developing and telling your story is what wins hearts and minds

Storytelling is the art of weaving a compelling narrative that entices and captures an audience. Undoubtedly there is at least one story, or one person's biography, that draws you in and absolutely captures you. Think back to your childhood and the people who captivated you, whether they were real, cartoon or imaginary. The human brain is wired to be ultra-responsive to captivating narratives, right down to the neurotransmitters released when we come across something that tickles our fancy. In this book you will learn exactly how that process works, and how powerful it is for your brand to have it founded on compelling narratives, be they brand stories, founder stories, user-generated content or employee stories. Every great story has a central theme that is woven throughout the narrative. For your brand, that central theme is your purpose and your values. By now you're beginning to see how powerful brands are.

Principle 6: Growth is cross-functional

As a brand owner or e-commerce professional, you know that in order for your company to grow, you need to find new ways to increase revenue and decrease expenses. That is rarely achieved through the practice of simple addition and subtraction. That is, adding new nodes to your growth stack to generate more revenue, or subtracting nodes to cut costs. To achieve real commerce growth, your task is to set your brand up for growth effects that are greater than the sum of its parts. For leverage. For symbiotic effects. That is the nature of cross-functionality. Every single node in the e-commerce growth stack is interconnected, interdependent and a prime fulcrum for leverage across the entire growth stack. Just like brands come together to create cross-functional symmetry from their specific and individual asymmetrical advantages, so too can each department and tactic in your e-commerce growth stack. Symbiosis is a close, long-term interaction between two different organisms that directly benefits both entities (Lang and Benbow, 2013).

Strategic planning and being able to spot interactive growth opportunities is what really scales business beyond linear growth. Cross-functional planning should be at the centre of your organization right from the beginning, and I suggest that you have regular meetings with this book as your guide, to brainstorm how the strategies and tactics within would look if implemented for your brand. Early-stage companies focus on optimizing single departments, or finding hacks to scale a channel like Facebook ads. But, to reach brand culture-defining heights, aligning the objectives and aims of different departments or functions within the organization to support the company's overall objectives is imperative. The biggest and best in e-commerce like Jack Ma and Jeff Bezos, or some of the best growth drivers in direct-to-consumer owe a large part of their success to recognizing the first principles of what makes consumers and commerce brands alike tick and being able to leverage cross-functional advantages from these very first principles. In this book you'll learn how to achieve cross-functional advantages from brands like Hero Cosmetics, Tony's Chocolonely, Kosmos Q and more.

Running an e-commerce brand, even if you're a sole founder and operator, is much like commanding an army – so there is much to be borrowed from strategic thinkers of old such as Sun Tzu, who among other things advocated for unity and cooperation among forces. Even as a sole founder, each department is like its own regiment or unit (Tzu, 2010). The opposing army, or force, is your competition. To beat out your competition, you must have unified forces. But, Tzu also advocated for speed and adapting to changing circumstances. Whereas a less seasoned general would be blindsided by a fast-changing environment, the seasoned general, with his thinking firmly founded in first principles thinking, is able to identify a course of action and adapt with ease (Tzu, 2010). It is such a first principles approach that I will teach you in this book. All of this, aided by your sentry, customer data, will mean that you're well equipped to navigate and conquer the e-commerce environment with relative first principles simplicity. The art of assessment, the art of unity and the art of adaptation – you will notice them all woven through the pages of this book. No trends, no fads, just core first principles and strategic execution.

Where most books would stop at social media marketing and search engine marketing, we will do all that and more, going deep into product development cycles and finance, as well as the specific psychology and sociology behind community building. Not to mention how to formulate your strategy based on the tried and tested in consumer psychology, as well as how to create digital maps of your consumers' thinking and behaviour using your customer data strategy.

References

Amazon (1997) Amazon.com, Inc announces initial public offering of 3,000,000 shares of common stock, Amazon Press Center, 14 May, https://press.aboutamazon.com/1997/5/amazon-com-inc-announces-initial-public-offering-of-3-000-000-shares-of-common-stock (archived at https://perma.cc/756C-3RMF)

Aristotle and Barnes, J (1998) *The Complete Works of Aristotle: The Revised Oxford Translation*, Princeton University Press, NJ

Bandura, AJ (1977) *Social Learning Theory*, Prentice Hall, Englewood Cliffs, NJ

Clear, J (2017) First Principles: Elon Musk on the power of thinking for yourself, https://jamesclear.com/first-principles#:~:text=Musk%20used%20first%20principles%20thinking,and%20building%20up%20from%20there. (archived at https://perma.cc/F79H-XDC9)

Descartes, R (1985) *The Philosophical Writings of Descartes* (J Cottingham, R Stoothoff and D Murdoch, Trans.), Cambridge University Press

Eldridge, A (2023) SpaceX, *Encyclopedia Britannica*, www.britannica.com/topic/SpaceX (archived at https://perma.cc/RB42-FE4R)

Johnson, S (2015) SpaceX: Bringing the costs of space back down to earth, *Technology and Operations Management*, https://d3.harvard.edu/platform-rctom/submission/spacex-bringing-the-costs-of-space-back-down-to-earth/ (archived at https://perma.cc/X25P-WVN4)

Lang, JM and Benbow, ME (2013) Species Interactions and Competition, *Nature Education Knowledge*, 4 (4), p 8

Marketing Accountability Standards Board (nd) Habitual Buying, definition, https://marketing-dictionary.org/h/habitual-buying-behavior/ (archived at https://perma.cc/MJ8Q-5A9Z)

McLeod, S (2016) Albert Bandura's social learning theory, *Simply Psychology*, www.simplypsychology.org/bandura.html (archived at https://perma.cc/3E8J-WRCL)

Tidy, J and Galer, SS (2020) TikTok: The story of a social media giant, *BBC News*, 5 Aug, www.bbc.com/news/technology-53640724 (archived at https://perma.cc/Z9GD-GQ38)

Tzu, S (2010) *The Art of War*, Capstone Publishing, Chichester

Vermeulen, F (2017) Many strategies fail because they're not actually strategies, *Harvard Business Review*, 8 Nov, https://hbr.org/2017/11/many-strategies-fail-because-theyre-not-actually-strategies (archived at https://perma.cc/B2UR-6W4T)

Walker, L (1998) Amazon gets personal with e-commerce, *Washington Post*, 8 Nov, www.washingtonpost.com/wp-srv/washtech/daily/nov98/amazon110898.htm#:~:text=Amazon.com%20has%20etched%20itself,30 (archived at https://perma.cc/S6CK-TNDU)

Yglesias, M (2013) Sweet sorrow: Coke won the cola wars because great taste takes more than a single sip, *Slate Magazine*, 9 Aug, https://slate.com/business/2013/08/pepsi-paradox-why-people-prefer-coke-even-though-pepsi-wins-in-taste-tests.html (archived at https://perma.cc/99JU-PCU9)

Zwass, Vl (2022) e-commerce, *Encyclopedia Britannica*, https://www.britannica.com/technology/e-commerce (archived at https://perma.cc/4SP4-MWGJ)

Further reading

Chan, KW and Mauborgne, R (2015) *Blue Ocean Strategy, Expanded Edition: How to create uncontested market space and make the competition irrelevant*, Harvard Business Review Press, MA

Rumelt, RP (2017) *Good Strategy/Bad Strategy: The difference and why it matters*, Profile Books, London

Willink, J and Babin, L (2018) *The Dichotomy of Leadership: Balancing the challenges of extreme ownership to lead and win*, St. Martin's Publishing Group, New York, NY

2

Collaborative cross-functional growth

The first step in your cross-functional journey

In the world of e-commerce, collaboration and cross-functionality are key to growing a successful brand. E-commerce involves a variety of teams and departments working together to create a seamless online shopping experience for customers. From marketing and sales to product development and customer service, each team plays a crucial role in driving growth and ensuring the success of the business.

In this chapter, I will introduce you, dear reader, to the most important nodes in the e-commerce growth stack and how they work together to support the growth of your brand. From understanding customer behaviour and developing effective marketing strategies to optimizing your website and delivering exceptional customer service, each of these nodes plays a crucial role in building a successful e-commerce brand.

In later chapters, together we will delve into each of these nodes in detail, providing you with a comprehensive guide to building your very own cross-functional growth roadmap. With this roadmap, you will be equipped with the knowledge and tools to drive growth and build a thriving e-commerce business.

The e-commerce growth stack

Growing an e-commerce brand requires critical layers integrally woven together that, when orchestrated in the right way, will create a flywheel effect that continually grows your customer base and, consequently, revenue.

FIGURE 2.1 Product and market

Products

Market

FIGURE 2.2 Critical functions under product and market

Products

Supply chain functions

Product development
and R&D
Sourcing
Manufacturing
Inbound logistics
Warehousing and fulfilment

Market

Marketing functions

Brand story
Audience building
Performance marketing
Lifecycle marketing
PR and WOM (word of
mouth)

At its most basic level, an e-commerce business comprises a suite of products and a market it sells these products to; this is fundamentally how marketplace businesses work. The marketplace provides merchants or e-commerce operators with a ready market of buyers. The operators need to develop unique products and promote these products within the marketplace.

But getting into the detail of the functions that bring the suite of products to life, as well as the functions that continually drive product innovation and iterations that deliver continual growth, is also quite a crucial factor for growth. **Marketing alone does not grow an e-commerce business.** It involves fundamentally establishing a strong product-market fit along with building competence in other supporting functions such as technology, finance and customer support.

Compared to a marketplace business, an e-commerce business that sells directly to customers must take on more marketing responsibilities. They must ensure they have a solid brand story, build an audience, capture a portion of that audience as prospects and customers, promote their products and offers through paid media, and nurture a relationship with their customers through lifecycle marketing.

On the other hand, making products available to a market requires a product development cycle, sourcing and manufacturing, inbound shipping, logistics, warehousing and order fulfilment. Without these critical functions established, an e-commerce business will be unable to grow.

An e-commerce business is like a puzzle with marketing and supply chain functions being two critical pieces. Two other important pieces that e-commerce operators and leaders must take seriously are technology and customer experience. Without these, the puzzle would be incomplete and the business would struggle to succeed.

The concept of an e-commerce growth stack comprises specific building blocks required to carry, grow and scale up your customer base and revenue. All e-commerce success stories have developed highly competent supply chain operations, deliver superior customer experience, understand their target market and have the technology stack to support each of these three critical functions. The underlying secret sauce to success across all of these functions is people. Their leadership, teams and company culture in each of these functions optimize for pre-selected KPIs that feed into other KPIs and consequently grow the business.

FIGURE 2.3 The full e-commerce growth stack

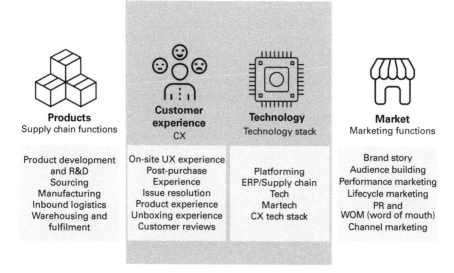

Products	Customer experience	Technology	Market
Supply chain functions	CX	Technology stack	Marketing functions
Product development and R&D	On-site UX experience		Brand story
Sourcing	Post-purchase	Platforming	Audience building
Manufacturing	Experience	ERP/Supply chain	Performance marketing
Inbound logistics	Issue resolution	Tech	Lifecycle marketing
Warehousing and	Product experience	Martech	PR and
fulfilment	Unboxing experience	CX tech stack	WOM (word of mouth)
	Customer reviews		Channel marketing

Critical business functions that deliver growth

Customer data

Customer data is the lifeblood of any meaningful e-commerce organization. It is crucial for building a deep understanding of customers and for making informed business decisions. Modern customer data has become so sophisticated that entire professions and industries have spawned as a result. It has become so necessary that possessing more customer data than competitors has become a significant competitive advantage. Knowing who your customer is is one thing, but knowing what they think and feel is another. Customer data can be collected through various methods, such as surveys, focus groups and ethnographic research. This data enables a brand to understand the consumer psychology of its target market and feed insights back through the value chain. On the more sophisticated end of utilizing customer data, companies like Sephora use quizzes to assist customers in finding items best suited to them. This data is then connected to post-purchase feedback and fed back into the recommendation engine (a machine learning algorithm) to improve it. In short, customer data is crucial for e-commerce businesses, as it enables them to make data-driven decisions and improve the customer experience.

The birth of the internet age, through to the dawn of the data age, has seen us progress from customer relationship management (CRM) systems to data management platforms (DMP) and now, to customer data platforms (CDP). Since the coining of the term CDP in 2013, customer data platforms are now an officially recognized software group by comparison and rating firms such as Gartner and Forrester and an integral part of e-commerce businesses operations.

In Chapter 5, we will dive deeper into the world of customer data and how e-commerce operators can use it as a growth lever. You'll learn about customer data layers like zero-party data and how it differs from third-party data, how data as a commodity and strategic asset leads to the creation of walled gardens, the ideal data structures and tech stacks for your business depending on its growth stages, how to adjust your data strategy over time and more.

Product development (R&D)

E-commerce is more than just marketing. The offer or product you're selling is a key component So, what goes into a good product?

Developing products that customers love is as much a science as it is an art. There are seven general stages of product development:

- Idea generation
- Idea screening
- Concept development and testing
- Market strategy and business analysis
- Product development
- Product deployment
- Market entry

But it's not all boring science labs and white lab coats. Although that is a part of it.

In crowded and competitive markets, innovation is often the key to finding gaps, expanding and pushing out competitors. You might not think that there is much room to innovate in the water industry, but LARQ saw things differently. The company was founded on the belief that there was a need for advanced technology and innovative design to address key issues with both reusable plastic bottles and tabletop filtration, such as contamination, difficulty cleaning and odours; their products use a multi-step purification process that combines a plant-based filter with PureVis UV-C technology to destroy contaminants at the molecular level (Klich, 2021; Silver, 2017; Steinberg, 2022; Harris, 2021). This innovative approach goes beyond traditional filtration methods and allows LARQ to offer a unique solution to the problem of contaminated drinking water. In addition to improving the user experience, LARQ is also committed to reducing our dependency on single-use plastic and providing people with access to clean water. The company's connected devices, such as the LARQ Pitcher, allow users to track water quality and filter replacements in their geography, further demonstrating their commitment to innovation in the industry (Harris, 2021). By focusing on innovation, LARQ has been able to find gaps in the market and push out competitors, making them a leader in the water industry. LARQ's mission and values-driven brand is also a textbook example of the brand core, which we will cover later in this book. Combining your brand's values and then having a clear enemy to rally against are critical elements to forming a tribe and a tight-knit community – something you will learn more about in my chapter on community building.

Then there's finance involved. Sure, R&D costs money. But there's also R&D funding and R&D tax credits to consider. In addition to that, you have questions about how much autonomy the R&D department has outside the 'way of thinking' of your head office. Some businesses even go so far as to intentionally create physical distance between their R&D departments and their main offices to foster this autonomy to experiment outside the constraints of what other stakeholders might think or feel about what they are doing. The number one online marketplace for buying and selling e-commerce stores and more, Flippa.com, while having its main office in Texas, has its R&D department in Melbourne, Australia, giving the team not only a huge amount of physical separation but time-zone separation as well (2X eCommerce, 2022a). Of course, perhaps the most important aspect: you need to **listen to your customers**. Your data and marketing teams need to be in sync with the kinds of questions that the R&D team is looking to answer. The R&D team needs to be in touch with marketing to know *what* they should be innovating on.

Operations

Advantages in e-commerce don't just come from better marketing or a better product. Building competitive advantages starts right at the beginning of the supply chain when raw materials are sourced, through to the last-mile operations required to get your products in the hands of your customers (and then back to you again if they return them, and many do, up to 25 per cent in some segments such as fast fashion) (Ader et al, 2021).

Perhaps no time has shown the importance of operations more than the Covid-19 pandemic and following events. Not only did this upheave our lives, it also led to rapid growth in operational requirements for e-commerce stores. Specifically, the equivalent of **10 years of growth in just three months**. We saw shipping ports gridlocked and unprecedented pressure in the supply chain (McKinsey, 2022).

Your brand needs collaborative operations

Cross-functional operations can mean the difference between winning and losing a **price war** because you can afford to go lower while maintaining your profit margins. Whereas a competitor without the supply chain efficiencies would go into the red selling at the prices you can still turn a profit on. After all, fulfilment costs can account for between 12 and 20 per cent of revenues for e-commerce brands; efficiencies here can make or break a company.

Operations efficiencies also allow more capital for product and R&D, which leads to innovation or to marketing where it enters the budget for a positive ROI marketing campaign. Slick operations ensure that your brand's most popular SKUs are **never out of stock**. Imagine your marketing team spends hundreds of thousands creating the most effective marketing campaign in the company's history, that is, until operational inefficiencies and supply chain miscalculations leave you without any units to sell.

Customer service

Customer service is a key part of your operations that has the potential to add value across all stages of the customer journey.

Readily available **customer agents** with the autonomy to assist customers in the manner they want and need will help you capture more revenue. But to achieve this, you need the symbiotic effects of management support, adequate financing and training, communication with logistics and marketing, and technological systems.

E-commerce operators shouldn't think of customer service as an **added cost of doing business** but rather as an integral part of the e-commerce growth stack. The customer that clicked your promotional email and is ready to buy but has that one question they need to be answered before they enter their credit card information... if there's a readily available customer service agent available via chatbot, they can get that question answered before they bounce from the store, never to come back again. In fact, 73 per cent of consumers consider customer service an important factor in their purchasing decisions, and 79 per cent would change retailers due to a poor experience (Puthiyamadam and Reyes, 2018; Bloomreach, 2021).

Is it the getting, or the keeping?

Often, a new e-commerce brand will focus heavily on acquiring customers, and not so much on keeping them. But what happens when the customer has post-purchase questions about how to use the product or how to return an item? **Your customer journey doesn't stop when your products arrive at the customer's door**. In fact, it's only just beginning, and runs the lifecycle of the product and beyond.

Delighting your customers is good for business. The average e-commerce business retains approximately 30 per cent of customers, and most often it's cheaper to keep a customer than to acquire a new one (Popescu, 2017). Besides, why would you do all the hard work to bring new customers in and communicate the equivalent of 'don't let the door hit you on your way out' after they've purchased? Research by VWO, a data analytics platform for businesses, shows that the probability of selling to a new customer is between 5 and 20 per cent (Gupta, 2022). The probability of selling to an existing customer, however, is 50 to 70 per cent. Just a 5 per cent increase in retention can yield a 25 to 95 per cent increase in profits (Reichheld and Schefter, 2000).

Recall Principle 2 from Chapter 1, 'Optimize experience for habitual purchase'. This means reducing friction and blockages at every stage of the customer journey. Your customer service team is the perfect business unit to handle the dynamic needs of your customer throughout both defined and unexpected stages in the customer journey.

Feedback loops

You also need your systems and customer service team integrated with your data and marketing teams to capitalize on rich sources of information for the business. Key metrics such as resolution times, as well as repeat purchase rate, loyal customer rate and revenue churn rate need to be tracked by your data team. From there, your customer service team can begin to build insights into how they can improve their performance.

Customer service also serves as a rich touchpoint for informal ethnographic research or other survey methods to feed back to marketing teams and other key stakeholders. Customer feedback is nothing new; the first recorded instance is from the 1750s when a dissatisfied customer left a merchant a clay tablet detailing their dissatisfaction (Standley, 2021). Today it's much easier to gather customer feedback; you have no excuse for guessing when you could just ask your customer. This information can be fed back into everything from marketing to product development.

Marketing

What is a book about e-commerce without marketing?

Marketing is an essential part of e-commerce, as it is the front-facing aspect your consumers interact with most. While social media channels, videos, articles, paid public relations, user-generated content (UGC) and brand communities may come to mind first, marketing actually starts with a lot of research, strategy and data. By the time you see a marketing campaign or piece of collateral, it has gone through the entire cross-functional value chain. The marketing team works closely with the product team and uses research and data to understand the target customer and create the perfect message that aligns with the brand's personality and customers' desires. The data team helps with pricing and campaign tracking, and the whole organization works together for a successful product launch or marketing campaign. In this way, marketing is the gravitational pull that determines whether customers will be drawn to the brand. As an investor and brand builder, I find this part of e-commerce particularly rewarding.

Throughout this book, you will learn about the marketing tactics used by top brands and successful brand builders. These companies, some of them 'unicorns', are known for their innovative and effective marketing strategies. One key aspect of their success is their ability to create a strong brand identity and consistently communicate it across all marketing channels. This includes using a unique and compelling brand voice, as well as visually appealing branding elements such as logos and colour schemes. These brands also excel at understanding their target audience and tailoring their marketing messages to appeal to them. This may involve conducting market research to gather insights into customer preferences and behaviour, as well as using data and analytics to inform their marketing decisions.

In addition to traditional marketing channels such as advertising and public relations, these brands often leverage the power of social media and other digital platforms to reach their audience. They are adept at creating engaging content that resonates with their followers and encourages them to take action, whether that's purchasing a product or simply engaging with the brand. Overall, the marketing tactics of these best-in-class brands and unicorn brand builders are a valuable source of inspiration and guidance for any business looking to improve their own marketing efforts. By studying their strategies and applying the lessons learned, you can improve the effectiveness of your own marketing and drive growth for your brand.

Finance

E-commerce operators rely on an in-depth understanding of their financials and communicating the implications of this to all key stakeholders within the company. I cannot highlight enough my absolute intention and specificity in calling this chapter 'Collaborative cross-functional growth'. Nor in including it so early in the book. To truly process and appreciate the rest of the book, you need to establish a certain mode of thinking first. But enough about the importance of connected business units and integrated strategies. What about the specifics of finance for e-commerce brands?

Know your metrics

While any e-commerce brand needs to be tasking the sexier marketing and retention metrics like average order value (AOV), customer lifetime value (CLTV), repeat purchase rate and all other metrics that can usually be found in your e-commerce analytics dashboard, it is up to the finance team to calculate critical metrics like earnings before interest and taxes (EBIT), free cash flow (which is the amount left after meeting operating expenditures and capital expenditures) and the working capital ratio (to name just a few).

It is also pertinent for e-commerce operators to get a grasp of the concepts of marginal and fixed costs. Whilst fixed costs include expenditures on things like your rent that do not change in relation to how many goods you produce or sell, marginal costs change as a result of you producing, scaling or procuring more units. Marginal costs, as the name suggests, will continually fluctuate. They include expenditure on things like employee salaries and equipment costs. As you make or ship new products you need more cardboard boxes and tape, more employees, more forklifts, etc.

Your costs come together to form your cost of products sold (COPS), sometimes called the cost of goods sold (COGS). To have a true understanding of your business, you need to know the COPS at an SKU (stock-keeping unit) level, which means you need to know your marginal costs, and your fixed costs need to be spread out across all your SKUs. Though there are some fixed costs you include (like the fabric used to make shirts) and others you don't (like marketing costs), so it is best to have a professional support you.

Learn from the best

Once operators have a handle on their revenue and various costs, they develop a clear understanding of their profit margin. It seems logical, then, to seek to maximize this. Increasing profits is, after all, a desirable outcome in business. However, you've read far enough to know that what might seem a logical decision or assumption is often not within the context of the collaborative cross-functional growth environment. Here, we have an opportunity to learn from the best.

While the same strategies and tactics may not work for every business, you can take heed to learn from some of the best and most well-funded e-commerce operations in the world. Or in this case, the largest at the time of writing in 2022 – Amazon. Jeff Bezos (who, the reader should note, operates a very large and public company, not a private one) favours free cash flow above all other metrics (SEC, 2004). Even percentage margin. As an innovator, free cash flow is something you can invest in new initiatives through your R&D, into high-ROI marketing campaigns that you've A/B tested for optimization or, importantly, in being able to delight customers. Bezos states that building loyalty and satisfying customers, even if it means lowering prices in the short term, will always lead to better free cash flow in the long term.

Financial growth traps

Underinvesting

It might be tempting to enjoy watching profits accumulate in the bank and create a safety cushion for your organization, and as a way to track your success – especially as a founder, for example, to take most of your profits as salary. Steer clear of this temptation. This trap is especially common for new e-commerce stores attempting to run lean and spend as little as possible. Even in large organizations, where the e-commerce arm is a new venture, you can find this lean mindset. The bottom line is that you need to be building systems that form symbiotic relationships to generate greater ROI. That means investing in marketing campaigns, R&D and operations.

Overinvesting

Like anything, the financial management of an e-commerce store requires strategic thinking with all business units in mind. Let's imagine you're a brick-and-mortar retailer selling furniture and not a small one at that. You're expanding into e-commerce, and it's going to require new distribution channels. That means new warehouses closer to your consumers and more. You'll need a new website too, of course. So how do you allocate your budget? Do you build your own warehousing and distribution (keeping in mind you lack the experience and intellectual capital in running B2C distribution), or do you outsource it to save money and invest more into your website and customer experience?

Overinvesting in the wrong areas is just as much of a growth trap as general underinvestment in the business. Strategic decisions at the financial level require a cross-functional growth mindset. Which will lead you then to questions like, 'Instead of building all this from scratch, can we merge with another company, or acquire another brand to add to benefit from already established systems, processes and competencies?' I will cover mergers and acquisitions (M&A) in more detail later in this chapter. But first, to technology stack.

Technology stack

It's no surprise that e-commerce is tech-heavy. After all, much of it takes place online. Why do I say 'much of it' and not all of it? Because if you've been paying attention, by now you'll know that there is much more to e-commerce than meets the eye from a web browser. It's people in factories and wheels on the road; it is finance teams crunching numbers in the background; and it's sales floor staff facilitating the last touchpoints of 'buy online, pick up in-store' orders.

A company's technology stack is the best opportunity to tie all the points of this chapter together. Effective technology solutions across the supply chain, product development and marketing, through to finance and operations, enable a brand to tie together a collaborative and cross-functional growth ecosystem. It is estimated that the MarTech (marketing technology) industry alone (the suite of technologies utilized for marketing operations) comprises an estimated 10,000 vendors and is worth approximately $344.8 billion (Learning Experience Alliance, 2022).

Brands rely on tech stacks comprising different systems for inventory management, customer data, e-commerce platforms (such as Shopify, SAP CX, Salesforce Commerce Cloud and BigCommerce), marketing, rewards, payments, credit, warehousing, delivery and returns (to name just a few), as well as organizational tools such as project management software, messaging apps like Slack and more. The tech stack, perhaps like no other section in this chapter, serves as an example of the need for holistic and integrated strategy and planning, and nuanced analysis of trade-offs and benefits with multiple factors in mind.

However, while complicated, the tech stack provides the opportunity to add value at every stage of the value chain. Your tech stack enables you to automate away human labour and remove the risk of human error, connect all stages of your value chain, improve your customer experience and gain a competitive advantage through data science (and more).

Questions you need to ask when choosing a tech stack, or adding a piece of software to your existing stack are:

- Does it meet performance requirements?
- Is it scalable?
- Is it compatible with the tools we already use?
- Will it create dependencies that make future changes to the tech stack more difficult?

To name a few...

Each piece of software or subscription service serves as a miniature merger or acquisition for your company, and your purchases should be vetted with the same thought and care as you would give to a substantial M&A deal. This brings me to our next section – mergers and acquisitions.

Mergers and acquisitions (M&A)

Mergers and acquisitions provide e-commerce organizations with numerous advantages over and above the acquisition of an additional cash-flowing asset. Advantages include:

- Customers
- Customer data
- Intellectual capital/knowledge capital
- Access to new resources
- Access to new markets
- Combining complementary skillsets and getting access to a company that has a strong track record in one area
- Economies of scale
- Reduce risk by spreading your business across markets and sectors

When it comes to M&A there are two main types – horizontal and vertical. A horizontal merger is when two companies in the same industry join forces (Osome, 2020). This is a great way to shore up a large market share under one organization. Although that certainly isn't the only benefit. Then there are vertical mergers, which are when two companies that operate at different levels but more or less in the same industry merge together.

One example of a horizontal merger is Disney buying 20th Century Fox, another media company, to expand its core business offering (Inci, 2019). An example of a vertical merger is Shopify when they acquired Deliverr, a fulfilment service for e-commerce brands (Marchese, 2022). This allowed Shopify to not only improve its fulfilment services for Shopify merchants, but also to acquire a business unit independently profitable with existing customers and contracts. Deliverr (owned by Shopify) enables fulfilment for Shopify, Walmart, BigCommerce and more (Rowe, 2022). Bring these M&A strategies together and you have what you could call an M&A roll-up strategy, an effective way to grow a brand fast when demand is high. Oren Schauble, an uber-successful founder and brand builder in the direct-to-consumer e-commerce space and 2X eCommerce podcast guest, used this exact strategy to quickly scale operations to meet the huge demand in the direct-to-consumer THC and cannabis products space in the United States. Many entrepreneurs will tell you that speed is key, and this is only amplified in fast-growing markets.

The M&A roll-up strategy involves acquiring multiple smaller companies in a particular industry and consolidating them into a larger entity. This may involve a combination of horizontal and vertical mergers, as it did in Oren's case – merging together with another established brand in another state, and adding into the mix the vertical aspect of a logistics acquisition to make it all possible. When done well, an M&A roll-up strategy allows the e-commerce organization to rapidly expand both its market presence and overall capabilities. As Oren (who went from graphic designer to owning a share in an $80-million-plus public company via mergers and acquisitions) says in 2X eCommerce podcast episode #358, their acquisitions strategy was instrumental in growing their business as rapidly and to such great heights as they did. A larger company has greater market share and is much more attractive to investors (2X eCommerce, 2022b). Oren says that the whole process from conception took about two years. First there was an initial merger with three companies and then a later merger with another series of companies. Initially there were four founders coming from a distribution company, and two different brands (a brand and a retail store). Later they brought in an experienced executive team to handle the public side of the business (that is, taking the business public and managing it). When Oren's company went public, at IPO it was valued at $80 or $90 million (2X eCommerce, 2022b). In 2021 alone, they did approximately $60 million in revenue.

M&A isn't just for new and fast-growing brands, either. Established retailers find market opportunity in these strategies, too. Boohoo group, at the time of writing in 2022, has 13 brands under its umbrella. One of those they founded (Boohoo in 2006). The rest came via acquisitions (i.e. a roll-up strategy), including Pretty Little Thing (2017), Nasty Gal (2017), Karen Millen (2019) and a big one, Debenhams, in 2021. Later came Burton of London and others (Boohoo, 2022). Their top brands, generating 80 per cent of their revenue, are Boohoo and Pretty Little Thing. These brands serve as what I call the mothership, enabling Boohoo Group to collect a host of other brands using the revenues and free cash flow from these huge established sources of income to pay a deposit on the new company. Brands then use the free cash flow from the new company to pay off the purchase amount, for example, a 20 per cent down payment using funds from the mothership, and free cash flow from the new company covers the rest. Boohoo, through their roll-up strategy, were able to acquire distressed companies and broaden their market share into different demographics. In their press release on 25 January 2021, they stated that the Debenhams acquisition is instrumental as a step toward achieving their goal of creating the United Kingdom's largest marketplace, assisting them to become a leader not just in fashion, but also in beauty, sport and homewares (Kamani, 2021). It's not just the obvious acquisition of stores and websites that makes acquisitions an attractive prospect. Consider also the intellectual property, customer data and related select contracts. Through their Debenhams acquisition alone, Boohoo gained access to 6 million beauty shoppers and 1.4 million beauty club members (Boohoo, 2021).

Of course, just because these integration strategies can be effective, it doesn't mean they're the right strategies for you. Knowing when to roll-up or vertically integrate requires a deep understanding of the market and your financials. For the smallest of stores, you're better off growing your main brand, though that doesn't mean there won't be opportunities to do your own smaller versions of vertical and horizontal integration. In fact, when you're small it's more likely you'll be fielding offers rather than making them. As McKinsey writes, companies sometimes don't do due diligence on the risks involved in mergers and acquisitions or integrations, even though these strategies are expensive and complex endeavours that are difficult to reverse (Stuckey and White, 1993). Not to mention that two-thirds of roll-ups fail to create additional value for investors or increase operating cash flows (Carrol and Mui, 2008). That's not to say not integrating doesn't come with its own risks. As *Forbes* points out, owning just one part of a broader system puts you at the mercy of suppliers and partners; one unexpected change could present a huge risk to your company's future (Harper, 2020). As always, you've got to know which cards to play and to do that you need to have an overview of the whole cross-functional growth ecosystem that is your e-commerce business (the cards you've been dealt).

Whichever strategy you pursue, you need to have a plan for adding value. This usually comes in one of four ways: first, reducing your overhead costs (for example rent for a warehouse); second, reducing your operating costs (for example marketing expenses); third, increasing price (without reducing volume); fourth, increasing volume (without decreasing price or increasing unit costs) (Gregory, 2021).

Time to take your next fateful step

In this chapter we have covered a wide range of topics related to the collaborative and cross-functional nature of e-commerce and growing a successful brand. From marketing and finance to M&A, we have discussed the various teams and departments that work together to support growth in the e-commerce arena.

In the next chapter we will delve into the topic of your brand's core, which is foundational for the long-term sustain growth of your e-commerce business.

From here on in we get serious and dive deep into the growth nodes I have mentioned throughout this chapter. Let's go!

References

2X eCommerce (2022a) S07, EP14, eCommerce business acquisitions are a vastly undervalued asset class – Flippa, https://2xecommerce.com/podcast/ep356/ (archived at https://perma.cc/W22Y-HBYR)

2X eCommerce (2022b) S07 EP16, 9-figure M&A roll-ups and product innovation, https://2xecommerce.com/podcast/ep358/ (archived at https://perma.cc/7ZE8-2TP4)

Ader, J et al (2021) Returning to order: improving returns management for apparel companies, *McKinsey & Company*, 25 May, www.McKinsey.com/industries/retail/our-insights/returning-to-order-improving-returns-management-for-apparel-companies (archived at https://perma.cc/CY55-49TJ)

Bloomreach (2021) The State of Commerce Experience 2021, https://visit.bloomreach.com/state-of-commerce-experience (archived at https://perma.cc/XX9F-GDJF)

Boohoo (2021) Strategic acquisition to develop online marketplace, 25 Jan, www.boohooplc.com/sites/boohoo-corp/files/all-documents/result-centre/2021/strategic-acquisition-release-jan-2021.pdf (archived at https://perma.cc/D94G-NEQA)

Boohoo (2022) Boohoo Group plc: Annual Report and Accounts, www.boohooplc.com/sites/boohoo-corp/files/2022-05/boohoo-com-plc-annual-report-2022.pdf (archived at https://perma.cc/5JA6-NWWN)

Carroll, P and Mui, C (2008) Seven ways to fail big, *Harvard Business Review*, Sep, https://hbr.org/2008/09/seven-ways-to-fail-big (archived at https://perma.cc/696J-QZJP)

Gregory, A (2021) E-commerce roll-ups are the next wave of disruption in consumer packaged goods, *TechCrunch*, 26 Mar, https://techcrunch.com/2021/03/26/e-commerce-roll-ups-present-the-next-wave-of-disruption-in-consumer-packaged-goods/ (archived at https://perma.cc/AS6L-56EJ)

Gupta, A (2022) 100 quick and snackable e-commerce statistics, *VWO*, 24 Oct, https://vwo.com/blog/ecommerce-statistics/ (archived at https://perma.cc/6QT5-ADCW)

Harper, S (2020) How vertical integration prevents existential threats to your business, *Forbes*, 4 Feb, www.forbes.com/sites/theyec/2020/02/04/how-vertical-integration-prevents-existential-threats-to-your-business/?sh=1e7814c865c0 (archived at https://perma.cc/B6N5-WNGL)

Harris, M (2021) Your water pitcher could be a source of contamination. This new smart-home pitcher prevents that from happening, *Forbes*, 3 Mar, www.forbes.com/sites/meggentaylor/2021/03/03/your-water-pitcher-could-be-a-source-of-contamination-this-new-smart-home-pitcher-prevents-that-from-happening/?sh=422c9106169a (archived at https://perma.cc/H347-Q6P7)

Inci, D (2019) Council Post: guide to mergers and acquisitions in e-commerce, *Forbes*, 20 Sep, www.forbes.com/sites/theyec/2019/09/20/guide-to-mergers-and-acquisitions-in-e-commerce/?sh=263573d47c6e (archived at https://perma.cc/3TL4-QCGC)

Kamani, M (2021) boohoo group plc announcements I boohoo group plc: STRATEGIC ACQUISITION, www.investegate.co.uk/boohoo-group-plc--boo-/rns/strategic-acquisition/202101250700076824M/ (archived at https://perma.cc/Z5NX-GHF8)

Klich, T (2021) After historic valuation on 'Shark Tank', LARQ expects revenue to hit $30 million in 2022, *Forbes*, 15 Nov, www.forbes.com/sites/tanyaklich/2021/11/15/larq-pitcher-water-bottle-shark-tank/?sh=4800a7324ab8 (archived at https://perma.cc/N5YG-4JF2)

Learning Experience Alliance LXA (2022) The State of Martech 2022/23, www.martechalliance.com/martechreport (archived at https://perma.cc/F5LJ-K2R3)

Marchese, A (2022) Shopify to buy e-commerce fulfillment specialist Deliverr for $2.1 billion, *The Wall Street Journal*, 5 May, www.wsj.com/articles/shopify-to-buy-e-commerce-fulfillment-specialist-deliverr-for-2-1-billion-11651765366 (archived at https://perma.cc/N986-AMRH)

McKinsey & Company (2022) The quickening, www.McKinsey.com/capabilities/strategy-and-corporate-finance/our-insights/five-fifty-the-quickening (archived at https://perma.cc/W7MJ-26MA)

Osome (2020) Horizon Merger, definition, https://osome.com/uk/term/horizontal-merger-uk/ (archived at https://perma.cc/9C3R-DBDV)

Popescu, R (2017) How to drive growth with ecommerce customer retention rate optimization, *OMNICONVERT*, www.omniconvert.com/blog/ecommerce-customer-retention-rate-optimization/ (archived at https://perma.cc/U4BM-4T2U)

Puthiyamadam, T and Reyes, J (2018) Experience is everything: here's how to get it right, *PwC*, www.pwc.com/us/en/advisory-services/publications/consumer-intelligence-series/pwc-consumer-intelligence-series-customer-experience.pdf (archived at https://perma.cc/D7M7-FX4K)

Reichheld, F and Schefter, P (2000) The economics of e-loyalty, *HBS Working Knowledge*, https://hbswk.hbs.edu/archive/the-economics-of-e-loyalty (archived at https://perma.cc/9NSG-GHPQ)

Rowe, A (2022) Shopify just bought the Deliverr shipping network for $2.1 billion, *Tech.co*, 6 May, https://tech.co/news/shopify-buys-deliverr-shipping#:~:text=twitter- (archived at https://perma.cc/NYB9-CKYD)

SEC (2004) 2004 Letter to Shareholders, www.sec.gov/Archives/edgar/data/1018724/000119312505070440/dex991.htm (archived at https://perma.cc/TXX7-7Z69)

Silver, C (2017) The LARQ water bottle cleans up your nasty tap water with UV-C light tech, *Forbes*, 7 Nov, www.forbes.com/sites/curtissilver/2017/11/07/the-larq-water-bottle-cleans-up-your-nasty-tap-water-with-uv-c-light-tech/?sh=bdf64996c8e2 (archived at https://perma.cc/MPG7-2DV9)

Standley, C (2021) The history of customer surveys, *Purple*, 22 Jul, https://purple.ai/blogs/the-history-of-customer-surveys/ (archived at https://perma.cc/TVQ3-XPAC)

Steinberg, D (2022) LARQ bottle filtered: The 200 best inventions of 2022, *Time*, 10 Nov, https://time.com/collection/best-inventions-2022/6222178/larq-bottle-filtered/ (archived at https://perma.cc/PUP2-T4GQ)

Stuckey, J and White, D (1993) When and when not to vertically integrate, *McKinsey & Company*, 1 Aug, www.McKinsey.com/business-functions/ strategy-and-corporate-finance/our-insights/when-and-when-not-to-vertically- integrate (archived at https://perma.cc/3X27-KUDA)

Further reading

Gerber, ME (1995) *The E-Myth Revisited: Why most small businesses don't work and what to do about it,* HarperCollins, New York, NY

Ghandour, J, Lange, T, Seyfert, A and Turco, A (2021) Consumer-goods companies must transform their planning end to end, *McKinsey & Company*, 24 Nov, www.McKinsey.com/industries/consumer-packaged-goods/our-insights/ consumer-goods-companies-must-transform-their-planning-end-to-end (archived at https://perma.cc/CUP6-KCYW)

Hill, K (2012) How Target figured out a teen girl was pregnant before her father did, *Forbes*, 16 Feb, www.forbes.com/sites/kashmirhill/2012/02/16/how-target- figured-out-a-teen-girl-was-pregnant-before-her-father-did/ (archived at https:// perma.cc/Z8TP-C366)

Puthiyamadam, T (2018) Experience is everything: Here's how to get it right, *PwC*, www.pwc.com/us/en/advisory-services/publications/consumer-intelligence-series/ pwc-consumer-intelligence-series-customer-experience.pdf (archived at https:// perma.cc/7G94-LY6K)

Recke, M (2021) Amazon, the pioneer of horizontal and vertical integration, *Next*, 18 Nov, https://nextconf.eu/2021/11/amazon-the-pioneer-horizontal-vertical- integration/#gref (archived at https://perma.cc/47MZ-FF2S)

Reichheld, F and Schefter, P (2000) The economics of e-loyalty, *HBS Working Knowledge*, 7 Oct, https://hbswk.hbs.edu/archive/the-economics-of-e-loyalty (archived at https://perma.cc/U3SR-VCVB)

Sullivan, D with Hardy, B (2020) *Who Not How: The formula to achieve bigger goals through accelerating teamwork,* Hay House, Carlsbad, CA

Wickman, G (2012) *Traction: Get a grip on your business*, BenBella Books, Dallas, TX

3

Brand core: the foundation for growth

When building a brand, you are essentially birthing a new personality into the world. This personality should reflect the demographic of your target audience, conveying the culture and values of your company. It is important to give your brand a human face, allowing customers to identify and relate to it in a personal way. This can be achieved by carefully choosing visuals, colours, and personalities that your target customers will identify with. Beyond that, and this is where it gets difficult, is that you need to consider what values, attributes and characteristics you want your brand to embody. What things does your brand do, say and believe in? What things doesn't your brand do, say or believe in? What is your brand for and what is it against? What things does it talk about and comment on and what things doesn't it? Is your brand the energetic and brightly coloured-clothing-wearing friend that is always up for something new? Or is your brand the mellow intellectual that prefers to stay in, read a book and talk politics? Once you've got that down, it gets even harder, because you have to formulate it in a way that your marketing team is able to begin to learn the script of your brand and put on that persona every day, much like an actor does. This chapter will teach you all that goes into brand, and give you a step-by-step toward building your own congruent and attractive brand.

Why brand?

Brand building forms the essential foundation for your entire cross-functional growth stack. The principles of branding and consumer psychology that you will learn in this chapter are evergreen growth tools that will, quite simply, through brand and culture building, make everything else you do so much easier. Not only that, but they will add a lot of value to your company. Apple's brand alone, not the business, but just the brand, is valued at over $400 billion (Interbrand, 2021). Other brands that you might be familiar with such as Tiffany & Co and Sephora are valued at almost $5.5 billion and just over $4.5 billion respectively (Interbrand, 2021). Again, that's just the brand, not the company, and is the result of leveraging the building blocks outlined in this chapter. In a world where consumers have an abundance of choice, and you have at least a dozen competitors in even the narrowest of niches, your brand is an essential differentiator. When you think of differentiation, you often think about things like making a better product with more features.

But, as Rory Sutherland, author of *Alchemy*, and a marketing veteran of over 30 years, including many years at Ogilvy, says that value can be created in the mind as much as it can be created in the factory – we value things not because of what they are, but what they mean. Having created some of the most compelling marketing campaigns of our time, he speaks from experience when he says that while engineering or science don't allow for magic, psychology certainly does (Sutherland, 2019). And what is brand building? Well, it is psychology. As branding pioneer and creator of brand identities for companies such as Levi Strauss and Fujifilm, Walter Landor says, 'Products are made in the factory, but brands are created in the mind' (Keegan et al, 1995). Often, the real challenge to securing new customers and retaining them is a psychological barrier, because the fact is, to consumers their purchases are about so much more than just products.

Brand

In almost any industry, you are engaged in a battle of the brands. You, your existing competitors and new entrants are all vying for a piece of the market share pie. While a brand can be something that seemingly just 'happens', the fact is that any e-commerce store needs to intentionally design their brand with the goals of maximizing brand equity, achieving profitable positioning and establishing a unique and consistent brand voice – because without a brand, you only have a product.

'Brand' comes from the Ancient Norse word 'brandr', which means to burn. In its original use, it was mostly used to describe a burning piece of

FIGURE 3.1 Brand strategy

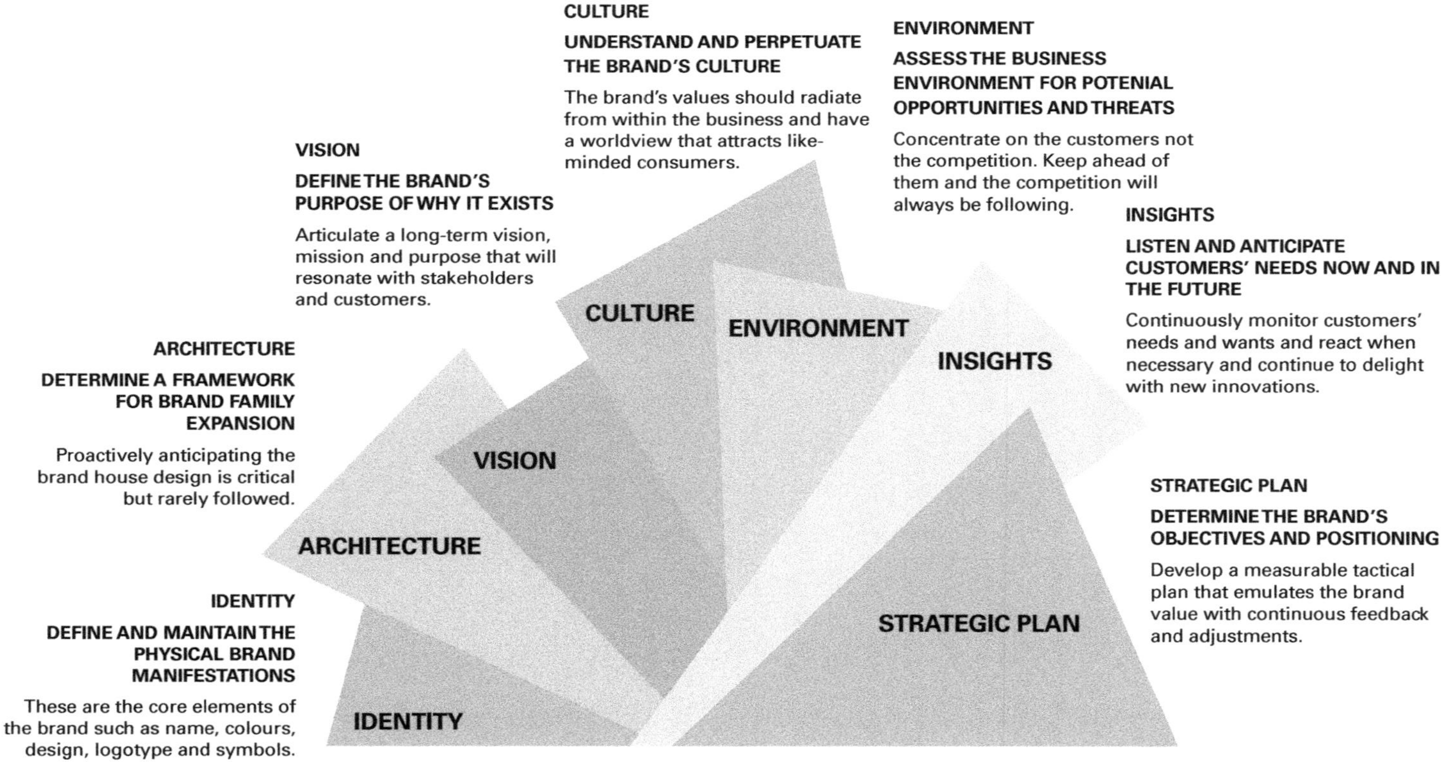

CULTURE

UNDERSTAND AND PERPETUATE THE BRAND'S CULTURE

The brand's values should radiate from within the business and have a worldview that attracts like-minded consumers.

VISION

DEFINE THE BRAND'S PURPOSE OF WHY IT EXISTS

Articulate a long-term vision, mission and purpose that will resonate with stakeholders and customers.

ARCHITECTURE

DETERMINE A FRAMEWORK FOR BRAND FAMILY EXPANSION

Proactively anticipating the brand house design is critical but rarely followed.

IDENTITY

DEFINE AND MAINTAIN THE PHYSICAL BRAND MANIFESTATIONS

These are the core elements of the brand such as name, colours, design, logotype and symbols.

ENVIRONMENT

ASSESS THE BUSINESS ENVIRONMENT FOR POTENIAL OPPORTUNITIES AND THREATS

Concentrate on the customers not the competition. Keep ahead of them and the competition will always be following.

INSIGHTS

LISTEN AND ANTICIPATE CUSTOMERS' NEEDS NOW AND IN THE FUTURE

Continuously monitor customers' needs and wants and react when necessary and continue to delight with new innovations.

STRATEGIC PLAN

DETERMINE THE BRAND'S OBJECTIVES AND POSITIONING

Develop a measurable tactical plan that emulates the brand value with continuous feedback and adjustments.

INSIGHTS

ENVIRONMENT

CULTURE

VISION

ARCHITECTURE

IDENTITY

STRATEGIC PLAN

wood that was used as a torch. However, later people began 'branding' cattle to mark ownership, and thus began the evolution toward the modern understanding of 'brand'. Today, brands are imbued with meaning, equity and emotion, and form the foundation of how consumers recognize you and attach emotion to you. But a good brand does more than allow recognition; it is a store of all the equity that you build up through your marketing and operations efforts. From your user-generated content and influencer marketing to your smooth last-mile processes, the actual utility and experience your products deliver, and your customer support. Your brand image holds all of these positive experiences and connotations within it.

Your brand is an encapsulation of micro-experiences.

Brand persona

As I said at the beginning of this chapter, bringing a new brand into the world is much like birthing a personality. Your brand persona is the foundation of that personality. And with values, story and tone of voice layered on top, you have your brand personality. Customer-centric brand personalities begin first with the customer, your target customer, and what they want to see and feel from interacting with your brand. Rolex is competent and sophisticated, whereas Volvo is competent and sincere. This results in two very different brand images and personas. So, you can see that you need to be very particular about your person to strike the right chord.

Diving deeper into two direct-to-consumer brands to illustrate brand persona and the elements of values and tone of voice that we are about to cover, we have Casper and Bombas. Casper is a DTC e-commerce brand that sells mattresses and other sleep products; its brand persona is often described as being modern, innovative and focused on wellness. Casper's values include a commitment to quality, comfort and customer satisfaction, and these values are reflected in its marketing campaigns, which often feature people enjoying a good night's sleep on Casper products. Casper's brand voice is often friendly and informative, reflecting the brand's focus on helping customers achieve better sleep (Casper Sleep Inc, 2023).

Bombas is a DTC e-commerce brand that sells socks. Its brand persona is often described as being innovative, comfortable and socially responsible. Bombas' values include a commitment to quality, comfort and giving back, and these values are reflected in its marketing campaigns, which often feature people enjoying the brand's comfortable socks and stories about the brand's efforts to donate socks to those in need (Bombas, 2023). Bombas' brand voice is often friendly and playful, reflecting the brand's focus on creating a fun and enjoyable shopping experience for its customers.

Now let's dive into how and why to build brand values, story and establish clear and consistent tone of voice for your brand.

Brand values

For e-commerce brands, having strong and clearly defined brand values can help to build trust and credibility with customers, as well as foster customer loyalty and engagement. When you think of a brand, the first things that probably come to mind are its logo, colours, products and influencers. For example, Nike's black and white tick logo, sportswear products and influencers like LeBron James, Rafael Nadal and Tiger Woods. But what you're really thinking of are the emotional associations with the brand – things like Nike's 'Just Do It' slogan evoking motivation and determination. These brand symbols are only powerful because of the emotions placed in them by consumers – emotions that have been built by brand values and brand story.

We are very lucky in the e-commerce world to have a wealth of examples to choose from when it comes to brand building done well, whether it be Gymshark taking the athletic wear industry by storm, or Warby Parker offering consumers stylish and affordable alternatives to designer prescription eyewear.

Let's take Warby Parker as an example. They already had a strong brand positioning by offering premium-quality eyeglasses, great customer experience and lower prices. But product and price aren't enough to overcome market inertia and get customers to switch to your company (Aaker, 2012). You need something more compelling. And in the eyeglasses market, where people have established and trusted sources and connections with medical professionals, getting customers to switch isn't easy. But Warby Parker brought a two-pronged approach to the eyewear industry. Not only did they offer stylish and affordable eyewear, they live their values through a brand mission. That mission is advancing access to quality eye care, whether you're a paid consumer who can't afford more expensive options or you can't afford glasses at all. They communicate these values and their commitment through initiatives such as their 'buy a pair give a pair' and 'pupil project' programmes, which have distributed over 10 million pairs of glasses globally to help solve the massive global issue of 2.5 billion people without the right glasses they need to see clearly. Some are left without glasses at all (Business Wire, 2022). The pupil programme has been operating since 2015 and is available in over 70 US school districts, providing free vision screenings, eye exams and glasses to schoolchildren (Business Wire, 2022). In 2021, the company launched the Warby Parker impact foundation to solidify their commitment to educating communities on the importance of eye health and providing them with the eye care they need to enjoy the full spectrum of joy that life has to offer. While you can compete on price or quality, or even both, winning brands recognize that they need a mission, real values and a cause to stand out and stand up for something. Only then can they build a tribe. The takeaway here is that any brand must fight or strive for something bigger than just the financials.

Brand story

A brand story is important because it helps consumers understand the value of a product or service. Just like a good book draws readers in and keeps them engaged, a strong brand story can capture a customer's attention and make them more likely to choose that brand over others. A well-crafted brand story can differentiate a company from its competitors and create an emotional connection with consumers. It can also help build trust and credibility, as customers learn about the history and values of the brand. In short, a brand story is like the heart of a company – it gives customers a reason to care about the brand and what it stands for.

A brand story also helps consumers understand the value of a product or service, even if they don't fully understand where the extra cost comes from. For example, luxury lingerie brand La Perla sells high-end items on the high street. They tend to be more expensive than many of their competitors, but why? The original La Perla garments were created in 1954 by Ada Massotti, an Italian corset maker known as 'Golden Scissors' (Bartlett, in Sutherland, 2022; La Perla, 2022). She started her own business to create garments for women, based on what they wanted and tailored to changing trends and desires. This consumer-centric approach has led to products that women can't find elsewhere. Today, the creation of every La Perla garment is overseen by a specialist to ensure the highest standards of quality. This brand story shows that consumers can trust La Perla's products to be of the highest quality, built on a foundation set by a pioneering woman in Italy. This brand story sets La Perla up to command the high prices that it does. If you were unfamiliar with the brand, the high price tag might send you quickly in the other direction. But, if you're of La Perla's target market AND you now know the story behind the brand, it might just compel you to spend the $400 or so to become part of the La Perla story and community. When you 'start with why', as author Simon Sinek puts it, you don't need to resort to manipulations like dropping the price of your product or using time-limited offer tactics; customers are ready and willing to pay more for your product (Sinek, 2011) and the brand substance behind it.

Negative stories

Do your brand stories always have to be positive? Obviously, it is natural to want to communicate your brand in the best light possible, but what about when something sounds too good to be true? Author and branding expert Rory Sutherland gives us the example of budget airlines. Have you ever wondered how these airlines offer such cheap fares in comparison to other airlines? Do they not service their engines? Are their staff not trained properly? Well, no, you probably haven't spent a lot of time thinking about these things, because low-cost airlines are very particular about telling you exactly what you don't get as part of the fare. For example, no meal and no free baggage allowance. These negative stories about the brand serve the purpose of preventing your mind from wandering to extremely negative things like maintenance issues or administration interns promoted to pilot. In this way, negative stories can serve to inoculate your consumers, to avoid worse assumptions being made about your brand, so keep them in your arsenal as a shield should it be wise for your brand to use them (Sutherland, 2022).

Brand equity

Brand equity, while certainly greater than the sum of its parts, is a combination of having an identifiable brand that is well known in your desired target markets, your consumers' perceptions of your brand, and their level of satisfaction built through positive experiences with your brand and your product (Vaidya, 2022). Your brand operates not only as a strong gravitational force that brings customers into your orbit, but also as a cushion for any shocks that would otherwise throw consumers out of your orbit. Consider, for example, in 2009 when the iPhone 4 had antenna issues that prevented users from making phone calls (Arthur and Halliday, 2010). Due to the huge brand equity that Apple had built up over the years, what could have been brand-ending was a simple hiccup that most people have probably even forgotten about by now.

According to branding strategist David Aaker, there are five key components to brand equity (Aaker, 2012):

- **Brand awareness:** how well known is your brand? Key metrics to track here could include not only brand awareness, but also prompted and unprompted brand recall and brand name search volume.
- **Brand loyalty:** exactly how loyal are your customers? Metrics like your customer retention will give you a measure of this; of course, you will need to benchmark it to know how you are performing.
- **Perceived quality:** does your brand have a reputation for delivering good-quality products?
- **Brand associations:** what do people feel when they see your brand?
- **Patents, IP and trading partners:** intellectual capital gives your brand a competitive edge against others.

Looking at Aaker's list, you begin to get a feel for how building brand equity requires the full commitment of the entire cross-functional growth stack. As an example, building awareness through your marketing channels, communicating authenticity through values as well as your UGC and influencers, and building trust and loyalty through effective post-purchase processes such as loyalty programmes and two-way customer service communications with smooth returns and exchanges. Not to mention building quality products via your R&D team and consumer research.

The three pillars of brand building

Once you have built your brand, there are three main aspects you need to communicate and establish in the hearts and minds of consumers: consistency, frequency and anchoring (Eisenberg and Eisenberg, 2006).

Consistency means consistent branding across products and channels, not necessarily sameness. A study by Lucidpress found that 85 per cent of brands had brand guidelines, but only 35 per cent used them consistently, causing two-thirds of companies to deal with off-brand content (marq, 2019). This is costly for brands, with an estimated 23 per cent average revenue increase from consistent branding (Hazzard, 2017).

Frequency means that you need to be establishing your brand as a publisher and a community hub to set the foundation for frequent interactions with your brand. As I mentioned earlier in this book, frequency is essential to establish a sense of familiarity and liking, which are two key elements of influence.

Anchoring means establishing an emotional anchor for customers to attach to, satisfying their social and status needs, and providing them with an unforgettable experience or the ability to rally with their tribe. When you have a well-defined brand image and voice, the emotions they evoke become anchored to your brand symbology (Airey, 2019).

Brand positioning

Brand positioning is understanding and engineering where your brand sits in relation to your competitors on aspects such as product benefits, price and consumer experience. Brand positioning is not something that should just come about without any conscious brand control on your part, which would lead to you potentially occupying a space in no-man's land where your product is not seen as optimally valuable by anyone. Brand positioning is something that needs to be engineered. And to engineer something, you need to work based on first principles. This section will give you ideas as to how you can position yours.

FIGURE 3.2   Brand positioning matrix

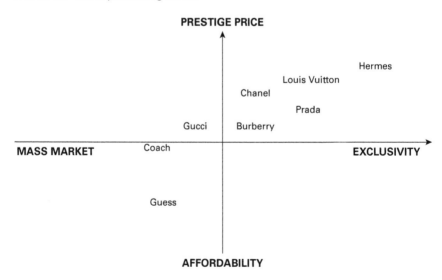

There are three main questions you need to ask yourself when positioning your brand:

- Who is my target market (and most importantly, what do they want)?
- How am I differentiated (through product characteristics, or brand)?
- How do I communicate this to my audience, so they get a sense for what my brand is, what it represents and, most importantly, what it stands for and why?

Huel positioning

Huel is a food and nutrition company that started out with an unfamiliar product, yet was able to grow at such a rapid rate it became the seventh-fastest-growing company in the United Kingdom (Huel, 2020). Typically, the diet and fitness space caters to one of the two main groups – people who want to bulk up, and those who want to slim down. You've probably seen and maybe even tasted both product offerings – bulk-up protein shakes built for the most serious of gym junkies and slim-down healthy meals suited for the most zen among yoga instructors. But Huel manages to do both with their product offering, in a big way. Huel's main positioning comes down to nutritional value and convenience. But they also win out with price, sustainability and plant-based meals, too.

First, convenience… to target anybody from firefighters working shifts to college students cramming for exams who need healthy meals at affordable prices. Customizable subscriptions facilitate habit forming and provide added convenience.

Second, you have nutrition… their products have everything from full meals with 27 vitamins and minerals to protein powders with gut-friendly prebiotics.

Good positioning doesn't have to be rocket science, it just has to find a gap in the market that customers want filled.

Brand voice and tone

Brand voice and brand tone are two elements of a brand's overall identity. While they are related, they are in fact distinct concepts. Brand tone and voice are important because they help a brand to establish its identity and differentiate itself from its competitors. A strong and consistent brand voice helps consumers to recognize and connect with your brand. With so many brands competing for consumers' attention, it's important to have a clear and distinct personality to stand out in a crowded market.

Your brand voice defines the words and language that your brand will use, and remains stable throughout its lifetime. Your brand tone, on the other hand, defines how you will use those words and can change based on your audience and situation. For example, your brand voice may be positive and inspiring like Nike, while your tone is friendly and informative when discussing health and lifestyle. Differentiating your brand with a strong voice is important, as a consumer who can differentiate your brand and is satisfied with your products is 51 per cent more valuable than a satisfied customer who cannot differentiate your brand (Magids et al, 2015). And remember, as Shopify VP of marketing Morgan Brown says, 'Brands that speak to everyone, speak to no one' (Collins, 2022). The fact is, brand voice is just as important as your product, as Lisa Gansky (entrepreneur and author of *The Mesh: Why the future of business is sharing*) says: 'A brand is a voice, and a product is a souvenir' (Air, 2021).

Brand tone, unlike brand voice, is the emotion and inflection that a brand conveys through its messaging. It can change depending on the situation or audience. An example of brand tone would be using a friendly and informative tone as opposed to a scientific and informative tone. The first is conversational, while the second will read more like a research report. Huel, for example, takes a friendly and informative tone when discussing nutrition.

Your tone might also change across platforms or in response to certain events, such as using a more educational and informational tone on platforms like Quora or Reddit, or switching to a more human tone in response to a natural disaster. You may even adjust your tone based on consumer research like British electrical retailer Currys, who found educational messaging to be more effective in getting consumers to purchase tech products than salesy messaging (Hubspot, 2021). This is because consumers wanted to feel like they had a base level of information about tech products before making a purchase. Here's an example:

> Important nutrients include fibre, vitamin K2 and phytonutrients ('phyto' means plant) which are not essential but do provide their own health benefits (Huel, nd).

What I want you to note here is that in brackets – we have 'phyto' and an explanation of what it means. This is perfectly on-brand copy for an accessible and informative tone of voice that is positioned to be as welcoming to the newcomer as it is to the established sports veteran. Adding this clause takes nothing away from the sports veteran's understanding of the text, but adds a world of context to the newcomer who may have never come across the term before. And while I can't show you here in this book, each term such as fibre, vitamin K2 and phytonutrients all contain hyperlinks to Huel-written articles about these specific topics for those that are interested or need to learn more to understand what exactly they are and why they're important (Huel, nd). As Gareth Jones, CMO at e-commerce giant FARFETCH, puts it, customers are busy and have lives to lead, brands need to use language that resonates quickly (Hubspot, 2021).

When it comes to building your brand's tone of voice and maintaining consistency, it is essential to build your brand personality into formalized documents that will help your marketing team act it out in the real world. This often comes in the form of simple dos and don'ts to illustrate where your brand does and does not stand. Like this:

- Don't use jargon or technical language that is difficult for the average person to understand. For example, instead of saying 'Our product utilizes a proprietary algorithm to optimize performance', say 'Our product is designed to help you work efficiently and effectively'.

- Don't use negative or confrontational language. For example, instead of saying 'Our competitors are inferior', say 'Our products offer unique features and benefits that set us apart from the competition'.

- Don't use language that is inappropriate or offensive. For example, avoid using language that is derogatory or that might be considered inappropriate in certain settings.

- Don't use language that is overly casual or informal. For example, avoid using slang or text speak in formal communications, such as emails or business proposals.

It is in this way, through to documentation and formalization of your brand, that your brand's personality begins to take shape, and your marketing team begins to feel the script and personality they are representing when they show up to work every day. It enables your brand to present a strong and unified front, engage with your consumers consistently and build a real relationship as a personality that your consumers can define and understand.

Visual identity

What is in visual identity design

In Chapter 8 we discuss the importance of building tribes and communities through visual identity design. Humans have a natural desire to differentiate themselves and connect with others through branding, and this has been evident throughout history, from local groups and sports teams to cities and countries. When creating your brand identity, it's important to consider the sensory elements of your brand, including the name, colour palette, logo, design and symbology. Packaging is a key aspect of this, as it brings all of these elements together in a physical form. Additionally, don't forget about the sound, smell and touch of your product and packaging. However, it's important to note that design is not just about creating something that looks good – it should also be functional and help achieve your brand goals. As Paul Rand, a renowned US art director, said in 1968, 'Design is the silent ambassador of your brand' (2016).

In today's fast-paced world, where consumers have many options, the physical characteristics of your product, particularly its packaging, play a crucial role in the early stages of their decision-making process (Clement et al, 2013). Even as an e-commerce store, it's important to stand out from the competition, especially on social media feeds where consumers are quickly scrolling through a vast amount of content and products. A great example of packaging that stands out is Who Gives A Crap. Their packaging is bold and easily recognizable, and their copy is consistent and differentiated, with lines like 'beyond the bottom line'. They are unapologetic about their focus on bowel movements and they align their brand values with their mission to use 50 per cent of their profits to build toilets in the developing world (Who Gives a Crap, 2022). Who Gives a Crap is a great example of a company that understands the power of branding and visual identity.

Unboxing and integrating visual identity with the cross-functional growth stack

Attractive packaging has been shown to activate regions in the brain associated with reward, and shut down regions linked to reflection (thinking about the purchase). It even increases the number of impulse buys that people make (Hubert et al, 2013). It really does pay to package your brand well. But it's not just the pre-purchase experience and conversion rates that can be improved with good design. The post-purchase experience is just as valuable to your consumer and to your brand. I bet you were always excited to unwrap any gifts you received as a child. And as a child, it was probably important to you which wrapping paper your gifts came in; maybe you liked cars or your favourite cartoon characters on yours. Well, good branding and packaging sets the stage for you to be able to deliver unboxing experiences to the consumer that excite and engage, just like when you were a child.

As an industry, e-commerce has the potential to be incredibly experiential. Any e-commerce purchase is an exchange of value, and that value is delivered in many different ways. So why stop at your product itself? Your unboxing experience can be one of them, if you do it well.

Smooth, attractive and exciting unboxing experiences will not only be satisfying for your customers as a post-purchase experience; it is something that you can use in your advertising too. That means user-generated content and influencer content showing off your brand's unboxing experience. Walk your consumers through the entire purchase flow with your brand. Show your exciting unboxing experience, or engaging and fun two-way messaging with your support team or chatbot. It's experiences like these that set your brand up to go viral.

Tips for superior unboxing experiences

First, you should definitely be using branded boxes. But go beyond that and make your packaging unique (but sustainable, as your customers are increasingly demanding this from you, and will appreciate that your values align with theirs). Use on-brand packing materials too, like a plain cardboard filler for a rustic feel, or a pink bubble wrap for a cute makeup product.

Don't stop there though. To leverage the concepts outlined in Chapter 6, 'Customer acquisition', provide free samples to not only promote cross-sells in the future, but to trigger reciprocity in your customers. As I will show in Chapter 6, this is a key pillar of influence, and will inspire purchase or repurchase. And to build upon Chapter 9, 'Lifecycle marketing and personalized experiences', include relevant inserts, like a prompt to scan a QR code and sign up for your SMS list. Think about how your unboxing experience can serve the other units of your e-commerce growth stack (and of course provide added value to your customers).

Building your brand

Because this book is focused on giving you not only the ways of thinking you need to form a first principles approach to e-commerce growth, but also the practical building blocks necessary for you to go out into the world and execute on your ambitious growth plans, I want to take a moment to give you a few starting points to begin structuring your own brand identity, resources that you can use in conjunction with this chapter to begin engineering and designing your own brand, to avoid commoditization and the competitive advantages that not building a brand forces you to forfeit. First, I will begin with some helpful models to get you started building your own brand architecture, and then I will show you what to look for in a designer or design firm to begin engineering your own visual identity.

Keller Brand Equity Model

Keller's Customer-Based Brand Equity Model is a useful tool for understanding how to create a strong psychological connection with customers. Its strength lies in its simplicity.

When consumers first encounter your brand in the crowded and competitive e-commerce landscape, they will likely have questions about who you are as a brand. The first thing they may see is one of your products in a video, along with any semiotic associations you have intentionally constructed for your brand image. In the second stage, consumers will evaluate whether your brand delivers on its promises, looking for indicators of performance such as reviews, user-generated content and testimonials. Semiotics will continue to be important to customers at this stage and beyond, even though the Keller model only addresses it in stage two for simplicity's sake.

At the third stage, customers will reflect on and make judgments about your brand, such as its trustworthiness and the experience of using your product (as mentioned earlier, good packaging can help bypass this reflective process and increase impulse purchases of your brand). If these judgments are positive and based on using your product, customers may begin to advocate for it at this stage. To track your performance here, you can use metrics such as Net Promoter Score. To capitalize on this, you can implement referral and affiliate programmes and loyalty programmes. Finally, in the resonance stage, you can secure your customers' loyalty as long as you have done enough to retain them, not just designing a compelling product, but also a compelling brand.

Another model that may be helpful is the Aaker model, also known as the Brand Vision Model or Brand Identity Model. Developed by David Aaker, a US marketing expert who specializes in brand strategy and is a professor emeritus at Berkeley's Haas School of Business, this model is slightly more complex than the Keller model, but you don't have to choose between them – you can benefit from both.

Hiring for visual identity design

Chances are, visual identity design is not something you are going to do in-house. That is typically reserved for the largest of companies. When hiring for visual identity design, consider more than just a company's portfolio. Look for signs of thought leadership, such as consumer psychology research and tactical design implementations, on their website. Also consider how big the company is and how many projects they are taking on at any given time. Do some deep due diligence to evaluate their processes and how well they understand your desired end result. It's a good sign if they require your involvement in each stage and if the process is iterative and tailored to your input. As Fred Hart, creative director and partner at Interact, says, 'A product and commodity just tell you what it is. A brand tells you who it is' (Hart, 2016). Choose a

FIGURE 3.3 Keller's pyramid

designer or branding firm that will help you avoid being commoditized in the market. Finding the right fit from a designer or branding firm is essential to avoid being commoditized in the market. Hart says there are a few things to be aware of when choosing between a freelancer or agency. The first comes down to the thought leadership that I mentioned before. A freelancer is just one person, with their perspective, and is potentially a generalist. An agency on the other hand is made up of multiple individuals, often with specialized niches, which is more likely to give you the well-rounded strategic approach you need to build a brand through visual identity (Hart, 2016).

When you get a commodity, your brand likely doesn't play a large part in the packaging. For example, with a product like coconut juice, with a commodity, the most prominent words on the packaging are likely just that, 'coconut juice'. Hart says that a company with packaging like this is just trying to move product – there's no brand building going on here at all (Hart, 2016). Contrast that with a product such as coconut water from 'Oasis' where on the packaging the brand name is the most prominent component – this is a company trying to build a brand.

Culture as part of your brand

Peter Thiel's most important piece of advice for Airbnb was to 'not **** up the culture' (Chesky, 2014). To the cross-functional e-commerce marketer, company culture is not only a tool for creating winning teams, products and customer service, but also an essential part of your brand image. Company culture is visible in everything your company does and produces. If used

FIGURE 3.4 Commodity vs a brand

wisely, it can provide the foundation for powerful brand stories and help realize your vision. For example, Gymshark's achievement-oriented brand image is reflected not only in their influencers and marketing campaigns, but in their company culture and R&D facilities. The relationship between your company culture and your brand is symbiotic, so it's important to find what binds them together and pay attention to engineering your culture as well as crafting your brand image.

It's no secret that a strong company culture attracts top performers to your business. In the cross-functional e-commerce growth stack, it's people that make the wheel go round. From manufacturing to distribution and everything in between, having top talent on your team sets you apart from the competition. Just as a great brand brings in new customers via referrals, a strong company culture does the same for your workforce. Over two-thirds of workers use referrals from current employees to learn about job opportunities (Pendell and Dvorak, 2018). Acquisition, retention and other stages of the customer journey also apply to your human resources. Advertising your open positions and hiring is acquisition, your onboarding processes are post-purchase flows, and retaining and engaging employees is just as important as retaining and engaging customers.

To attract top employees, you need to have a compelling answer to questions like 'How will I learn and grow at this company?' and 'What does this company stand for?' Gymshark's strong culture has allowed them to attract over 500 specialists to their new Solihull HQ (Cook, 2020), even though Solihull is a town with less than 220,000 residents at the 2021 census (ONS, 2022). Every action you take as a brand introduces something to your company culture, whether positive or negative. A healthy culture, founded on your brand mission, values and story, gives your team meaning, which has been shown to increase the quality of their work (Chandler and Kapelner, 2013). At the end of the day, it's talent, people, that make up your company core and your brand core.

Wrapping up

Congratulations on reaching the end of your journey in learning the fundamentals of building a powerful brand identity. It's definitely a unique skill that will set you apart as a marketer and as a brand. Now that you have a strong foundation in brand tone, voice, visual identity design and more, it's time to put your brand to work and start scaling. In the next chapter, we'll be diving into customer behaviour, which will transform the way you view people and their buying behaviours all through the e-commerce sales funnel. So let's get started!

References

Aaker, DA (2012) Win the brand relevance battle and then build competitor barriers, *California Management Review*, 54 (2), pp 43–57, doi:10.1525/cmr.2012.54.2.43 (archived at https://perma.cc/C2MN-Q88T)

Air (2021) 35 branding quotes to inspire your next design project,16 Jun, https://air.inc/blog/branding-quotes (archived at https://perma.cc/3UQY-CH5L)

Airey, D (2019) *Identity Designed: The definitive guide to visual branding*, Rockport Publishers, Beverly, MA

Arthur, C and Halliday, J (2010) Apple shares dip amid iPhone 4 recall uncertainty, *The Guardian*, 14 Jul, www.theguardian.com/technology/2010/jul/14/apple-shares-dive-iphone4-criticism (archived at https://perma.cc/5ARS-CAER)

Bombas (2023) About Us, https://bombas.com/pages/about-us (archived at https://perma.cc/T946-WW9R)

Business Wire (2022) Warby Parker publishes its 2021 Impact Report, *Yahoo! Finance*, 21 Apr, https://au.finance.yahoo.com/news/warby-parker-publishes-2021-impact-152500055.html (archived at https://perma.cc/R9JJ-SANL)

Casper Sleep Inc (2023) Our Story, https://casper.com/about.html (archived at https://perma.cc/U7HF-ZMD8)

Chandler, D and Kapelner, A (2013) Breaking monotony with meaning: Motivation in crowdsourcing markets, *Journal of Economic Behavior & Organization*, 90, pp. 123–33, doi:10.1016/j.jebo.2013.03.003 (archived at https://perma.cc/DRW9-HUEL).

Chesky, B (2014) *Don't Fuck Up the Culture*, Medium, 20 Apr, https://medium.com/@bchesky/dont-fuck-up-the-culture-597cde9ee9d4 (archived at https://perma.cc/KF3L-ATMG)

Clement, J, Kristensen, T and Grønhaug, K (2013) Understanding consumers' in-store visual perception: The influence of package design features on visual attention, *Journal of Retailing and Consumer Services*, 20 (2), pp 234–39, www.academia.edu/16724679/Understanding_consumers_in-store_visual_perception_The_influence_of_package_design_features_on_visual_attention (archived at https://perma.cc/CGE8-JYJK)

Collins, A (2022) What is brand voice and how to create one for your business, *Shopify*, 9 Mar, www.shopify.com/au/blog/brand-voice (archived at https://perma.cc/GZ5D-ESEB)

Cook, J (2020) How Gymshark became a $1.3 billion brand, and what we can learn, *Forbes*, 17 Aug, www.forbes.com/sites/jodiecook/2020/08/17/how-gymshark-became-a-13bn-brand-and-what-we-can-learn/?sh=2007570476ed (archived at https://perma.cc/RB73-SM39)

Eisenberg, B and Eisenberg, J (2006) *Waiting for Your Cat to Bark?: Persuading customers when they ignore marketing*, Thomas Nelson, Nashville, TN

Hart, F (2016)) What your branding partner needs from you Fred Hart, Creative Director, Interact, YouTube, 4 Aug, www.youtube.com/watch?v=VWVJSOb6EEw (archived at https://perma.cc/5LJV-VKWR)

Hazzard, TL (2017) If you want to make 23% more money, then get consistent: From the experts, everything you need to know on branding consistently for higher visibility and more revenue, *Inc.com*, www.inc.com/tracy-leigh-hazzard/boost-profit-with-constant-brand-consistency.html (archived at https://perma.cc/NE52-T6Y5)

Hubert, M, Hubert, M, Florack, A, Linzmajer, M and Kenning, P (2013) Neural correlates of impulsive buying tendencies during perception of product packaging, *Psychology & Marketing*, 30 (10), pp 861–73, https://onlinelibrary.wiley.com/doi/abs/10.1002/mar.20651 (archived at https://perma.cc/5S75-H7NP)

Hubspot (2021) Brand voice comes of age: as culture, technology and mindsets evolve, https://f.hubspotusercontent20.net/hubfs/4094824/Brand_Voice_Comes_of_Age_OP.pdf (archived at https://perma.cc/7RZ9-ACQ9)

Huel (2020) Huel are the 7th fastest growing private company in the UK, 20 Dec, https://discuss.huel.com/t/huel-are-the-7th-fastest-growing-private-company-in-the-uk/19738 (archived at https://perma.cc/RVE8-W4JD)

Huel (nd) Why you should care about a nutritionally complete diet, https://huel.com/pages/why-you-should-care-about-a-nutritionally-complete-diet (archived at https://perma.cc/7BLV-LH5H)

Interbrand (2021) Best Global Brands, https://interbrand.com/best-global-brands/ (archived at https://perma.cc/T736-2Y4L)

Keegan, TR, Moriarty, WJ, Duncan, S and Duncan, T (1995) *Marketing*, Prentice Hall, New York, NY

La Perla (2022) Breaking the bias: let's celebrate International Women's Day, Beautybylaperla, www.beautybylaperla.com/blog/breaking-the-bias-let-s-celebrate-international-women-s-day?setCurrencyId=1 (archived at https://perma.cc/7DCT-X824)

Magids, S, Zorfas, A and Leemon, D (2015) The new science of customer emotions, *Harvard Business Review*, Nov, https://hbr.org/2015/11/the-new-science-of-customer-emotions (archived at https://perma.cc/MKP4-SSPK)

marq (2019) Brand consistency – the competitive advantage and how to achieve it, 12 Nov, www.marq.com/blog/brand-consistency-competitive-advantage (archived at https://perma.cc/X5MW-W2GW)

ONS (Office For National Statistics) (2022) How the population changed in Solihull, Census 2021, ONS, 28 Jun, www.ons.gov.uk/visualisations/censuspopulationchange/E08000029/ (archived at https://perma.cc/243M-ASE8)

Pendell, R and Dvorak, N (2018) Culture wins by attracting the top 20% of candidates, *Gallup*, 28 Jun, www.gallup.com/workplace/237368/culture-wins-attracting-top-candidates.aspx (archived at https://perma.cc/H9L3-WDYL)

Rand, P (2016) *A Designer's Art*, Princeton Architectural Press, NJ

Sinek, S (2011) *Start with Why: How great leaders inspire everyone to take action*, Portfolio, New York, NY

Sutherland, R (2019) *Alchemy: The surprising power of ideas that don't make sense*, WH Allen, London

Sutherland, R (2022) The Diary of a CEO: the marketing secrets Apple & Tesla always use: Rory Sutherland, Apple Podcasts, 31 Jul, https://podcasts.apple.com/us/podcast/e165-the-marketing-secrets-apple-tesla-always-use/id1291423644?i=1000574601018 (archived at https://perma.cc/6FHS-XTVW)

Vaidya, D (2022) Brand equity, *WallStreetMojo*, www.wallstreetmojo.com/brand-equity/ (archived at https://perma.cc/BF4A-3KZZ)

Who Gives a Crap (2022) Meet our impact partners, https://blog.whogivesacrap.org/home/gooddeeds/who-give-a-crap-charity-partners (archived at https://perma.cc/YG23-K9S6)

Further reading

Godin, S (2018) *This is Marketing: You can't be seen until you learn to see*, Portfolio/Penguin, New York, NY

Gosset, S (2021) Exploring Semiotics in Marketing, *Builtin*, 2 Mar, https://builtin.com/marketing/semiotics-examples (archived at https://perma.cc/4U6E-Z3UJ)

Ingrassia, L (2021) *Billion Dollar Brand Club: How Dollar Shave Club, Warby Parker, and other disruptors are remaking what we buy*, St. Martin's Griffin, New York, NY

Malinic, R (2019) *Book of Branding: A guide to creating brand identity for start-ups and beyond*, Brand Nu Limited, Kingston upon Thames

Miller, D (2017) *Building a Storybrand: Clarify your message so customers will listen*, HarperCollins Leadership, New York, NY

Rozdeba Brand & Co. (2020) The who, what, how & why of a brand, *The Startup*, 17 Mar, https://medium.com/swlh/the-who-what-how-why-of-a-brand-2d56fafab14 (archived at https://perma.cc/UYX2-WQA5)

Sign Salad (2016) What is Semiotics?, https://signsalad.com/our-thoughts/what-is-semiotics/ (archived at https://perma.cc/4WTN-AZA5)

Sinek, S (2011) *Start With Why: How great leaders inspire everyone to take action*, Portfolio/Penguin, New York, NY

4

Consumer behaviour

This book approaches growing an e-commerce business or digital-native consumer brand from two fundamental perspectives: the first is that growth does not only hinge on marketing alone but is a cross-functional growth effort, and the second is that of customer-centricity – meaning your operational optimization should focus on profitably improving the experience of your customers.

Customer-centric e-commerce growth must absolutely start with a deep understanding of your customer. Without a deep behavioural understanding of your audience's pain points, values, wants, needs and desires, sustained growth would be impossible. This chapter is probably the most important in the entire book because it lays in the fundamental principles in psychology and neuroscience that address customer behaviour in the context of transactional e-commerce experiences.

I have broken down the fundamental customer-centric principles along the line of a standard e-commerce sales funnel: **Awareness > Consideration > Action**.

Consumer behaviour is a study of the decision-making process that individuals undergo when making purchases, and so is a fine blend of neuroscience, psychology and economics.

How our brains are fundamentally wired

With the rise of e-commerce, consumers are no longer limited to shopping within a certain radius of their home. This means that their pool of choices has become almost infinite. The study of consumer behaviour is not new, but it has become increasingly important in the era of e-commerce. In the past, a brand's success could be based on its proximity to consumers, rather than on a competitive advantage derived from a deep understanding of consumer psychology. Today, with millions of online stores and marketplaces available to customers, consumer behaviour and understanding human psychology are essential for success. There are no competitive advantages to be gained from geographical proximity.

The competitive advantages of today come from psychological proximity. Without the constraints of geography, consumers are becoming more attuned to which brands truly satisfy their psychological needs and desires and which do not. When we think of intelligence, we often think of great minds from the past and present, such as Musk, Nietzsche, Tesla and others. These are the products of our neocortex, the part of the brain that controls logic, analysis, rational thought, language, morality and the regulation of emotions. However, the human brain is much more than that. In fact, the neocortex is the most recently developed part of our cognitive architecture. Older parts of the brain, often referred to as the 'lizard brain' because of their early development and more primitive nature, control our basic needs such as breathing, temperature, hunger, thirst, danger avoidance, territoriality and reproduction.

Between the neocortex and the lizard brain is the mammalian brain, which controls memory, sociability and emotions such as anger, maternal love, anxiety and jealousy. These areas of the brain, the lizard and mammalian brains, make up a significant part of our cognitive architecture and serve as the foundation for our survival. They are also the areas that marketing typically targets. However, this was not always the case. In the past, the marketing industry followed the general population in its admiration of logic, analysis and rational thought. (In truth, many marketers still fall into this way of thinking today, but it is not the only ingredient in a successful marketing strategy, nor is it the most important.) In 1994, Antonio Damasio, a neuroscience professor, published a book titled *Descartes' Error: Emotion, reason and the human brain* (Damasio, 1994).

To call out Descartes, one of the most famous philosophers of all time, is no small feat. Damasio's book marked the beginning of the emotional renaissance in fields such as neuroscience and highlighted the importance of emotion not only as a standalone function, but as a part of reasoning. Emotion aids and enhances our ability to reason and can even take over

FIGURE 4.1 Three brain systems that control your behaviour: reptilian, limbic, neocortex

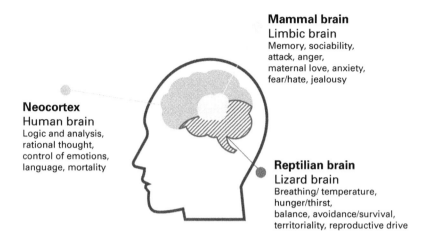

Mammal brain
Limbic brain
Memory, sociability,
attack, anger,
maternal love, anxiety,
fear/hate, jealousy

Neocortex
Human brain
Logic and analysis,
rational thought,
control of emotions,
language, mortality

Reptilian brain
Lizard brain
Breathing/ temperature,
hunger/thirst,
balance, avoidance/survival,
territoriality, reproductive drive

when there is no time for thinking and reasoning. Damasio's findings showed that people with damaged brains who were unable to process emotions also struggled to make decisions, even those that were based on logic and reasoning. This was because they lacked the emotional component that would have made them feel good about their decisions.

So, what does this mean for the marketing and advertising world? Does it mean that decision making is all about emotions? This is what many people took away from Damasio's book, but it is not true. Decision making is not 100 per cent emotional and 0 per cent rational. However, without emotion, it is difficult to engage customers and even harder to convert them. If this helps you in your marketing efforts, then great, but remember that emotion and reason are not mutually exclusive. They are both essential components of a successful marketing strategy.

To map the needs and cognitive functions of the lizard and mammalian brains and the neocortex, let's take a look at Maslow's hierarchy of needs, the brainchild of Abraham Maslow, a US professor of psychology. The lizard brain is highly attuned to concerns of physiology and safety, the mammalian brain to not only love and belonging but our emotions in general, as well as esteem needs. And the neocortex, just as this part of the brain developed to enable us to become more than we were, is concerned with actualization and helping us become the most that we can be.

FIGURE 4.2   Maslow's hierarchy of needs

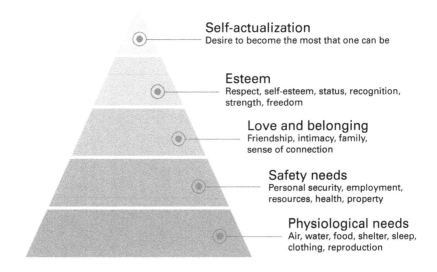

To map these needs to selling a consumer brand in a digital environment, you need both an understanding of the emotions that could underpin a purchase decision and an understanding of your target market and how they might relate to your offering. As an example, some of the basic emotions typically targeted in marketing are pride (or status), greed, fear, love and guilt. Dan Kennedy, one of the most revered copywriters and marketing consultants in the world, in his book *No B.S. Marketing to the Affluent* shows just how these emotions translate to a product and a prospect match, i.e. your offer and your target market (Kennedy, 2015). And when you understand your customer, you can be much more granular with the emotions targeted. As an example, Dan shows that a luxury customer buying a new Ferrari likely has some very specific emotions that can be linked very much to the esteem level of Maslow's hierarchy of needs, exactly where you would expect someone wealthy enough to consider buying a Ferrari to be (Kennedy, 2015). Emotions like insecurity with new social status, the fear of being found out to be a faker (i.e. not deserving their social status), to affirm their self-esteem or as a personal reward as recognition of their hard work. They may even see the new Ferrari as a way to achieve love and intimacy, or to achieve a sense of belonging with a new social group such as a car enthusiasts' club (Kennedy, 2015).

Other things that you can use to target customers who are concerned with higher-order needs are:

- Competition: 'My neighbour just bought a new Porsche, so I need to one-up him with a new Range RO.'

- Trendsetting: 'The new iPhone just came out, I need to get one.'

- Instant gratification: 'I'm bored or feeling down, I need something to lift my mood.'

- Leadership: 'Patagonia is changing the world for the better. I think everyone who can afford to support Patagonia should support their cause, so I'm going to lead the way.'

- Time: 'Since the Tesla is self-driving, I'll be able to get back an hour each day by answering my emails on the way to work and back.'

FIGURE 4.3 Balanced messaging across function and emotion is most likely to drive sales regardless of brand type

Ads with messages that are both emotional and rational see slightly better results

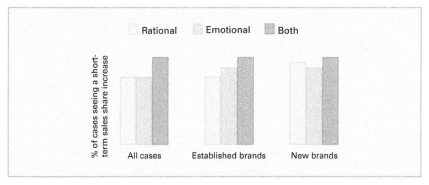

- For NEW brands, ads with rational messages tend to show a very slightly higher likelihood of success than those with purely emotional messages.
- For ESTABLISHED brands, the opposite is seen.
- For ALL brands, however, the highest likelihood is seen where the messages communicated are both rational and emotional in nature.

Bases : All cases = 1795: Established brands = 1359; New brands = 436. The relevant CS team determine the nature of the messages communicated.
Research by Kantar Millward Brown

SOURCE Kantar

But again, it's not all emotions. Empirically speaking, a mixture of both rational messaging and emotional messaging outperforms either strategy alone. This holds true for both small and established brands. In fact, for small brands, emotion alone can be less effective than marketing messaging based on rationality.

Just be careful with emotions like guilt or shame, because they involve self-accountability, which can stir up negative emotions. And while negative emotions are memorable, negative emotions attached to self-accountability can repel consumers. Although, on the other hand, it is self-accountability that can spur action – so when using emotions like guilt or shame, make sure you walk the consumer to the power of self-accountability and the potential desirable future they can have. Don't simply leave them wallowing in self-pity with negative associations of your brand (Janssen, 2018).

Your funnel psychology

Rather than fill this chapter with a lot of tips, tricks and psychological hacks and have you finishing it with a whole lot of new knowledge but no road-map for actually applying it, in this chapter I will break down each stage of the e-commerce funnel and show you how to optimize it. Having problems at the top of your funnel? Come back to the attention and awareness section of this chapter. Having trouble with acquiring new customers? Come back to the decision/action section. Having trouble with retention? Come back to the retention section. The three main steps you need to take your customer through to get the sale are attention and awareness, consideration and decision/action. First, I will break down your general strategy for each stage of the funnel, and then we will move into the specific psychological hacks that bring consumers closer into your orbit and eventually turn them into part of your tribe.

Attention/awareness

FIGURE 4.4 Psychology and neuromarketing toolset at the brand awareness phase

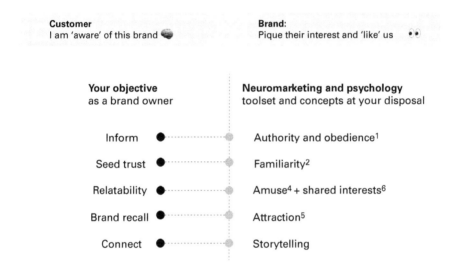

1. Inform from a point of Authority to trigger Obedience
2. We like and trust people who are members of our own social group more than we like outsiders or strangers. This in-group effect is so powerful that even random assignment into small groups is sufficient to create a sense of solidarity (https://hbr.org/2009/06/rethinking-trust)
3. The Psychology of Attention: 10 lessons for web writers from Deez Nuts (www.orbitmedia.com/blog/the-psychology-of-attention/)
4. It has long been known that experiences that elicit arousal are more likely to be remembered than experiences that do not evoke an emotional response. This emotional memory enhancement has been demonstrated across a range of paradigms and using a variety of stimuli (www.ncbi.nlm.nih.gov/pmc/articles/PMC2676782/)
5. & 6. We like people who are similar to us (www.psychologytoday.com/gb/blog/close-encounters/201812/why-do-we-people-who-are-similar-us)

Typical channels awareness takes place:

- Social advertising
- Recommendations from influencers
- Podcast mention or podcast ad
- Video: YouTube
- Article
- WOM (word of mouth)
- Search ad
- Product discovery on a marketplace or another channel

Psychologist William James wrote that attention is the mind being taken possession of, in a clear and vivid form, by one single train object out of many potential trains of thought (Lindsay, 2020). The human brain is bombarded with almost endless amounts of information throughout the day. Whether we like it or not, there is always something vying for our attention. This can include the conditions and other drivers on the road, billboard advertisements or the push notifications on our phones. Apps like TikTok expose us to dozens of advertisements per minute, whether they are explicit paid ads or user-generated content. When selling consumer packaged goods, it is important to stand out from competitors or risk being drowned out by them. The stakes in e-commerce are high, with the level of marketing seen during peak shopping periods becoming everyday reality.

The attention and awareness stage is crucial in the customer journey. In addition to capturing the initial attention of the consumer, it is important to seed information that will be discussed in more detail later in the funnel. During the awareness stage, the consumer needs to be informed, trust needs to be built, relatability and connection need to be established, and brand recall needs to be generated. To set the brand up for success, authority, familiarity and relatability must be established, and the customer's heart and mind must be captured. This can be achieved through various channels and tactics, such as paid ads, podcasts, videos, written content like blogs, word of mouth or channel strategy.

Attention begins with searching or scanning, during which people decide if something is interesting to them or not, often in less than a second. If the consumer decides that the content is worthy of their attention, they move into sustained attention, giving the brand a chance to seed the full suite of conversion tools that will be built upon throughout the funnel. In order to satisfy the conscious or unconscious desires of an awareness stage customer, it is important to make them feel informed, able to trust the brand, connected to the brand and its story, and to establish a degree of relatability between the brand and the customer. In the following section, we will break down how to do this for an awareness stage customer.

The key insights into satisfying the conscious or unconscious desires of an awareness stage customer are:

- Consumers want and need to feel informed
- People need to trust you to buy from you
- They also want to feel a degree of relatability between them and your brand
- It's important that they feel connected to your brand and its story

Information needs in today's digital age are satisfied by all kinds of content – content marketing strategies should be tailored to the needs of the audience, and specifically to the concerns and pain points they might have during their journey. Throughout this book you will uncover a myriad of tools at your disposal to achieve this, such as SEO, social media and email marketing. But these tools are nothing without a core understanding of the consumer psychology that you need to target them towards. Later in this book you will also learn about the key foundational elements of brand persona, values, story and voice. In essence, when building an e-commerce brand, you are birthing a new personality into the world – that is no easy task. All the personality you have, the personal values, the aspirations, everything you're for and against – it's a lot. How you speak, the predominant mannerisms. There's a lot of there. And to build a brand you have to imagine this for your company and then, the hardest part, bring it into being. So, just getting attention is no easy task. It takes a lot of work to even get there. And then you've got to get people to actually consider your brand, which is what we will cover next.

Consideration

FIGURE 4.5 Psychology and neuromarketing toolset at the consideration phase

CONDSIDERATION **2**

At this stage, brand owners should focus on demonstrating as much **value as possible to shoppers and their audience.** Brands are essentially selling the future pleasure that would be derived from consuming this brand's product. In commerce, **value = future pleasure**

Customer:
I know the brand, should I buy
from them?

Brand:
How can we demonstrate and
deliver value?

Your objective
as a brand owner

Neuromarketing and psychology
toolset and concepts at your disposal

Problem restatement[1] ●·············● Amplify pain

Demonstrae value[2] ●·············● Stimulate pleasure or sell the idea
that your brand or product delivers a
solution or pleasurable experience

Reinforce trust ●·············● Social proof[3]

Instant gratification[4] ●·············● Your offer must include the option
to deliver your value or pleasure
as promptly as possible; like
availability in-store or on Amazon

1. 7 common examples of customer's pain points (https://sellingrevolution.com/blog/7-common-examples-of-customers-pain-points/)
2. Recognizing it as valuable validates those who choose to pursue the interesting, and also opens up a new dimension of value that can enrich our lives. Most of us know there is more to life than pleasure, yet it is all too easy to choose our experiences for the sake of pleasure. For many of us, though, interesting experiences are more rewarding than pleasurable experiences, insofar as their intrinsic value is a product of multifaceted aspects of our engagement. Interesting experiences spark the mind in a way that stimulates and lingers. They can also be easy to come by – sometimes just a sense of curiosity is needed to make an activity interesting. Look around, feel the pull and cherish the interesting (www.fastcompany.com/90247237/what-makes-a-person-or-experience-interesting)
3. The selling power of social proof (www.bigcommerce.com/blog/social-proof-examples/)
4. How Freud's pleasure principle works (www.verywellmind.com/what-is-the-pleasure-principle-2795472)

Typical channels consideration takes place:

- Website

- Marketplace or other channel

- Owned marketing channels: website, email, social media pages

- Influencers demonstrating product

- Product demos

- Articles, tutorials, guides

- Product pages

- Owned marketing channels: website, email marketing, social profiles

- Retargeting

- Consumer carting deeper research

- Search engine result page

- Additional recommendations

- Brand/product seen again on a marketplace or other channel

At the consideration stage, the customer understands that they have a problem that they would like to solve. This problem could be anything from back pain to boredom to a desire for greater social connection. However, the customer may not know exactly how they want to solve it. This means that competition at this stage is much broader than just competing with direct competitors who sell similar products. It also includes all available solutions that the customer is aware of. For example, a person with back pain could choose to use a back-straightening device that buzzes when it senses bad posture, pain-soothing gel, ultrasound therapy or an exercise programme. This means there are many available options.

As a brand owner, it is important to focus on demonstrating as much value as possible to the audience, satisfying their informational needs and amplifying key marketing messages. Amplify the pain point that is driving the customer to consider making a purchase, stimulate the pleasure that the brand delivers, communicate the values behind the brand and show why the customer should choose it. Ideally, do all of these things and add some social proof for good measure. Don't forget lessons from Freud – we like instant gratification, so communicate that the customer will get the value or pleasure they seek as soon as possible. At the consideration stage, it is important to utilize the full suite of conversion-optimizing touchpoints.

This means engaging and optimizing the website, email marketing and social media profiles – all of what we call 'owned' marketing channels. Retargeting should be used to keep customers in the consideration stage (and not buying from someone else) and an omnichannel retail strategy should be implemented to recognize the power of distribution in creating new organic options for retargeting. This will have the customer coming across the brand on multiple touchpoints because the distribution strategy has been successful. Later, in Chapter 12, we will show you exactly how to do this. The consideration stage is critical because even though the customer's search will begin with the initial set of brands they are aware of and can recall, the set of available brands may actually expand during their research and consideration stage (Court et al, 2009). Earlier in the awareness stage, the brand was fighting for attention, but now the real competition begins. Consumers put the brand through an increasingly demanding set of evaluations to see if it is the right brand for them.

Decision/action

FIGURE 4.6 Psychology and neuromarketing toolset at the decision and action phase

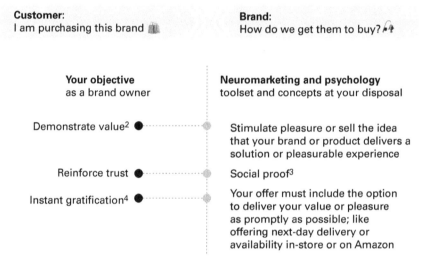

3 ▶▶▶ **DECISION/ACTION**

At this stage, brand owners should focus on converting **shoppers into their customers**. Figuring out the intrinsic motivation for the potential purchase will unlock ways to softly persuade a conversion

Customer:
I am purchasing this brand 🛍

Brand:
How do we get them to buy? 📢

Your objective
as a brand owner

Neuromarketing and psychology
toolset and concepts at your disposal

Demonstrate value[2] ●·············○ Stimulate pleasure or sell the idea that your brand or product delivers a solution or pleasurable experience

Reinforce trust ●·············○ Social proof[3]

Instant gratification[4] ●·············○ Your offer must include the option to deliver your value or pleasure as promptly as possible; like offering next-day delivery or availability in-store or on Amazon

1. 7 common examples of customer's pain points (https://sellingrevolution.com/blog/7-common-examples-of-customers-pain-points/)
2. Recognizing it as valuable validates those who choose to pursue the interesting, and also opens up a new dimension of value that can enrich our lives. Most of us know there is more to life than pleasure, yet it is all too easy to choose our experiences for the sake of pleasure. For many of us, though, interesting experiences are more rewarding than pleasurable experiences, insofar as their intrinsic value is a product of multifaceted aspects of our engagement. Interesting experiences spark the mind in a way that stimulates and lingers. They can also be easy to come by – sometimes just a sense of curiosity is needed to make an activity interesting. Look around, feel the pull and cherish the interesting (www.fastcompany.com/90247237/what-makes-a-person-or-experience-interesting)
3. The selling power of social proof (www.bigcommerce.com/blog/social-proof-examples/)
4. How Freud's pleasure principle works (www.verywellmind.com/what-is-the-pleasure-principle-2795472)

Typical channels awareness takes place:

- Website checkout flow
- Marketplace or other channel
- Shoppable link, video and other channels

At the decision stage, you are compelling your *potential* customer to take action. Key channels for your brand at this stage, and key areas for optimization, include your product detail page (PDP), website checkout flow, your marketplace listings, packaging or other 'last-mile' channels that enable your customers to purchase from the channels they prefer and that are most convenient for them, and any other directly shoppable channels like shoppable social media and videos.

Your key objectives at this stage, as a brand owner, are to convert your customer, reinforce instant gratification and reinforce trust.

To get your customers over the line, though, you may need to make use of psychological tactics like scarcity and time-limited offers to evoke fear of missing out (FOMO) and compel them to make a buying decision. Just don't use fake scarcity; having a limited-time sale is fine, so is offering an exclusive time-limited discount – telling people that there are only five items left when in fact there are 500, however, is not.

The psychological building blocks of a brand strategy

Capturing attention

Our brains are hardwired to pay attention to things that signal danger, suggest entertainment or arouse curiosity. This is because our brains have evolved to help us avoid pain and seek pleasure. Anything that suggests either pleasure or pain will capture our attention, whether we are in the African savannah facing lions and hippos, in a shopping mall enjoying the sights and sounds, or online being targeted by advertisers who seek to persuade us to buy their products by appealing to our fears and insecurities.

Danger

When we see something that might be dangerous, we instinctively go into high alert and focus our attention on the potential threat. This response likely saved our lives on the savannah, and while we have learned to turn off or slow down this response in modern environments, our brains still have an attraction to danger. This is evident in our online behaviour, where headlines with negative tones aimed at avoiding pain receive an average click-through rate that is over 60 per cent higher than headlines with positive tones suggesting the acquisition of something pleasurable. Brands can capture our attention by conveying danger through shocking statistics, disastrous potential consequences and highlighting pain points.

Entertainment

Entertainment is any situation or activity that provides pleasure (Zillman and Bryant, 2004 in Shrum, 2004). The need for entertainment is strong, as demonstrated by a US study showing that respondents would require at least one million dollars in compensation to give up watching television (Mazzocco et al, 2003 in Shrum, 2004). Sigmund Freud, the founder of psychoanalysis, believed that the human psyche consists of an id, ego and superego. Freud's psychoanalytic theory of personality suggests that the id is driven by the pleasure principle, which is the desire for pleasure and the avoidance of pain (Evan, 2022; Cherry, 2022). In other words, our psyche pushes us toward entertainment and other forms of pleasure. All of this holds great power for the e-commerce marketer who knows how to wield it effectively. It can even make a potato peeler the hottest product in New York and make the man selling them a multimillionaire.

What am I talking about? I'm talking about one of the greatest illustrations of entertainment as a tool for garnering attention and gaining the time to get your target market to consider your product. Joe Ades, known as the 'Gentleman Grafter', was able to turn a potato peeler into a highly entertaining product on the streets of New York for many years. His charismatic character and entertaining vegetable peeling routine earned him millions and allowed him to put his granddaughters through college. Ades was known for making the mundane extraordinary, and his daughter Ruth recalls working with him selling bed sheets at a market in Wales, where he famously said, 'you put these on your bed and you'll be on a second honeymoon' (Bergner, 2009). Ades' success may seem surprising, given that he was operating in a city with a population of around 7–8 million, but he was already driving a Rolls-Royce in Australia, where the largest city at the time had a population of around only 2 million (Bergner, 2009). Ades' pitch was simple and effective: 'Just come up a yard, I want to show you how this works, I won't ask you for money' (CBS, 2010). He then demonstrated the value of his product by slicing sunflower-shaped pieces from carrots. He also understood his customers and addressed their concerns, saying, 'you do that for the kids, they'll eat their vegetables' (Bergner, 2009). Ades' ability to combine value propositions and entertainment made him successful, and his approach is still relevant today. Modern marketers who use engaging and entertaining routines on platforms like TikTok can drive millions in revenues for their clients, just as Moshe Saraf, a guest on episode 251 of the 2X eCommerce podcast, does with his performance marketing powerhouse, Pareto Solutions, which promotes brands such as Eko, Fiverr, Nectar Sleep and Mixtiles.

Inform

In the current era, known as the information age, we have access to almost immediate information on any topic. This has changed the way brands and consumers interact. In the past, if a consumer wanted to compare products, they would need the support of a knowledgeable sales representative. Now, consumers can research all the information they need online and may never have to interact with a person throughout their entire customer journey. However, while a salesperson can adapt to a consumer's needs in real time, digital content cannot. To provide a personalized customer journey, brands need to replicate the role of the salesperson in digital form. This requires customer journey optimization with explicit consideration of a consumer's informational needs as they traverse the digital landscape at different stages of the buying journey. Not to mention that different segments will have different informational needs altogether. But it's not about just bombarding customers with all the information you can throw at them. In the information age, the power really is in the consumer's hands. But with great power comes great responsibility, and consumers are often faced with the tyranny of choice, find themselves gripped by analysis paralysis and deal with more complexity than ever before – this makes it even harder for consumers to make decisions (The Economist, 2010). Too much information and choice is just as bad as not enough. As a brand owner, you are the facilitator of consumers' informational search processes – often this means your task is not to provide more information, but to assist your consumer by providing only the most relevant information.

Let's take an example from Dan McGaw, founder of McGaw.io and customer data specialist. Dan worked with a vegan food brand, but not just any vegan food brand – a mission-based vegan food brand. What is the difference between a vegan food brand and a mission-based vegan food brand, you might ask? A vegan food brand might be content selling to vegans. A mission-based vegan food brand is driven to convert as many potential consumers into vegans as possible. But everyone who comes to their site is at a different stage in their vegan journey, and the only way to know where is to ask them – only then can a relevant customer journey, complete with relevant information flows, be presented to the customer. The informational needs for a first-time vegan shopper versus a vegan veteran are night and day. The complexity of the recipes, where in the flow you offer for them to join your community, which community you offer them to join first, everything.

Consumers are looking for three main things from your brand when it comes to the information you provide. They want:

- Informativeness: that means you cover all the features and benefits that are most important to them.

- Ease of understanding: it's one thing to have a comprehensive and informative content strategy, but if it is not easily understood, then the effect you have will be negligible and may even turn your customers off.

- Involving qualities: your content needs to engage, by satisfying the very core psychological needs we outline in this chapter.

Authority

Authority is rated as one of the three most persuasive aspects of marketing messaging (Moore et al, 2018). The other aspects, by the way, were *authenticity* and *likeability*.

When it comes to authority there are two general ways to go about building it. You can either build it yourself through thought leadership and building your brand into a recognized and desirable player in your industry, or you can borrow it from an already established authority figure. The latter, borrowing authority, is one of the core reasons brands engage in celebrity endorsements and build an army of influencers. Of course, as a brand, you should be doing both. Subtle ways brands use authority in their marketing include Apple's 'Genius Bar', which uses the pre-built authority inherent in the cultural associations we typically have with a genius. It communicates not only expertise in the product, but also a level of intellect exceeding the average person.

Trust

Trust is the constant across all stages of the funnel. In the beginning, you will be seeding trust and then building on that foundation, and finally, after the sale is made, solidifying the customer's decision to trust you. How well you seed and build upon trust at one level will affect the level of trust you are able to generate at the next stage in the funnel and will significantly influence the success you have in getting your customers to make important decisions like purchase and repurchase.

When consumers begin browsing, they're looking for signs that they can trust your brand. Things like site reviews, product reviews and customer recommendations all signal social proof. Social proof is a heuristic that reduces the cognitive load of our decision-making processes, it boosts the reputation of your brand and product in the eyes of consumers, and has bundled within the suggestion of many other desirable characteristics (Amblee and Bui, 2011). Make sure your rating- and review-gathering process is efficient, and that they are displayed prominently on your site and social channels. You should also build trust into your offer with things like money-back guarantees and warranties. Some other ways you can generate trust and reduce perceived risk include:

- case studies
- testimonials
- expert reviews
- guaranteed delivery dates
- try before you buy
- security badges on your site
- SSL certificates
- trial offers – first month of a subscription might be a free + shipping offer

Good brand visual identity and website design also give your brand heightened credibility and trust (Lowry et al, 2013). What you are aiming to do when communicating your trustworthiness on your website is move the relationship between you and your customer from being one of faith ('I believe in the goodness of others') to trust ('I trust that this company will deliver') to confidence ('I know that this company will deliver').

Relatability

By providing customers with content that is useful and relevant to their needs, you will be able to establish yourself as an authority in your niche. But it is through creating a brand persona that resonates with your customers and creating stories that show your values, that customers will be able to identify and relate to your brand. Having a consistent set of traits that your target customer segment enjoys will help increase your brand equity and influence. By understanding your customers' needs and providing them with content that speaks to them, you will be able to increase your influence, make more sales and, most importantly, build a community.

Consider how Patagonia's marketing speaks to their customers and how it is very much a 'heart on your sleeve' statement to all out there. If you don't know what I am talking about, Patagonia is a mission-driven brand trying to take on waste in the clothing industry. How? By using over 80 per cent recycled materials in their clothing, and donating 1 per cent of all sales to charity – it's their self-imposed earth tax (Matthews, 2021; Patagonia, 2022). Everything about Patagonia's brand comes together to show that they are relatable, in line with their customers' values, and that they just 'get' their customers, because, well, they think and behave just like their customers do when it comes to the environment.

Attraction/liking

You may have noticed that you are more likely to go the extra mile for someone you like. This could be a crush from school, your best friend or even a complete stranger who has charmed you into doing them a favour. You are not alone in this; humans are generally more likely to comply with a request from someone we like. But what makes us like someone in the first place? Saying 'make your customers like you more to get them to buy' is not particularly useful advice. Instead, we need to break it down into its component parts so we can learn how to use 'likeability' to our advantage. According to Robert Cialdini, who some call the godfather of persuasion, there are five main elements of 'liking': physical attractiveness, similarity, compliments, contact and cooperation, as well as conditioning and association (Cialdini, 2006). Conditioning and association typically use a combination of other psychological tools to borrow the positive attributes of others or existing cultural symbols associated with objects. When it comes to borrowing the positive attributes of others, it might be the attractiveness and likeability of an influencer or the authority of a doctor.

Wrapping up

In this chapter, we've explored how the three key regions of the brain fundamentally work the world of consumer psychology and have examined concepts like social proof, trust and influence. These psychological phenomena play a crucial role in how consumers make decisions, and understanding them is essential for building successful brands. This will set the foundation for the remaining chapters of this book and enable you to utilize the tools and tactics within to maximum effect.

In the next chapter, we will delve deeper into the world of branding and look at how personas, brand stories and brand values can be used to create a powerful and lasting brand. Just as a person's character is made up of their unique qualities and traits, a brand's character is built from its personas, story and values. By crafting a compelling brand character, you can attract consumers and win their loyalty.

References

Amblee, N and Bui, T (2011) Harnessing the influence of social proof in online shopping: The effect of electronic word of mouth on sales of digital microproducts, *International Journal of Electronic Commerce*, 16 (2), pp 91–114, doi:10.2753/jec1086-4415160205 (archived at https://perma.cc/4742-RVEU)

Bergner, D (2009) Joe Ades: Peeler Peddler, *The New York Times*, 23 Dec, www.nytimes.com/2009/12/27/magazine/27ades-t.html (archived at https://perma.cc/S6YS-WFZZ)

CBS (2010) A most appealing street peddler, *CBS NEWS*, 22 Mar, www.cbsnews.com/news/a-most-appealing-street-peddler/ (archived at https://perma.cc/3ZZ6-RCJT)

Cherry, K (2022) Id, Ego and Superego: Freud's elements of personality, *Very Well Mind*, www.verywellmind.com/the-id-ego-and-superego-2795951 (archived at https://perma.cc/AQ7R-56LH)

Cialdini, RB (2006) *Influence: The psychology of persuasion*, revised edition, Allyn and Bacon, Boston, MA

Court, D, Elzinga, D, Mulder, S and Vetvik, OJ (2009) The consumer decision journey, *McKinsey & Company*, 1 Jun, www.McKinsey.com/capabilities/growth-marketing-and-sales/our-insights/the-consumer-decision-journey (archived at https://perma.cc/HG4H-U8MM)

Damasio, AR (1994) *Descartes' Error: Emotion, reason and the human brain*, G.P. Putnam, New York, NY

Evan, JM (2022) 'Sigmund Freud', *Encyclopedia Britannica*, 19 Sep, www.britannica.com/biography/Sigmund-Freud (archived at https://perma.cc/8K9B-VBUC)

Janssen, D (2018) Emotions: an important factor driving consumer behavior, *Neurofied*, 6 Aug, https://neurofied.com/emotions-important-factor-driving-consumer-behaviour/ (archived at https://perma.cc/74JZ-7WMW)

Kennedy, DS (2015) *No B.S. Marketing to the Affluent: The ultimate, no holds barred, take no prisoners guide to getting really rich*, Entrepreneur Press, Irvine, CA

Lindsay, GW (2020) Attention in psychology, neuroscience and machine learning, *Frontiers*, 16 Apr, www.frontiersin.org/articles/10.3389/fncom.2020.00029/full (archived at https://perma.cc/B5YG-X76F)

Lowry, PB, Wilson, DW and Haig, WL (2013) A picture is worth a thousand words: source credibility theory applied to logo and website design for heightened credibility and consumer trust, *International Journal of Human-Computer Interaction*, 30 (1), pp 63–93, doi:10.1080/10447318.2013.839899 (archived at https://perma.cc/HQ53-243C)

Matthews, R (2021) 10 reasons why Patagonia is the world's most responsible company, *The Green Market Oracle*, 10 Sep, https://thegreenmarketoracle.com/2021/09/10/10-reasons-why-patagonia-is-worlds-most/# (archived at https://perma.cc/7FZA-5STS)

Moore, A, Yang, K and Kim, HM (2018) Influencer marketing: Influentials' authenticity, likeability and authority in social media, *International Textile and Apparel Association Annual Conference Proceedings*, 75 (1)

Patagonia (2022) Patagonia Outdoor Clothing & Gear, www.patagonia.com/activism/ (archived at https://perma.cc/7GR3-P4TM)

Shrum, LJ (2004) *The Psychology of Entertainment Media: Blurring the lines between entertainment and persuasion*, Lawrence Erlbaum, Mahwah, NJ

Further reading

Ash, T (2021) *Unleash Your Primal Brain: Demystifying how we think and why we act*, Morgan James Publishing, New York, NY

Beard, R (2012) Trust in advertising – paid, owned and earned, *Nielsen*, Sep, www.nielsen.com/insights/2012/trust-in-advertising--paid-owned-and-earned/ (archived at https://perma.cc/T779-L55K)

Delgado, M (2008) To trust or not to trust: ask Oxytocin, *Scientific American*, 15 Jul, www.scientificamerican.com/article/to-trust-or-not-to-trust/ (archived at https://perma.cc/53F2-DESU)

Demangeot, C and Broderick, AJ (2010) Consumer perceptions of online shopping environments: A gestalt approach, *Psychology and Marketing*, 27 (2), pp 117–40, doi:10.1002/mar.20323 (archived at https://perma.cc/45MH-S9PP)

Grcic, J (2008) The Halo Effect Fallacy, *Electronic Journal For Philosophy*, ISSN 1211–0442

Greene, R (2018) *The Laws of Human Nature*, Profile Books, London

Helm, C and Morelli, M (1979) Stanley Milgram and the Obedience Experiment, *Political Theory*, 7 (3), pp 321–45, doi:10.1177/009059177900700303 (archived at https://perma.cc/9CUL-XAMJ)

Kensinger, EA (2009) Remembering the details: effects of emotion, *Emotion Review*, 1 (2), pp 99–113, doi:10.1177/1754073908100432 (archived at https://perma.cc/AY8A-SN7M)

Kramer, RM (2014) Rethinking Trust, *Harvard Business Review*, Jun, https://hbr.org/2009/06/rethinking-trust (archived at https://perma.cc/K7PG-46LV)

Magids, S, Zorfas, A and Leemon, D (2015) The new science of customer emotions, *Harvard Business Review*, Nov, https://hbr.org/2015/11/the-new-science-of-customer-emotions (archived at https://perma.cc/8NGA-VYLT)

The Economist (2010) The tyranny of choice: You choose, 16 Dec, www.economist.com/christmas-specials/2010/12/16/you-choose (archived at https://perma.cc/UAY7-BFV9)

Zak, P (2013) How stories change the brain, *Greater Good*, 17 Dec, https://greatergood.berkeley.edu/article/item/how_stories_change_brain (archived at https://perma.cc/5C5K-XMFX)

5

Customer data

The lifeblood of any successful business is data, and this is especially true in e-commerce. This chapter will explore the importance of customer data for e-commerce stores and how it can be used to create personalized experiences and drive growth. By understanding and utilizing customer data, e-commerce businesses can steer their operations in the right direction and accelerate their success.

Customer data is what helps you understand your customers, both in aggregate and individually, and enables you to provide a more personalized shopping experience. This is important because, according to Segment's 2022 State of Personalization report, 49 per cent of consumers are likely to become repeat buyers with a retailer if they're given a personalized shopping experience. However, only 47 per cent of brands are using personalized communications based on real-time customer actions, and only 37 per cent use their first-party data to deliver personalized customer experiences (Segment, 2022).

In this chapter we will provide an overview of the customer data space and its importance in a collaborative, cross-functional growth environment for e-commerce brands. We will also share insights that you can use to fine-tune your data strategy and improve your systems, processes and campaigns. This information is broken down for different retailers at different stages in their growth journey and is backed by some of the biggest names in e-commerce.

One example comes from Dan McGaw of McGaw.io – a data veteran who has worked with many of the world's top e-commerce brands and founder of McGaw.io and URM.io. He's also a multiple-time guest on my 2X eCommerce podcast (2X eCommerce, 2021). In 2X eCommerce podcast episode #297, Dan tells us how in working with RealThread.com, a t-shirt-printing company, he and his team were able to increase orders by 51 per cent by building a data strategy enabling better customer tracking, which in turn enabled better communication with the customer, more personalization of brand touchpoints and all-in-all a better customer experience.

My goal in this chapter is to help you understand not only why customer data is important and how you can use it to improve your business, but also how to create cross-functional advantages within your growth stack based on the data-gathering and interpretation systems you put in place for different nodes in the growth stack, and how each team leverages them. By leveraging your customer data effectively, you can increase orders, improve customer satisfaction and drive growth. Let's explore the customer data landscape for e-commerce stores and learn how to get real-world results from your customer data.

Being customer-centric starts with your data

As marketers, we can get caught up in what we want to do with our campaigns and brand. But the most important question to ask is what our customers want from us. To answer that, we need to be customer-centric and gather feedback from them. This can be done through website analytics and data collected through automated methods, as well as through questionnaires, quizzes and focus groups. We need to become so customer-centric that we can even answer questions our customers can't explicitly give us. Answering customers' questions isn't just about writing content that speaks to them, it's in how your brand behaves and how your site is to interact with. It's in how you behave as an e-commerce brand, aligning every touchpoint with customer needs and desires to satisfy their pain points, smooth experiences, and provide memorable engagements with your brand because you just 'get it' and know what your customers want. This requires segmentation and personalization, which can be achieved through data and a solid strategy.

Despite common misconceptions, one of the data-driven marketer's favourite tools, multi-touch attribution, is not customer-centric, and it is not customer-journey tracking. It tracks what customers click on and attributes that mathematically to a campaign, providing insights into campaign performance and costs. Customer journey analytics, on the other hand, tells you how a customer interacts with your brand and marketing beyond those narrowly defined touchpoints. It provides a deeper understanding of the customer experience and can help identify potential friction points in the customer journey. Common multi-touch attribution models include:

- linear (all touchpoints are given the same credit)
- time decay (last touches given higher preferences)
- position-based (40 per cent to first and last touch, 20 per cent spread between the middle)
- data-driven (Shapley, Bayesian, Markov attribution)
- first touch, and last touch

Don't get me wrong, these are great data points to be tracking, but they don't go far enough to create customer-centric experiences.

Understand what you are optimizing for

In e-commerce, there are complex cross-functional interactions between departments, and there are pros and cons to any action. So, it's crucial that you understand exactly what you are optimizing for. As an example, the marketing team may want to move the shipping cost information from the view cart stage to the checkout stage to increase the number of people making it to the checkout. However, this change may also decrease the number of people actually buying products. That's why it's so important to understand what you are optimizing for and to always dig deeper into the end effects on that metric, so that you can catch an unprofitable change sooner and rectify it, not to mention focus on what you really want to achieve right from the beginning.

As you will also learn in this chapter, when compiling your data strategy, it is important to understand not only data, but also yourself. Just like there is no one-size-fits-all model that will please all your customer segments, there is also no one-size-fits-all best solution for e-commerce brands of different sizes or in different industries. Some things I talk about here in this chapter will not be suitable for small brands. Others will be well in the past for larger brands. I will break down the strategies available to your brand specifically segmented by lifecycle stage, and present a roadmap for growth for smaller stores that need to progress from seven to eight figures and beyond.

Collecting company data (infrastructure)

Data is tough for retailers. Over two-thirds say that the integration and synthesis of customer data is their greatest roadblock to achieving personalization; over two-thirds also say that they don't have the right tools for personalization (Lindecrantz et al, 2020). McKinsey outlines eight stages to effective data operations. All of these rely heavily on infrastructure (Lindecrantz et al, 2020). McKinsey's advice: start small, test and learn, and focus on getting the right data rather than every last scrap. Their ideal data system for retailers is:

- **Foundations:** Customer data management.
- **Decision making:** Customer segmentation and analytics, a playbook of campaigns to match to customers and campaign coordination systems to prevent inconsistent messaging.
- **Design:** A cross-functional team and the right capabilities.
- **Distribution:** Tech enablement, and testing and learning.

To collect customer data, you should first have the right infrastructure in place. This may include your customer management system (CMS), enterprise resource planning (ERP), enterprise data management (EDM), and analytics platforms for smaller stores or a customer data platform (CDP) for larger ones. Extract transform load (ETL) operations can help you bring data between these systems, and a data management platform (DMP) may be necessary to handle large volumes of third-party data. Once you have collected and stored your data, you can use it to improve your business. Machine learning models can help you make the most of your data.

Again, there is not a one-size-fits-all approach for all e-commerce brands. It's perfectly fine for a smaller store just establishing itself to not have a CDP. But you do need to know that they exist, and have it in your growth road-

TABLE 5.1 CDPs vs DMPs

CDPs	DMPs
Used for all types of marketing efforts	Used mainly for advertising efforts
First-party data priorty	Third-party data priorty
Identity resolution	Anonymized data
Long-term data retention	Short-term data retention

map so that you can transition to this solution in a timely manner and avoid the technical bloat that comes from layering systems on top of systems for the life of the business. Using the same strategies that worked when you were small will only create high software costs and dependencies that require deep experience with the company's tech stack. In short, it becomes frustrating, time consuming and expensive.

Your end goal should be to form a single view of the customer through a single source of truth.

Collecting customer data (methods)

Customer data is more than just the information found in your Google Analytics dashboard or e-commerce platform. It includes focus groups, questionnaires and quizzes, as well as customer feedback gathered from post-purchase surveys. It also includes purchased data from third-party vendors and data enrichment services that use machine learning algorithms to fill in gaps in your data. Additionally, customer data includes clicks and customer journeys tracked on your website through first-party cookies. However, it's important to note that customer surveys and questionnaires have their limitations. For example, questions can inadvertently tell people what to think about, change how people think and 'lead the witness' by using subtle language to influence answers. In some cases, market research can be simply wrong.

The success of your data strategy can be heavily influenced by the quality and type of data you have. To avoid getting stuck with bad data when it comes to training machine learning models and implementing more expensive solutions, it's important to have a data analyst with experience in marketing and e-commerce analytics oversee and inform your strategy early on. Additionally, it's worth having a market research professional on your team. Up to 80 per cent of the success of your data strategy comes down to the quality and type of data that you have (Courtheoux, 2003). Research by Amperity, a leading customer data platform, found that consumer companies often misidentify up to 23 per cent of their best customers, who are responsible for over 50 per cent of their revenue (Amperity, 2022). This is often due to issues with cookies, tracking and not having a single view of the customer, which are technical considerations that can be addressed with the right expertise.

A market research professional will be able to guide you in the softer skills of data collection, while your data team (analysts and engineers) will be able to guide you in the technical aspects of collection and interpretation. It's important to be aware that customer surveys and questionnaires are not always reliable. Philip Graves, in his book *Consumerology: The market research myth, the truth about consumers, and the psychology of shopping* (2010), highlights the main flaws of survey and questionnaire-based methodologies when it comes to customer research. These include:

- questions inadvertently tell people what to think about
- questions change what people think
- questions 'lead the witness' by using subtle language to influence answers
- sometimes market research is simply wrong

It's worth noting that the subtleties of good survey design are many, and it's important to have experts in survey methods on your team, such as a specialist market research professional.

Collecting customer data (types)

There are several ways in which information about customers can be collected, such as automatically during their browsing journey, directly from the customer or through the purchase of data from another party. This leads to the concept of zero-, first-, second- and third-party data, and offers insight into the goals for each type.

One way to categorize these data types is to group them into retention- and acquisition-focused groups. Zero-party and first-party data is collected and owned by you, and typically involves some level of interaction with the customer. For example, if a customer fills out a form on your website, that data becomes your first-party data. This type of data is focused on retention, but can still inform your acquisition strategy through analysis of your existing customer segments. Second- and third-party data is acquisition-focused when it comes to advertising, but can also be used to inform retention strategies when it comes to things like market research and data enrichment. This can be especially useful for segmenting and personalization:

- **Zero-party data:** customers' preferences and interests, as indicated by their responses to a survey or quiz on the e-commerce store's website.

- **First-party data:** customers' browsing and purchase history on the e-commerce store's website, as well as information entered during checkout (such as name, address and payment information).

- **Second-party data:** data that you collect about your customers using assets from third parties, such as cookies, and can include voluntarily shared information with your data partner.

- **Third-party data:** typically purchased from a data vendor or enrichment service, and while it becomes your data after purchase, the methodology used to generate it remains with the enrichment service. Because consumer preferences and behaviours change over time, you will always be reliant on third-party sources for up-to-date information.

The changing landscape of customer data, including limitations on third-party sources and emerging first-party data limitations related to customer privacy, political and legal environments, will be discussed later in this chapter.

The changing landscape of data gathering

With great data comes great responsibility, and also great legal obligations. The trend is definitely towards user data protection and is unlikely to reverse. This means that companies are restricted not only in the information they can gather through third-party means, but also through first-party methods.

There are, however, nuances and solutions for savvy marketers. First, there is the political and legal landscape, with the introduction of laws such as the EU's General Data Protection Regulation (GDPR), which gives individuals in the EU the right to access, control and even delete their data, even if they have given permission for the company to access it. Other regions, such as the United States, do not have comprehensive national laws, but rather industry-specific ones such as HIPAA for healthcare, as well as state-specific laws such as the California Consumer Privacy Act (CCPA).

This creates a complex data collection environment for global e-commerce operations. At the time of writing in 2022, companies that breach the GDPR can be fined up to 2 per cent of their annual global turnover, or €10 million, whichever is greater (Wolford, nd). So, it is serious business.

Then there is the technological landscape. Andrew Seipp from mcgaw.io provides an overview of recent changes leading up to 2022 (Seipp, 2022). In March 2020, Apple's ITP enhancements implemented the blocking of third-party cookies across iOS and iPad OS devices and the Safari browser (Wilander, 2020). In September 2021, Apple, along with their iOS 14 update, announced that apps must ask users for permission to track them. By opting out of tracking, Apple will not share the IDFA of these users (Wulfsohn, 2021). Since 2020, Google has been taking steps to replace third-party cookies with a privacy sandbox system, limiting the information available to advertisers to indicators of interest in topics and removing information such as gender. The Chrome browser is used for almost two-thirds of internet browsing (Milmo, 2022; Temkin, 2021). UTM data, however, is not affected by changes to things like your Facebook pixel or third-party cookies. UTM data is fed to your analytics tool, and enables you to collect information on traffic sources as well as conversions (Seipp, 2022).

Changes like these do make formulating an effective data strategy harder. In fact, research by Epsilon in conjunction with Phronesis Partners showed that 67 per cent of marketers felt confused, disappointed and overwhelmed by changes to the IDFA and other data privacy laws and systems (Epsilon, 2020). It is no surprise that the impact has been so strongly felt. Eighty per cent of marketers say they are either moderately or very reliant on third-party cookies for their marketing strategies (Epsilon, 2020). But they do not make it impossible. By focusing on 'the customer is front and centre', you need to improve your customer experience in a way that makes your customers want to engage with you and share their data. From there, creating first-party cookies is another step you can take to improve your customer-centricity. These allow you to save, manage and utilize your data in the most effective and profitable way, as opposed to third-party cookies, which are completely at the mercy of third parties.

However, first-party cookies are not the answer to every problem. While you have ownership of the data collected by your first-party cookies, you are unlikely to be tracking users across other sites (other than yours). Your first-party cookies will remember things like preferences, login details, cart items and actions taken by the customer, such as clicks (to name a few) (LaFleur, 2022). This means that your first-party data will only be effective for personalization on your own site. If you want to track users across the web, you will need to use third-party cookies or another method.

Putting your data strategy into action

First of all, your customer data strategy is going to depend on the size of your business. It's only natural. Larger companies have more resources at their disposal to do things like build custom machine learning models to truly utilize their customer data to its maximum potential. Smaller e-commerce companies just starting out have a vastly different set of opportunities in front of them. However, if you fall into this category, there are many steps that are not only accessible but effective as well.

For any brand, the goal is to segment your customers and provide unique, personalized customer journeys to improve the customer experience for each of them. Because there is no one-size-fits-all model for what makes a good customer experience. Each segment has different preferences, habits and behaviours.

Ivan Mazour, co-founder of Ometria, has some insights for us on this topic that come from 2X eCommerce podcast #31 titled 'Scaling Mid-Tier E-commerce with Customer Lifecycle Data and Personalization' (2X eCommerce, 2015). Ivan studied mathematics at Cambridge, and has an incredible amount of experience with e-commerce companies, and Ometria is a customer intelligence and cross-channel marketing platform that uses proprietary AI to deliver customized marketing plans to retailers, including personalization (Mazour, 2022). So, you would think that Ivan would say that you need to get started with serious personalization in the form of machine learning-optimized automated marketing right away. But that's not the case. Ivan says that until you have an initial list of contacts built up, in the form of email addresses or remarketable customers, with actual names and other customer information attached, then you're better off focusing your budget on customer acquisition to build that up. For some businesses, that list might only be 1,000 people, and for others, they may need 100,000 or more – it all depends on the average order value (AOV) and hence the value of each contact. Once that list is in place, then investing in a highly personalized CRM strategy becomes much more effective and starts to take over from acquisition in terms of ROI. In 2X eCommerce podcast #31, Ivan says the same goes for A/B testing and personalization on your website. At a conference a few years ago, he sat through a speech on A/B testing, but the audience was mostly smaller e-commerce stores. He points out that a smaller store with a $2,000 marketing budget just does not have the resources to spend $1,000 per month on an A/B testing program. Nor do they likely have the web traffic to justify it. A few hundred visitors a day isn't enough to get useful or even accurate insights from A/B testing. Instead, Ivan recommends focusing on customer acquisition first to build up a list, then implementing an initial basic email strategy, and then once the list is big enough, investing in advanced customer data, personalization and CRM techniques to ensure those customers stay loyal, keep coming back and keep increasing their lifetime value.

There are, however, platforms that enable personalization in online and marketing experiences for any brand. Solutions like Nosto and Fresh Relevance offer personalized on-site product recommendations and post-purchase up-sell suggestions, as well as email personalization and A/B testing on a 'pay as you grow' pricing model. For small businesses, though, retaining customers is key. Expensive personalization tools and website A/B testing can wait. Instead, opt for simpler but effective solutions. Your main task when starting out is to grow acquisition and reach 10,000 names. To learn more about the specific things you can do to achieve just that, read Chapter 6 on demand generation and capture across owned, paid and earned media channels. Chapter 10 will show you what that looks like in the search engine landscape, and Chapter 11 will show you how paid social comes into the cross-functional mix. The strategies and principles discussed will help you grow your customer base and improve their experience.

Advancing your data strategy through segmentation and personalization (starting out)

As I mentioned, there is no one-size-fits-all model for an e-commerce brand. Simply put, some solutions are going to be too expensive for a smaller and growing brand. And that's okay; every brand has had to work within budget limitations.

One example of accessible personalization for e-commerce brands is the power of a simple questionnaire. This idea comes from Ben Parr, co-founder of Octane AI, a zero-party data platform for Shopify stores. For those that don't know, Ben is an award-winning entrepreneur, investor, journalist and the author of the best-selling book *Captivology: The science of capturing people's attention*. He really knows his stuff. In episode 322 of my 2X eCommerce podcast, Ben discussed how Doe Lashes, a brand owned by Jason Wong, used a quiz to personalize the entire shopping process for their customers (2X eCommerce, 2022). Doe Lashes realized that many of their customers were new to using fake eyelashes, so they introduced a quiz to ask users if they were a newbie or not. This enabled Doe Lashes to personalize their product recommendations and post-purchase email flows, leading to increased revenue and customer satisfaction. New users got way more information about the different types of lashes available, what might be best for them and, importantly, how to use them.

This is a great example of using customer data and segmentation in a way that is accessible for any store, regardless of size or budget. The data you need isn't hard or expensive to collect, you just need to be customer-centric and put yourself in your customers' shoes. If you're struggling to do this, conduct focus groups and engage with your customers or potential customers to gain valuable insights. To implement these tactics, you only need three tools: a CMS like Shopify, an EDM and SMS platform like Klaviyo, and a method to implement the quiz such as Octane.ai. All it takes is some creativity and a focus on the customer to improve the shopping experience and optimize your marketing efforts.

Here are some simple segmenting ideas that will be available even on simple tech stacks:

- Geographic
- Purchase history (product types purchased)
- Product viewed on site
- Cart abandonment
- Checkout abandonment
- VIP segments
- High or low AOV
- Time of last email open (for example, has opened an email in the past three months)
- Custom quiz-based segmentation

Preparing for advanced tactics and strategies

Once you've reached a certain level of growth in your e-commerce business, you may want to explore advanced strategies like deep segmentation based on machine learning insights and automated personalization across customer touchpoints. To do this, you'll need to create a single source of truth for your customer data using a customer data platform (CDP).

Google Analytics is a great tool for e-commerce , but it lacks the key data needed for effective segmentation and personalization. Google Analytics is anonymized and doesn't provide customer names, so you can't create personalized experiences with the data it provides. It's a good high-level view of your website traffic, but it's not designed as a full-service platform for e-commerce stores.

A CDP allows you to create a single view of your customer with names and emails. Instead of integrating multiple tools and dealing with compatibility issues, you can put everything into your CDP and create a unified language for your data. You can then integrate your CDP with your existing tech stack and other services that need access to your customer data. Machine learning algorithms can work on your data in the background, creating new variables that your CMS and other tools cannot produce.

Once you've set up your CDP, you can use data enrichment services to get even more information about your customers. For example, if you put an email address from your first-party data into a data enrichment platform like Experian, you can get a wealth of information about your customers, such as their interests and lifestyle. Dan McGaw, a regular guest on my 2X eCommerce podcast, put his wife's corporate email into Experian and was surprised by the amount of information the platform provided.

Brinks Home, a sister company of Brinks that offers smart home solutions, used data enrichment to combine customer data from its security business with data from its smart home business. This allowed the company to segment its customers and create personalized experiences for them, going from two or three A/B tests daily to over 50,000 – resulting in a 9.5 per cent increase in revenue (Edelman and Abraham, 2022).

By using a CDP and data enrichment services, you can create a single view of your customer and segment them effectively to create personalized experiences. This can result in increased revenue, as seen with Brinks Home. However, it's important to note that these advanced strategies take time and resources to set up, so they may not be suitable for smaller e-commerce businesses. But even if you're not at the stage yet where you're ready for a CDP, you need to know that this is a logical next step for a business. Otherwise, you'll continue doing things the way you have always done since the start, blissfully unaware that there is a better way.

Advancing your data strategy through segmentation and personalization (growing)

Creating personalized experiences through intelligent customer segmentation is essential to retaining customers. But how can this be achieved on a large scale? Using a CDP and a customer intelligence and cross-channel marketing platform like Ometria can help. Once data is collected and attributed, machine learning models can be used to predict important metrics for acquiring and retaining customers. These can be segmented and easily understood by marketers and e-commerce brands. CDP platforms use proprietary AI technology to apply Bayesian statistical models to every data point for a customer. This allows you to answer questions like 'How do I acquire more email subscribers?' You can then use this information to change your campaign and website, promote your blog and test the results. By understanding what makes VIP customers unique and how you acquire them, you can personalize their experiences and increase profits. You can also predict when customers are most likely to make a purchase and what the most likely AOV is. This can help you increase revenues and build more profitable strategies. So, dig deep into your analytics and begin to answer these kinds of questions.

Finding which customers are most likely to purchase, and even when they are most likely to purchase, is nothing new. Peter Fader, a pioneer in customer-centric marketing and author of *Customer Centricity*, shows in a 2004 research paper (with Wendy Moe) that using stochastic and Bayesian models it was possible to predict not only which customers were more likely to convert, but also the time at which they were most likely to convert (Fader, 2020; Moe and Fader, 2004). Fader analysed data from Amazon (back when they only sold books) and CDNOW to prove that changes in visit frequency were predictors of conversion probability over and above the general baseline visit frequency of the customer. To illustrate, previously it was thought that only gross frequency mattered in distinguishing who would convert and who would not. That is, a customer displaying high average visit frequency was more likely to buy than a customer displaying low visit frequency. This usually calculated average visit frequency, and separated segments into high and low groups. Fader's model went further to show that even within a segment, subtle changes in visit frequency predicted the probability of conversion. A customer who had above-average baseline visit frequency but is showing decreasing frequency of site visits is less likely to convert. A customer who has low baseline frequency of site visits but is showing increasing frequency is more likely to convert. Previously, the 'low visit frequency on average' (though with an increasing trend in visits) customer would have been ignored as a low purchase probability customer.

Fader is a long-time advocate for customer-centric marketing and customer-centric measurement methods and his work is definitely worth checking out for any customer-centric brand. In *The Customer Centricity Playbook* (2018), Fader and co-author Sarah Toms illustrate the turnaround of Electronic Arts (EA), which went from being the worst company in America (two years in a row, would you believe) in 2013, beating out Bank of America and Comcast, to the global juggernaut you see today (Tassi, 2013). According to the SEC, in 2013 EA's global revenues came in at just under $3.8 billion (SEC, 2013). For FIFA games fans out there, the title FIFA 13 accounted for 17 per cent of EA's revenue in that year. That might sound like a lot of revenue. But for a company like EA, it was not a good place to be. Their flavour of 'customer-centric marketing' was that there is a customer, and we are going to throw 22 per cent of our revenue into simply blasting them all with the same messages. Luckily, some astute data professionals caught on to how ineffective EA's spray and pray marketing strategies were, and implemented a true customer-centric strategy that focused on making experiences as amazing as possible for the customer, rather than blasting their customers with as much marketing collateral as their budget could afford. And, of course, they used data to drive this strategy. Fast-forward to today, and EA is no longer America's worst company, and their revenues for fiscal year 2022 reached just over $7 billion (almost doubling a billion-dollar company in less than 10 years is no small feat). The FIFA title alone generated $1.34 billion in revenue for EA in 2021 (Evenden and Reseburg, 2022; Byers, 2021).

Now, you may not be an EA-sized company. But, as a smaller player, your potential for even larger growth in terms of raw percentages is much higher. A billion-dollar company is like a cargo ship, while a smaller e-commerce brand is agile like a jet ski and fast like a speedboat. Customer-centricity is your fuel.

Advanced segmentation opportunities

- Behavioural data gathered from first-party cookies – things such as browsing time and scroll depth. Are they browsing the entire store or going deep on one category?

- Demographic data (such as age and sex).

- Educational background.

- Psychographics (lifestyles and values).

- Predicted most likely time of next purchase

The bottom line on customer-centric data

Being customer-centric is about bringing boutique and bespoke experiences to digital in a way that is automated and optimized for effectiveness. It's about knowing your customer well enough to be able to recommend the perfect products and tailor the experience to them. This is achieved through customer data and detailed product data, which enables the use of machine learning models to replicate and optimize the in-store salesperson experience on a mass scale. Just as a ship cannot sail without a proper navigation system, an e-commerce store cannot thrive without customer data as its guide. By understanding your customers and their behaviour, you can create personalized experiences that will win their hearts and minds. In the next chapter, we will delve deeper into the world of customer acquisition and how customer data can help you acquire new customers and retain existing ones. By understanding your customers and utilizing data to target them effectively, you can increase your customer base and drive sales. We will explore various tactics and technologies that can help you acquire new customers and retain them for the long term. This chapter will provide an overview of the key techniques for acquiring customers in the e-commerce space, as well as practical tips and best practices for implementing these strategies.

Looking to improve your customer data strategy? The 2X eCommerce site offers a wide range of guides and resources that can help. From best practices to step-by-step guides, our resources are designed to provide valuable insights and practical advice that can help you get the most out of your customer data. By following best-in-class, cross-functional aligned data strategies, you can avoid costly data mistakes and headaches. Whether you're just starting out or looking to take your customer data strategy to the next level, 2X eCommerce resources can provide valuable support and guidance. Head to 2xecommerce.com/book/chapter5 to access them today.

References

2X eCommerce (2015) EP31, Scaling mid-tier e-commerce with customer lifecycle data and personalisation w/ Ivan Mazour, Ometria, https://2xecommerce.com/podcast/ep31/ (archived at https://perma.cc/L7KM-C5EK)

2X eCommerce (2021) S06 EP23, Building your first-party data martech stack for eComm, https://2xecommerce.com/podcast/ep297/ (archived at https://perma.cc/2JUT-QWXN)

2X eCommerce (2022) S06 EP48, Zero and 1st party data for Q4, https://2xecommerce.com/podcast/ep322/ (archived at https://perma.cc/CS95-PEDM)

Amperity (2022) The pitfalls of misidentifying customers – and how to avoid them, https://amperity.com/resources/think-you-know-your-customers-think-again (archived at https://perma.cc/B8ZY-5AZX)

Byers, J (2021) EA pockets $1.62B from Ultimate Team, *Front Office Sports*, 3 Jun, https://frontofficesports.com/electronic-arts-pockets-1-6b-from-ultimate-team/# (archived at https://perma.cc/A63H-Q526)

Courtheoux, RJ (2003) Marketing data analysis and data quality management, *Journal of Targeting, Measurement and Analysis for Marketing*, 11 (4), pp 299–313, https://link.springer.com/content/pdf/10.1057/palgrave.jt.5740086.pdf (archived at https://perma.cc/CX9Z-XHBH)

Edelman, DC and Abraham, M (2022) Customer experience in the age of AI, *Harvard Business Review*, Mar–Apr, https://hbr.org/2022/03/customer-experience-in-the-age-of-ai (archived at https://perma.cc/E3CH-P6PX)

Epsilon (2020) Research Summary: preparing for a world without third-party cookies, www.epsilon.com/us/insights/resources/research-preparing-for-a-world-without-third-party-cookies (archived at https://perma.cc/P2JY-JC28)

Evenden, C and Reseburg, J (2022) Electronic Arts Reports Q4 and FY22 Financial Results, *Electronic Arts Inc*, 10 May, https://ir.ea.com/press-releases/press-release-details/2022/Electronic-Arts-Reports-Q4-and-FY22-Financial-Results/default.aspx (archived at https://perma.cc/FH5R-6R54)

Fader, P and Toms, S (2018) *The Customer Centricity Playbook: Implement a winning strategy driven by customer lifetime value*, Wharton School Press, Philadelphia, PA

Graves, P (2010) *Consumerology: The market research myth, the truth about consumers, and the psychology of shopping*, Nicholas Brealey Publishing, Boston, MA

LaFleur, G (2022) First-party vs third-party cookies: what's the difference? *TechTarget*, 3 Mar, www.techtarget.com/searchcustomerexperience/tip/First-party-vs-third-party-cookies-Whats-the-difference (archived at https://perma.cc/XY8C-NN8K)

Lindecrantz, E, Tjon Pian Gi, M and Zerbi, S (2020) Personalizing the customer experience: driving differentiation in retail, *McKinsey & Company*, 28 Apr, www.McKinsey.com/industries/retail/our-insights/personalizing-the-customer-experience-driving-differentiation-in-retail (archived at https://perma.cc/57NB-EF92)

Mazour, I (2022) About Ivan Mazour. A young entrepreneur in London, http://www.ivanmazour.com/about-me/ (archived at https://perma.cc/5X2B-BTYY)

Milmo, D (2022) TechScape: Google is changing how it tracks us online – but who benefits? *The Guardian*, 2 Feb, www.theguardian.com/technology/2022/feb/02/techscape-google-chrome-cookies (archived at https://perma.cc/U2RU-BBGW)

Moe, WW and Fader, PS (2004) Capturing evolving visit behavior in clickstream data, *Journal of Interactive Marketing*, 18 (1), pp 5–19, doi:10.1002/dir.10074 (archived at https://perma.cc/R5TU-HVXT)

Parr, B (2015) *Captivology: The science of capturing people's attention*, HarperOne, New York, NY

SEC (2013) Electronic Arts Inc. Form 10-K 2013, www.sec.gov/Archives/edgar/data/712515/000071251513000022/ea20130331-10kdoc.htm (archived at https://perma.cc/GR3B-E7ZY)

Segment (2022) The State of Personalization 2022, https://segment.com/state-of-personalization-report/ (archived at https://perma.cc/6GQT-K5VS)

Seipp, A (2022) The end of third-party tracking, the rise of iOS14 ITP, McGaw.io, 27 Aug, https://mcgaw.io/blog/end-of-third-party-cookies-ios14-itp/#gs.c5g0v9 (archived at https://perma.cc/Z6GX-PYEM)

Tassi, P (2013) EA voted worst company in America, again, *Forbes*, 9 Apr, www.forbes.com/sites/insertcoin/2013/04/09/ea-voted-worst-company-in-america-again/?sh=1bd152c7aebe (archived at https://perma.cc/G54U-ALGB)

Temkin, D (2021) Charting a course towards a more privacy-first web, Google, 3 Mar, https://blog.google/products/ads-commerce/a-more-privacy-first-web/ (archived at https://perma.cc/TV99-CEDZ)

Wilander, J (2020) Full third-party cookie blocking and more, *WebKit*, 24 Mar, https://webkit.org/blog/10218/full-third-party-cookie-blocking-and-more/ (archived at https://perma.cc/L8W5-KPHJ)

Wolford, B (nd) What are the GDPR fines? *GDPR.eu*, https://gdpr.eu/fines/ (archived at https://perma.cc/4JFB-D7Z7)

Wulfsohn, J (2021) Council post: how Apple's IOS 14 will change the advertising landscape, *Forbes*, 16 Apr, www.forbes.com/sites/forbesagencycouncil/2021/04/16/how-apples-ios-14-will-change-the-advertising-landscape/?sh=249cb6771c7b (archived at https://perma.cc/GB7K-R3HE)

6

Customer acquisition

Since the Paleolithic period, when people were largely hunter-gatherers, hunting has been a feature of human history. These hunter-gatherers were often small, nomadic communities who, for nourishment, would go on wild animal hunts and collect herbs and berries. This way of life is not drastically different to the practice of actively searching out new customers and persuading them to make a purchase in an e-commerce context. However, thanks to our connectedness through social platforms, scalable programmatic advertising systems and data-driven targeting strategies, companies may adopt a more focused and planned approach to customer acquisition and span out across the globe from the comfort of their office in New York or Singapore, rather than traversing hundreds of kilometres of plains and steppe.

Customer acquisition is driven through tools and channels in your marketing arsenal like video, content, influencers, advertising, retargeting and leveraging psychological and sociological drivers like social proof and influence. All of which we will cover in this chapter, your first-principles primer on how to attract and convert customers for your e-commerce brand.

Every e-commerce brand should have both demand generation (typically through the form of media-driven awareness and engagement marketing campaigns that introduce your brand and products to new audiences) and demand capture (that either compels the mentally converted segment of your target audience to purchase your product or provides direct access to your store when existing or potential customers are in buy-mode). This typically happens through the medium of search engines. As an example, someone actively looking for noise-cancelling headphones could, on the one hand, have watched a few 20-minute YouTube reviews about a product, visited the website of the brand, joined their email and SMS list and, five days after their initial website visit, responded to a retargeted ad campaign that only focused on converting an audience segment comprising website visitors that visited the specific headphone page in the last 30 days. The first part of this journey encapsulates demand generation activities (the influencer seeding campaign with YouTubers that produced content about their new model leading to email capture that added this new contact to their email and SMS list, retargeting list and community, where demand could further be seeded) and then finally, demand capture through the retargeting campaign. Demand capture could also be in the form of their search engine marketing campaigns catering to either specific searches about their products or broader search terms related to the product category (in this instance 'noise cancelling headphones') on their favourite search engine.

This chapter covers both demand generation and demand capture to prepare you to integrate everything you learn throughout this book into a comprehensive and full-funnel marketing strategy. Today, in the fast-paced e-commerce environment full of rich media content, video is not only the primary medium of communication and broadcast but also one for generating maximal reach and engagement, so we cover this in detail, too. Not from a technical perspective but from a strategic one. All brands are struggling with rising advertising costs, but many are suffering more than they need to be because they haven't been able to adjust their video marketing strategy to the new e-commerce, social media and advertising environments. Competition is heating up and it calls for a new and, in my opinion, better approach to video marketing. Like all challenges, this has led to an improvement in the overall video marketing landscape in terms of quality and customer-centricity, at least from brands that have been paying attention.

This chapter will give you a 30,000-foot view of the critical components that should be in your demand generation and demand capture marketing plans, with a focus on the demand generation aspects you need to set the foundation for comprehensive demand capture and customer retention strategies we cover in later chapters such as Chapter 7, 'Retention for long-term growth', Chapter 9, 'Lifecycle marketing and personalized experiences', Chapter 10, 'Search engine marketing'. We then circle back to demand generation to put the icing on the cake of your full funnel strategy with Chapter 8, 'Audience and community building' and Chapter 11, 'Paid social advertising'. Without further ado, let's get started with what your demand generation strategy should look like.

Demand generation

Demand generation, as the name suggests, is about creating awareness, desire and demand for your brand's products. That could be the desire to be a part of your brand community for the exclusivity and status it brings, as it does for many sportscar owners, or it could be due to the overwhelming utility of your product, which convinces the market yours is definitely the solution they need to scratch their particular itch. The point is that there are many ways to generate demand and it will require a good understanding of what exactly your consumers value. And those values could be multifaceted – like the environmental activist who also feels a tinge of joy from being part of an exclusive group of Tesla owners rather than driving a more mainstream electric vehicle. The result of demand generation should be brand recall in the form of intentional awareness about your brand, likeness for the brand and its values and, ultimately, trust for your brand to facilitate a purchase transaction in the medium to long run. For low-priced items and for no- and low-cost trial offers, demand generation campaigns could trigger an immediate purchase.

Before the internet, television was the primary channel consumer brands relied on to create demand. Today, as much as TV advertising still plays a significant role in brand building and selling products and services, social media has become the central battleground for creating brand awareness and communities as well as for reinvigorating desire for brands and products.

Today, demand generation, much like during the predominance of television, relies heavily on video as its central medium. Later in this chapter we will explore the video economy and offer guidance for organizing your demand generation functions like a media company through what I term 'edutainment'.

Influencers and creators play a crucial role in social media and the video economy. As a brand owner, your task is to penetrate communities through their leaders (the influencers or creators) to help your brand establish credibility and social proof and generate sales (especially first-time sales). As you structure your media strategy, you should task them with creating content around specific topics and, in turn, build communities and audiences around these themes. They should be creating product reviews, tutorials or how-to's, behind-the-scenes peeks and more about specific themes and lifestyle elements. A clear strategy is key.

Direct response advertising, another tool in your arsenal, is a powerful and necessary way to generate demand for e-commerce brands. Social media is the most accessible paid media channel for demand generation and, with the right strategy, it can help e-commerce businesses attract potential customers, optimize ad campaigns and drive awareness, traffic and sales. Other channels include direct mail, display and TV. Chapter 11 focuses on the benefits of leveraging social media advertising to grow and scale your brand, so take what you learn here in this chapter as a foundational primer – we'll dig into details later.

The final layer in your demand generation strategy should be amplifying your *brand story* through these media channels. Product is one thing, but to truly get cross-functional growth from your marketing efforts, you need to layer in brand story. This means not only utilizing social media platforms, which are going to be heavily product focused when it comes to your paid campaigns (using paid to promote your brand story in any significant way is going to take away from your product marketing budget, which means less demand capture, at a very high ad cost), but also exploring other platforms more suited to brand story and values initiatives. That means establishing thought leadership initiatives (publishing articles or whitepapers that showcase your company's expertise in a particular field) and traditional public relations campaigns – this will get you into media publications like magazines and newspapers, and onto television via news stories or popular talk shows as just a few examples. By taking advantage of these channels, you can build an engaged community of followers who feel connected to your brand and its values, without having to spend a cent or penny on paid ads which would be better spent driving and capturing demand for your product.

Become a cross-functional full-funnel marketing specialist

Every customer acquisition strategy requires knowing, understanding and mastering the dynamics of a fully cross-functional e-commerce marketing funnel.

The essential nodes of this funnel, like media, influence, advertising, brand story, word of mouth (WOM), search engine marketing (SEM), search engine optimization (SEO), retargeting and messaging, are the building blocks required to create an acquisition strategy that not only drives commercial results for your business but also builds a community of fans and customers that lean on your brand values and love your products.

As you grow and scale in e-commerce, at each growth iteration, each of these nodes will be in a constant state of flux and realignment.

The demand generation and demand capture customer acquisition e-commerce funnel framework shown in Figure 6.1 consolidates the principles covered in this chapter, and the reference chapters I mentioned in the first section of this chapter serve as a roadmap for your community-centred customer acquisition strategy.

FIGURE 6.1 Demand generation and demand capture e-commerce funnel

Demand generation and demand capture e-commerce funnel

Demand Generation
Edutainment

Media: Visual, audio, short and long-form video

Influence: Influencers and building authority

Brand: Amplifying brand story and values

Advertising: Performance-driven product-first

Community: Your owned audience

Referral Marketing
3rd party sales

WOM: Amplifying word of mouth

Affiliate marketing: Performance-driven incentivized sales

Search Engine Marketing: SEO and PPC on search platforms; Google, YouTube, TikTok or Amazon

Demand Capture
Search

Brand name search and brand equity: From demand-generation activities

Retargeting: Looping back lost conversions

Messaging: 1:1 communication with audience

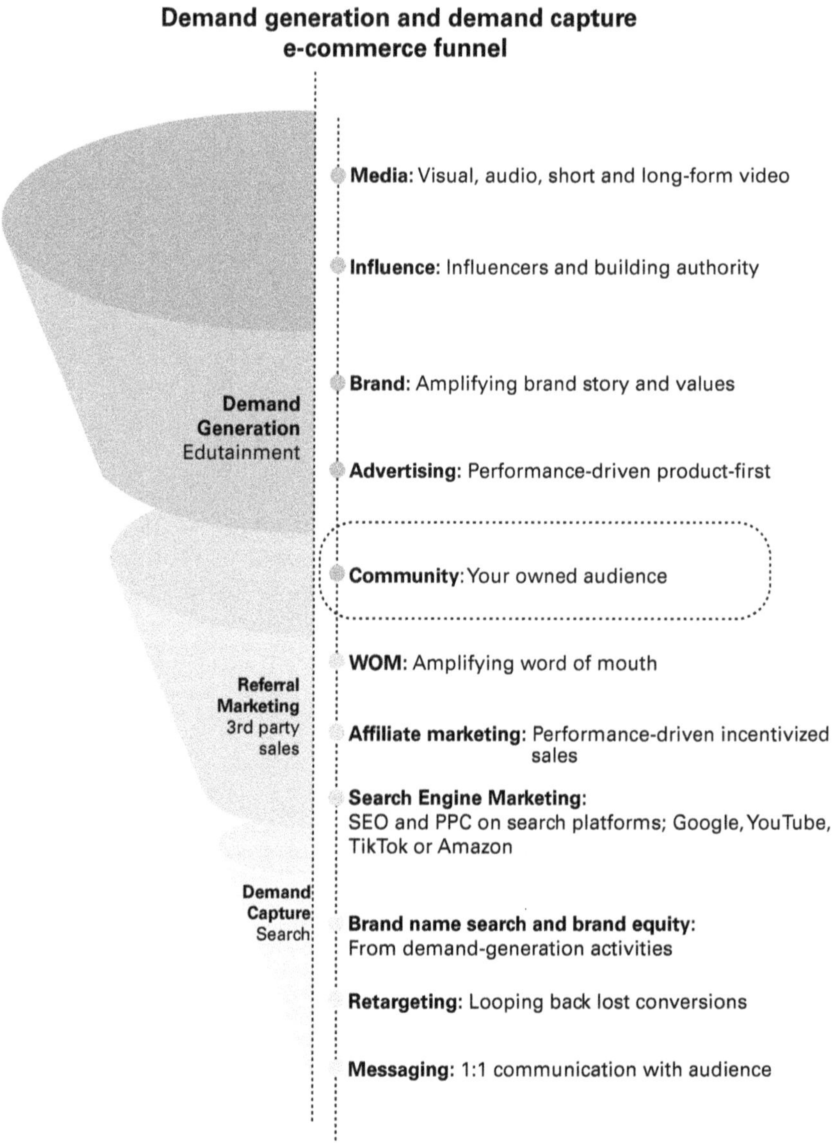

TABLE 6.1

	Objectives	Medium and Channels
Media	Visuals Audio Short-form video Long-form video	Social media videos & visuals Product demo videos UGC videos How-to videos Brand story videos Vlogs Entertainment videos Product photography Podcasting
Influence	Influencer Building authority	Nano influencers 1–10k Micro influencers 10–50k Macro influencers 500k–1M Mega influencers 1M+ Mid-tier influencers 50–500k
Brand	Amplifying brand story and values	PR Social media Thought leadership
Advertising	Performance-driven product-first	Social advertising Direct marketing Display advertising Retail media Streaming TV ads TV advertising
Community	Your owned audience	Email SMS Social media followers Private groups
Word of mouth (WOM)	Amplifying word of mouth	Referral marketing Reviews User-generated content
Affiliate marketing	Performance-driven incentivized sales	Affiliate networks Influencer-driven affiliate marketing
Search Engine Marketing	Leveraging search for capture demand on key platforms: Google, YouTube, TikTok, Amazon	Pay-per-click (PPC) advertising Search Engine Optimization (SEO)

(continued)

TABLE 6.1 (Continued)

	Objectives	Medium and Channels
Brand name search	Brand equity from demand-generation activities	Search platforms
Retargeting	Looping back lost conversions	On-platform retargeting Site retargeting Search retargeting Email retargeting
Messaging	1:1 communication with audience members	Email capture, Email marketing automation Promotional email campaigns Messaging app automation and campaigns Live chat

Now, let's start off by diving into video. From social media videos and product demos to how-to videos and brand story videos, video content helps to engage and inform your target audience. In the modern e-commerce environment, it's a skill that your brand cannot afford not to master.

The video economy

It's official, video is in! The online video landscape has developed rapidly since platforms like YouTube, Vine, Twitch and Instagram were in their infancy in the early 2010s. Today, 90 per cent of marketers say that video is a key part of their strategy, and that it gives them a positive return on investment, compared to only 3 in 10 in 2015 (Hayes, 2022). While the numbers will surely fluctuate over time, recent research shows that video posts are getting roughly 1.6 times more engagement than regular text-based posts, and make up over three-quarters of the top 500 posts on Facebook (Peters, 2019).

Perhaps this should come as no surprise. As humans, we developed visual imagery before we developed written language. We didn't have video, but we did have sequences of visual imagery. Our first stories were told as a rolling series of paintings and engravings across stone cave walls. The earliest of these are shown to be at least 30,000 years old, in contrast to the oldest indications of written language estimated to date back to 3,400 B.C. – the Sumerian script (Marchant, 2016; Brown, 2021). We evolved to print, screen and digital video. At first, only experts or the very rich could create video content. Then with technological innovations, the majority were able to create grainy but authentic home videos; with the advent of the smartphone and easy-to-use video editing applications, all of a sudden the majority of people had a full-scale video production studio in the palm of their hand. Today, 'Vlogger' or 'YouTuber' has become a valid, popular and lucrative profession accessible to anybody.

At the time of writing in 2022, since 2018 consumers have nearly doubled the amount of video they watch, now consuming 19 hours of video content each week on average (Wyzowl, 2022). Obviously, this trend can't go on forever – we only have so many hours in a day after all – but it goes to show that consumers are putting their attention where their interests are and voting in numbers for video content. Brands stuck in their old ways of thinking that aren't scaling their video production will see the digital native world pass them by in a flash. The competition is already tough, too, and the quality of video needed to break into the video space is high. This is evidenced by a mere 10 per cent of videos on YouTube accounting for 80 per cent of all views (Cha et al, 2009), showing us that to really compete in the space requires true customer centricity, so that you can decode exactly the kind of content your customers want to see.

Here are some ideas to kick off your video strategy.

User-generated content: some estimates suggest user-generated content (UGC) is 8.7 times more impactful for consumers than influencer marketing (Nosto, 2022). It also beats out branded content in the hearts and minds of consumers, being rated as 6.6 times more impactful (Nosto, 2022). Definitely don't ditch influencers, that's not what I'm getting at, but certainly don't snooze on UGC either.

Edutainment and social selling: in 2021 the social commerce market was valued at $584.9 billion, and by some estimates is expected to grow at a compound annual growth rate (CAGR) of 30.8 per cent until 2030 (Grand View Research, 2022). Try out live shopping events where you educate and promote.

I also highly recommend parlaying any of your video content into on-site video assets, whether they be customer reviews and testimonials, explainer videos or simply a short clip to highlight the value proposition of your product. It will engage, increase dwell time, which will boost your SEO ranking and, most importantly, convert your customers. Which brings me to something incredibly important when it comes to your video assets, or any of your paid efforts. While throughout this book, I am downloading into your ways of thinking, the importance of brand, story, values and more, your paid strategies, in most cases, are not the place to be walking your consumers through these important aspects.

Your paid strategies, especially video, should get straight to highlighting your product and its value proposition. If your brand sells a vibrating device that sits on people's backs and helps them maintain a healthy posture, immediately show the device in action in the first few seconds of the video, and highlight the benefits of it like better posture and appearance, reduced pain, etc.

Don't spend the first 10 seconds of your ad showing people hunched over with bad posture in the office, only to show at the end that your product is the solution to a problem that your customer may have not even caught on to until you presented your product and they put the pieces of the puzzle together. This insight and many more came from Moshe Saraf of Pareto Solutions, a builder of unicorn brands through his effective creative and advertising campaigns, at the Commerce Accel 2022 conference.

Building a community-first content platform

Content marketing is the process of creating and distributing relevant and valuable content to your target audience in order to attract and engage potential customers. It should be at the centre of your customer acquisition wheelhouse as it is an essential part of any successful marketing strategy. Content marketing helps to establish your brand as a trusted authority, it builds relationships with customers and it boosts your sales. Content should be tailored to your target audience and should focus on presenting them with valuable information. Content can be in the form of YouTube video series, blog posts, infographics, videos on social platforms, podcasts and more. Content marketing is a great way to reach people who may have not heard of your business before, as well as to build relationships with existing customers. Content is the foundation of any successful community and is part of your top-of-funnel marketing efforts. Content serves as the driving force behind a community, providing a reason for people to come together and interact. Content can be used to spark conversations, share ideas and create a sense of belonging. Content also acts as a source of information, offering users valuable insights and advice. Without content, there would be no community and no interaction. Content is the lifeblood of any community, and marketers must ensure that they create high-quality, engaging content that their audience will find interesting and useful.

Building a content platform means building a macro community of *trusted* nodes on social media that actually LIKE your brand, and then tapping into that affinity to create attention for your brand and products. Not only can you generate attention, you'll also be able to control the narrative in 'dark social' environments (like messenger apps and private groups) and be privy to more of the conversations surrounding your brand as users gravitate to you and your channels, rather than going completely dark in their own private groups and messaging apps.

So, before you go further, understand that this chapter is all about connecting with your customers on a human level, engaging with them in ways that are meaningful to them, and building a community for them to engage and interact with around your brand. It's not about blasting out content and campaigns to get as many views and clicks as possible. That would be trying to reach an *audience*, which is not the same thing as building a community. The distinction being that an audience is something you have to keep reaching out to. **A community is something that sustains itself even when you're not there.** An audience is customer personas and ad targeting. A community is a place that is tailored to the needs of members, a place where people come to learn new things and share information, to connect and engage.

A community happens whether you build or facilitate one or not and can continue long after a brand ceases to exist. An audience on the other hand only exists for as long as you keep projecting content to it. That is the key distinction between the two.

We'll dive deep into what it means to build a community and why it is such a successful strategy for brands based on core psychological and sociological principles in Chapter 8. For now, just know that strategies such as content marketing, social media marketing, email marketing, direct mail and personalization can be used to build relationships with customers and create an engaged customer community. The keywords here being 'build relationships' and 'engaged community'.

Build communities as a go-to-market strategy

One of the biggest future trends in e-commerce will be the emergence of new brands from publishers, who have the knowledge and expertise to grow and engage audiences. These publishers will leverage their existing platforms and audiences to launch successful e-commerce ventures, often in niche markets where they have a deep understanding and passion.

Take a moment to put yourself in your customer's shoes. It shouldn't be hard, because as a human you do buy things, too, from time to time (I'm assuming that you are human, although this book may well see things that I could never imagine). Why would you, with a plethora of alternative options available, choose to buy your brand above all others? It's the connection that sets brands apart. Why do you feel more connected to one brand than the other? Probably, even if you didn't consciously realize it, they created a too-good-to-resist recipe from the principles I've outlined here in this chapter. Don't think a community is a valid go-to-market strategy? Oh have I got news for you.

Take Glossier, for example, a billion-dollar brand that started out as a, you guessed it, community. Emily Weiss's blog was a hobby, giving her a platform to connect with other young millennials and share beauty recommendations. Starting in 2010, Weiss began posting tips and beauty routines. Fast-forward four more years to 2014 and her blog was attracting over 10 million views every month. So, what did she do? Weiss did what any community-led go-to-market strategist would do, and she launched Glossier, a direct-to-consumer beauty product line. At the time of writing in 2022, Glossier is valued at over $1 billion (Rangan et al. 2021).

Think you don't have a community? Think again. An email list, that's a community. It might only be between your brand and one consumer, but that's a community. An Instagram page with 100 followers, that's a community. Or at least, the potential for one if you engage them in the right ways, instead of just projecting content at them as if they were simply an *audience*.

Whether you're building your go-to-market strategy, or are an established brand – community is key to generating demand for your product. Then, from those communities, build sub-communities of advocates who will take your brand out into the broader world of connected nodes, of family and friends. By recruiting others to do so, and then having them recruit more to do the same, you put the power of network effects behind your brand. How do you do that? With official referral and brand advocate programmes, of course. If you think that nobody would be interested, think again. Almost two-thirds of consumers say they would be likely to join an advocate community to create content for a brand (Nosto, 2022).

Influencer marketing

One of the key benefits of influencer marketing is the ability to reach a highly targeted audience. Influencers have built up their followings by providing valuable content and building trust with their audience – the exact same things you are trying to do as a brand. By engaging influencers you can leverage this foundational audience and community-building work done by others, as well as the core principles of influence (liking, authority and social proof) that you will learn later in this chapter to increase your customer acquisition.

Influencer marketing is nothing new. We've been swayed to give our attention to brands and even purchase their products by sportsmen, actors, actresses and even doctors for hundreds of years now. But with the democratization of content creation that technological advances have allowed, a new breed of influencer has sprung forth, known affectionately as the micro-influencer, but their impact is anything but small. While their sheer reach may have you believing so, it's not just the super influencers, the actors, actresses and celebrities that have all the pull in the online world. For many consumers, **micro-influencers** are incredibly influential nodes in their purchase decision-making network. This is because the smaller following of micro-influencers feels more personal and real for consumers. It's intimate and consumers feel more like a friend than a fan. And this added relatability and connection manifests in 60 per cent higher engagement with consumers (Main, 2017). Video of course is the ideal medium for influencer marketing, as these micro (or macro) celebrities can have their faces seen and recognized by their fan base and engage with them through creative and entertaining content.

But before you think that the big names aren't worth it, they definitely are; just know that a Kim Kardashian serves a different purpose than your smaller-scale beauty blogger. Very few people in the world have the recognition that someone like Kim Kardashian does. For example, at the time of writing I could probably simply say 'Kim K' and a majority of readers would know who I was talking about. Now, of course in several years' time, that may not be the case – but there will be a new set of influencers that have the same level of recognition. Celebrity may just be as old as time, as old as the first rock cave paintings mentioned in the introduction of this chapter, or older still. The authority that a macro-influencer lends to your company, as well as the interest they generate, is not something a micro-influencer can do for your brand, usually.

But a micro-influencer *can* add to your brand's authenticity and relatability and add authority within their much smaller circle. Look at macro-influencers as your top of funnel, attracting consumers to you. Your micro-influencers are who your customers turn to for their product use, research and post-purchase deeper connection and engagement needs. So, the point of this section is not to play one off against the other, but to illustrate how the two general types of influencer function *together* in your growth stack. Comparing the two directly as if it were a one or the other decision is almost like comparing apples and oranges.

One example of the power of micro-influencers, which will be especially relevant for up-and-coming brands without the big budgets of their competitors, is Gymshark. Ben Francis of Gymshark recognized the power of user-generated content and influencer marketing early, and is now at the time of writing in 2022 a near-billionaire. The company got its start largely through the help of influencers (and building communities) – not huge names either, just trusted nodes in networks that kept spreading the Gymshark brand gospel and singing its praises. It was with this strategy that Francis took his store from doing $450 a day to $45,000 a day (Sternlicht, 2020). From small beginnings with local influencers at local events, Gymshark now pays (at the time of writing in 2022) approximately 80 athletic influencers from $6,000 to $100,000 per year to live the Gymshark lifestyle and promote their product (Sternlicht, 2020).

So, a small brand can still grow big on micro-influencer marketing. Research by Andreas Bayerl (University of Mannheim), Jacob Goldenberg (Reichman University and Columbia University), and Andreas Lanz (HEC Paris), illustrates the nature of both micro- and macro-influencers. They found that the revenue generated per dollar invested for micro-influencers is actually higher than it is for macro-influencers, almost three times higher at €20 versus €7 (Bayer, A et al, 2022). However, macro-influencers get much greater reach and present an attractive option even if micro-influencers (seemingly) have a much larger impact on your bottom line. For example, you need only find one macro-influencer to generate a large impact for your brand. But you will need to find dozens if not hundreds of micro-influencers to generate a similar impact. This brings with it large costs and teams or agencies dedicated to sourcing and managing your influencers. Not to mention the brand awareness and social proof your brand gains from the huge reach and influence of a macro-influencer. The potential reach for a macro-influencer is approximately 26 times higher than for a micro-influencer, on average (Bayer, A et al, 2022). Additionally, views are 19 times higher, and engagement is almost 10 times higher. So, as always there are trade-offs well beyond the surface-level aspects of which type of influencer generates the best immediately attributable return on investment.

As always, when engaging in any campaign, be it a more intimate micro-influencer promotion or a large-scale celebrity push, consider your entire cross-functional e-commerce growth stack, for example your marketing team's capacities and finance team's budgets. Not to mention your supply chain's capacity to handle the huge upsurge in customers that an influencer campaign might bring. There would be nothing worse than running out of stock when hungry customers are lining up to get a piece of your brand!

The power of influence

Before we go further, I will first establish within the reader the core fundamental knowledge and ways of thinking required to wield the tool that is *influence* in the digital world. Because it is one thing to talk about influencers, user-generated content and tactics for growing your brand, but it is another thing to understand the fundamental *why* of the specific tactics we choose and the specific ways we implement them. This fundamental knowledge will also help you step beyond the bounds of what is outlined in this book, and move from copying my playbook to developing unique plays of your own based on the core first principles I have outlined for you throughout.

For this chapter we will turn to a man known in some circles as the 'Godfather' of persuasion, having written the book on influence, titled *Influence: The power of persuasion*: Robert Cialdini. In his book, Cialdini developed the six principles of persuasion: reciprocity, commitment, social proof, authority, liking and scarcity. Four of these are particularly relevant for this chapter's discussion: reciprocity, social proof, authority and liking (Cialdini, 2006). In this chapter I will show you how the principles of persuasion can be leveraged to create marketing campaigns that resonate with your audience and turn them into adoring fans.

Reciprocity is when people feel obligated to return a favour that was done for them – for example, when someone offers to help you with a task, you feel more obligated to help them in return. **Social proof** is when people look to the actions and beliefs of others to decide what to do – for example, when a product is popular, you may be more likely to buy it. **Authority** is when people follow the advice of an expert or respected figure – for example, when a doctor recommends a specific medication, you may be more likely to take it. Lastly, **liking** is when people are more likely to be persuaded by someone they know or like – for example, a friend's recommendation may influence you more than a stranger's. With the core principles of influence, as outlined by Cialdini himself, covered, we now move to the more practical aspects of leveraging influence in your e-commerce marketing.

Word of mouth

Referral marketing is a powerful way to get new customers. It involves leveraging your existing customers to bring in new ones. The idea is to incentivize your existing customers to refer new customers to your business. This could be done through discounts, rewards or other incentives. A referral programme should be designed to track and increase referrals and reward customers. The more customers who refer, the more successful the programme will be. By utilizing referral marketing, you can grow your customer base exponentially. Word of mouth (WOM) is the lifeblood for e-commerce businesses with a great product. Ogilvy Cannes found that three-quarters of consumers are highly influenced by word of mouth when making a purchasing decision (Coffee, 2014). But as an e-commerce brand you can't just wait for your product to start doing the talking for you; you need to actively build desire in a customer. This is based on the simple fact of human nature when it comes to e-commerce, and almost anything; when we see a group of people congregating around a brand and showing interest in it, we become interested in it ourselves. Not to mention the huge influence that trusted others have over our buying decisions.

While not being completely free, referral marketing in its many forms is very cost effective. In the new digital native era, consumers more than ever have access to more than just friends and family. They have access to people in communities on the internet, social media influencers. They're influenced by anybody online that consumers can feel a connection and similarity to. I want those two words to really sink in: connection and similarity. Because later I will cover the power of brand and why it is essential for demand generation as an e-commerce store. Data shows that referred customers are more loyal and spend more than non-referred customers (LaPlante-Dube, 2022). They're also more likely to then refer your brand to more people.

There are many ways you can rev up this growth engine for your e-commerce store:

1   **Referral programmes:** The most obvious is to set up an official referral programme. A simple incentivized refer-a-friend campaign is enough to do the trick. But adding an incentive to say thank you, like a mutual discount for both parties, will not only serve as a motivator but will also kick in the reciprocity effect.

2   **Get an affiliate army:** Take Sephora for example – its affiliate programme is particularly popular due to its 5 per cent commission and lack of restrictions on which products affiliates can choose to promote and earn commission on. Affiliates get perks like free shipping, free samples with every order, special offers and promotions that are only available to affiliates, and exclusive sneak peeks of new products (Sephora, 2022). This turns every customer into a potential marketer and customer acquisition specialist for your company. Affiliate marketing drives 16 per cent of e-commerce revenues in the United States (Insider Intelligence, 2016). But don't leave your affiliate strategy to chance. This is going to require a dedicated manager who can oversee and guide your affiliate strategy toward on-brand content that meets your brand image and guidelines. Affiliate marketing needs to be managed systematically for it to be effective, just like any other marketing channel needs to be. Affiliate team leaders

FIGURE 6.2   A referral programme banner

Refer a friend

GET **$25** OFF

Kunle, your word counts. Spread it for more rewards. Tell a friend about us and send **$25** their way.

You'll get **$25** off your next order once they have made a purchase

REFER A FRIEND

should be in charge of recruiting affiliates, settling terms and commissions, monitoring sales and performance, and supporting affiliates, as well as the general promotion of the affiliate programme. Your affiliate programme is essentially another product you are selling, only with a different and specific target persona. This means that your affiliate programme needs to be attractive to your target market, which can be done via things beyond the commission, like special perks, freebies, access to exclusive insider communities and more. Importantly, your affiliate managers are necessary to ensure affiliates have all the tools, resources and support they need – and are advertising goods in a manner that is compatible with the company's image.

3 **Ratings and reviews establish social proof:** Customers trust online reviews and use them to make decisions, with over two-thirds reading between one and six reviews before purchasing (Herman, 2017). A strong review strategy is important, with products rated 4–5 stars making up 94 per cent of purchases (Millwood, 2015) and 70 per cent of consumers using review filters (Reviewtrackers, 2021). Eighty-four per cent of consumers trust online peer reviews as much as they do reviews from family and friends (Bloem, 2017).

Demand capture

Finally, it's time to reap the rewards of all the hard work you've been doing. Once you have your customers' interest, through all of your brand awareness and demand generation marketing, you need to capture all the demand you have generated. This is what we call demand capture, or bottom-of-the-funnel marketing.

Demand capture sits at the bottom of the e-commerce marketing funnel – representing the stage of the customer journey where you are either nudging the customer to buy with promotional content such as product-focused ads and promotions, or simply facilitating their navigational searches through paid branded search so they can easily find your store at the top of the search engine. If you have laid the right foundations during demand generation, you will get a lot of branded search terms coming through, and this is great, because it shows not only brand awareness but brand recall – people remember your name – and for e-commerce stores that brand recall is very good for your bottom line.

For a deeper understanding of funnel dynamics, let's take a look at the kind of content you would be producing at each stage if you were a retailer selling a heart health device direct to consumers – a blood pressure monitor with electrocardiogram capabilities (the same kind of feature that's in many Apple watches, that will tell you if it recognizes problems with the electrical system in your heart). Whereas appearing in search engines for top-of-the-funnel search queries looking for answers to questions such as 'What does ECG stand for?' is fine, the customer doesn't really know a lot about electrocardiogram capabilities and benefits, but they might have seen it mentioned alongside a heart rate monitor they saw online. They may even simply be searching for something like 'How do I prevent cardiovascular disease?' or 'How do I reduce my risk of having a heart attack?' In this case they don't even know about blood pressure monitors with electrocardiogram capabilities. Middle of the funnel is getting closer to purchase; here you might be publishing content about 'How often should I do a check-up with an ECG machine?' And finally, bottom of the funnel looks like 'What is the best blood pressure monitor with electrocardiogram capabilities?' or 'Which heart rate monitor with ECG is better, A or B?' At this stage, bottom of the funnel, there is now real buying intent. The pinnacle of bottom of the funnel, though, is what we call brand name search. This is when you have already generated enough demand for your specific product and brand that the customer seeks you out directly by typing your brand name into the search bar, or something like 'your brand + product type'.

As I alluded to, search is a vital component of demand capture (as well as demand generation). At any stage of the funnel, you have access to both paid and organic strategies – both of which we will cover in due course, in later chapters of this book. Another key aspect is advertising and retargeting. Utilizing your customer data, be it through lookalike audiences generated based on your existing customer base, or first-party data which tracks your viewers or browsers of your content, it becomes an incredible highly targeted demand capture tool. A majority of your customers just aren't ready to buy when they visit your site for the first time, so without a dedicated retargeting strategy you're going to be letting a lot of customers slip through the cracks – in fact some estimates show retargeting campaigns converting 10 times better than a simple targeted advertising campaign (Google, 2022; Wishpond, 2022).

Retargeting is a marketing tactic that includes presenting personalized adverts to website visitors or those who have previously expressed interest in your brand. This is frequently accomplished through the use of first-party data, which monitors website users' online activities and enables businesses to show them relevant adverts when they explore other websites.

There are several ways that you can utilize retargeting for your own brand:

- **Display advertising:** display ads show up on websites or social media platforms and are one of the most popular methods of retargeting. People who have seen your brand's website or demonstrated interest in it can be found across the internet and shown your ads.

- **Email marketing:** if you give shoppers the ability to sign up as email subscribers on your site, and you can utilize first-party data to track when users visit your site, a cart abandonment or checkout abandonment email is about one of the best and cheapest retargeting methods there is. With approximately 40 per cent of abandoned cart emails being opened and, of those that are opened, 20 per cent receiving a click-through, email retargeting is a great way to capture demand and close on the sale (Moosend, 2023).

- **Paid search:** another way to do retargeting is through platforms like Google Ads, which allows companies to display ads to people who have previously visited their website as they search for related terms on Google.

All in all, retargeting is a powerful tool for businesses aiming to enhance conversion rates and return on their marketing investments. With it your brand can ensure it is capturing maximum value from its demand-generation activities.

Wrapping up

Just as the hunter-gatherers of old were faced with no easy task, needing to work together, against the odds, with a plethora of tools and techniques to land their next meal, the modern e-commerce brand does not have it any easier. They need to employ a full suite of connected experiences to herd and corral their potential consumers into favourable ground (that is, your brand's ecosystem) and persuade them to buy. The marketing funnel begins with demand generation, which includes edutainment and influencer marketing to build authority and trust, and advertising to reach new audiences. Once demand is generated, referral marketing can be used to amplify the power of the current audience, adding social proof and further generating interest in and desire for your products. Demand capture follows, which includes search engine marketing to capture existing demand in the market on what we call non-branded queries and optimizing brand name search to capture potential customers with navigational or purchase intent queries (you will learn more about this in Chapter 10, 'Search engine marketing'). Of course, Rome wasn't built in a day, and you shouldn't expect your customers to convert in such a short time period either. Retargeting is used to loop back lost conversions and, in many cases, it's a matter of third, or even seventh time lucky, before your customer converts. To land that conversion, you will likely need a full arsenal of tools for 1:1 communication with audiences, including email capture and marketing automation, promotional email campaigns, messaging app automation and campaigns and live chat. All of these steps work together to create a cohesive marketing strategy that drives engagement once your customer is in your brand's ecosystem and increases conversions. Here's how it all looks broken down into the modern e-commerce marketer's demand-generation and capture funnel.

In conclusion, customer acquisition is a crucial aspect of any successful business. Broken down into its component parts as you see in Figure 6.1, it seems quite simple, and it is. But by no means is it easy. Creating on-brand messaging and experiences across all these channels and touchpoints alone, not considering all the other aspects involved in your e-commerce business, is a mammoth task. By implementing effective strategies and utilizing the right tools, you can attract new customers and add to your customer base. However, it is equally important to focus on retention and ensuring that your existing customers continue to be satisfied and engaged with your brand. In the next chapter, we will delve deeper into the topic of customer retention and explore strategies and tactics that you can use to keep your customers coming back for more. By mastering both customer acquisition and retention, you can create a strong and loyal customer base that will help drive the growth and success of your business.

References

Bloem, C (2017) 84 percent of people trust online reviews as much as friends. Here's how to manage what they see, *Inc.*, www.inc.com/craig-bloem/84-percent-of-people-trust-online-reviews-as-much-.html (archived at https://perma.cc/7SF9-G4LP)

Brown, S (2021) Where did writing come from? *Getty*, 27 Apr, www.getty.edu/news/where-did-writing-come-from/ (archived at https://perma.cc/F6N7-TAB8)

Cha, M, Kwak, H, Rodriguez, P, Ahn, Y-Y and Moon, S (2009) Analyzing the video popularity characteristics of large-scale user-generated content systems, *IEEE/ACM Transactions on Networking*, 17, pp 1357–70, doi:10.1145/1665838.1665839

Cialdini, R (2006) *Influence: The psychology of persuasion*, Harper Business, New York, NY

Coffee, P (2014) Ogilvy Cannes study: behold the power of word of mouth, *Adweek*, 19 Jun, www.adweek.com/performance-marketing/ogilvy-cannes-study-behold-the-power-of-word-of-mouth/ (archived at https://perma.cc/7GXU-VXD4)

Comscore (2010) Comscore study with ValueClick Media shows ad retargeting generates strongest lift compared to other targeting strategies, www.comscore.com/Insights/Press-Releases/2010/9/comScore-Study-with-ValueClick-Media-Shows-Ad-Retargeting-Generates-Strongest-Lift-Compared-to-Other-Targeting-Strategies (archived at https://perma.cc/YQ5B-3GQ3)

Google (2015) Marketo sees 10x higher conversion rate vs traditional display remarketing with Google Analytics, *Think With Google*, www.thinkwithgoogle.com/_qs/documents/506/marketo-scores-10x-higher-conversion-rate-with-google-analytics.pdf (archived at https://perma.cc/3LQH-BJBK)

Grand View Research (2022) Social commerce market size, share and trends analysis report by business model (B2C, B2B, C2C), by product type (personal and beauty care), by platform/sales channel, by region and segment forecasts, 2022–2030, Market Analysis Report, *Grandviewresearch*, p 109, www.grandviewresearch.com/industry-analysis/social-commerce-market# (archived at https://perma.cc/73NW-9TEM)

Hayes, A (2022) What video marketers should know in 2023, according to Wyzowl Research, *Hubspot*, 26 Jul, https://blog.hubspot.com/marketing/state-of-video-marketing-new-data (archived at https://perma.cc/54ZC-EZKJ)

Herman, Z (2017) Why customer reviews are crucial to your small business, *Inc.*, www.inc.com/young-entrepreneur-council/why-customer-reviews-are-crucial-to-your-small-business.html (archived at https://perma.cc/ZH8C-RTTB)

Insider Intelligence (2016) Omnichannel Strategy Bundle: your guide to engaging with shoppers on multiple channels, *Business Insider*, 19 Dec, www.businessinsider.com/omnichannel-marketing-strategy-and-research-e-commerce-and-online-sales-2016-11?IR=T (archived at https://perma.cc/VAY6-R59M)

LaPlante-Dube, M (2022) How to build a strong customer referral program, *Hubspot*, 16 Jun, https://blog.hubspot.com/service/customer-referral-program (archived at https://perma.cc/M8BD-LEA6)

Main, S (2017) Micro-influencers are more effective with marketing campaigns than highly popular accounts, *Adweek*, www.adweek.com/performance-marketing/micro-influencers-are-more-effective-with-marketing-campaigns-than-highly-popular-accounts/ (archived at https://perma.cc/8MR5-977C)

Marchant, J (2016) A journey to the oldest cave paintings in the world, *Smithsonian Magazine*, Jan, www.smithsonianmag.com/history/journey-oldest-cave-paintings-world-180957685/ (archived at https://perma.cc/T72Q-VSRZ)

Millwood, A (2015) How star ratings influence customers' behavior, *Yotpo*, 5 Apr, www.yotpo.com/blog/star-ratings-influence-customers/ (archived at https://perma.cc/FY5E-JP5U)

Moosend (2023) Shopping cart abandonment stats you'll need for 2023, https://moosend.com/blog/cart-abandonment-stats/ (archived at https://perma.cc/A5TQ-J3SR)

Nosto (2022) Consumer behavior stats 2021: the post-pandemic shift in online shopping habit, *Nosto*, 7 Apr, www.nosto.com/blog/consumer-behavior-stats/ (archived at https://perma.cc/4VE8-WECW)

Peters, B (2019) What 777,367,063 Facebook posts tell us about successful content in 2019 (new research), *Buffer Resources*, 10 Jan, https://buffer.com/resources/facebook-marketing-2019/ (archived at https://perma.cc/28HL-CDJQ)

Rangan, VK, Corsten, D, Higgins, M and Schlesinger, LA (2021) How direct-to-consumer brands can continue to grow, *Harvard Business Review*, Nov–Dec, https://hbr.org/2021/11/how-direct-to-consumer-brands-can-continue-to-grow (archived at https://perma.cc/H7B3-NZQK)

ReviewTrackers (2021) Online Reviews Statistics and Trends: A 2022 Report by ReviewTrackers, 1 Dec, www.reviewtrackers.com/reports/online-reviews-survey/ (archived at https://perma.cc/DFK3-P9BX)

Sephora (2022) Sephora Affiliates, www.sephora.com/beauty/affiliates (archived at https://perma.cc/U3T4-Q82D)

Smith, KL (2022) What is the most viewed video on TikTok? Here are the Top 10, *POPBUZZ*, 4 Apr, www.popbuzz.com/internet/viral/most-viewed-video-tiktok/# (archived at https://perma.cc/MS74-U8H7)

Sternlicht, A (2020) How a former Pizza Hut delivery guy used TikTok and Instagram to build Gymshark into a billion-dollar sportswear brand, *Forbes*, 2 Dec, www.forbes.com/sites/alexandrasternlicht/2020/12/02/how-ben-francis-used-tiktok-and-instagram-to-build-gymshark-into-a-billion-dollar-sportswear-brand/ (archived at https://perma.cc/YZQ4-B3SW)

Wishpond (2022) 7 incredible retargeting ad stats, https://blog.wishpond.com/post/97225536354/infographic-7-incredible-retargeting-ad-stats#close-overlay (archived at https://perma.cc/MYC8-6YGB)

Wyzowl (2022) Video marketing statistics 2022 (brand new data), www.wyzowl.com/video-marketing-statistics/ (archived at https://perma.cc/A8TP-MR39)

Further reading

2X eCommerce (2019) S04 EP11, e-Commerce SEO and the impact of E-A-T with Marie Haynes, https://2xecommerce.com/podcast/ep180/ (archived at https://perma.cc/BD8G-UAJ8)

Ackerman, B (2019) 3 unexpected reasons baby boomers are turning to YouTube, *Think With Google*, Jan, www.thinkwithgoogle.com/marketing-strategies/video/baby-boomer-youtube-trends/ (archived at https://perma.cc/UZ9L-Z5T9)

Auxier, B, Anderson, M, Perrin, A and Turner, E (2020) 2. Parental views about YouTube, *Pew Research Center*, 28 Jul, www.pewresearch.org/internet/2020/07/28/parental-views-about-youtube/ (archived at https://perma.cc/3GQY-XM2K)

Ogilvy, D (2007) *Ogilvy on Advertising*, Prion, London

Seaman, JT and Smith, GD (2012) Your company's history as a leadership tool, *Harvard Business Review*, Dec, https://hbr.org/2012/12/your-companys-history-as-a-leadership-tool (archived at https://perma.cc/R3XH-7BF8)

Switch, W (2019) No. 314: On linear commerce, *2PM*, https://2pml.com/2019/04/22/on-linear-commerce/ (archived at https://perma.cc/XHN3-PE8M)

Tellis, GJ (2004) *Effective Advertising: Understanding when, how and why advertising works*, SAGE Publications, Thousand Oaks, CA

Think With Google (2017) Baby boomer YouTube behavior statistics, www.thinkwithgoogle.com/consumer-insights/consumer-trends/baby-boomer-youtube-behavior-statistics/ (archived at https://perma.cc/RJU4-VK86)

Zak, PJ (2014) Why your brain loves good storytelling, *Harvard Business Review*, 28 Oct, https://hbr.org/2014/10/why-your-brain-loves-good-storytelling (archived at https://perma.cc/UC7S-MTL8)

7

Retention for long-term growth

Now that you have learned what it takes to acquire customers, it's time to focus on how to keep them coming back for more. After all, customer retention is just as important as customer acquisition. In this chapter, we cover how to deliver experiences that delight, whether it be through customer experience, messaging and email marketing, or building on the omnipresent underpinnings of human psychology to keep customers in your orbit. This chapter will build into the next, where we cover community building and the fundamental sociological realities that e-commerce brands can leverage to create long-term sustainable brand growth.

Why retention matters: the numbers

Introduction to retention

RETENTION AS AN INNOVATION

It might be hard to imagine today, with supermarket shelves full of farmed grains and vegetables, but at one point in the short history of humanity we had to roam vast expanses of land to hunt, fish and forage if we wanted to eat. But at some point (estimates suggest somewhere around 14,500 and 12,000 BP (Before Present) in Southwest Asia) we began to collect wild plants such as barley on a large scale. Around 12,000 BP domesticated versions of some plants were seen in the Levant (a region corresponding to modern-day Syria, Israel, Lebanon and Jordan), and thus began our transition to agriculture (Britannica, 2022). Slowly but surely we switched from being nomadic hunter-gatherers, to farmers with permanent settlements. In Mexico it was squash, in China it was rice. Something so simple, but that changed the course of our history in ways unimaginable. Now, not all of us have been domesticated by agriculture – some still are primarily hunter-gatherers, like the Hadza of Tanzania, but they are few and far between. Or are they? Perhaps we've still got the same hunter-gatherer itch and we've just found new ways to express it now that we can enjoy the relative comfort that agriculture brings. One modern arena where we see both hunting and gathering, and farming, is e-commerce.

To bring in new customers requires the hunter-gatherer mindset. If you want to eat, you have to go out and find your food; it might be a long way away, and it could take a lot of effort. But if you want to survive... well, you have no choice. Customer acquisition is going out into the vast expanses and depths of the internet and finding shoppers. The scent on the trail is thrown by a series of third-party cookies and our weapon of choice is the targeted ad campaign. An e-commerce brand that isn't actively bringing in new customers is slowly starving. But we've wised up a little since our hunter-gatherer days. We've realized that by building settlements and tilling the land, we can comfortably enjoy the fruits (and vegetables) of our labour. We know that if we put in the work, we can reap what we sow right from our own backyard. Because all that hunting and gathering can be tiring. In the e-commerce world, the agriculture equivalent is customer retention. It's things like building communities, loyalty programmes and post-purchase email automations. It's events and experiential marketing. It's save and subscribe, and replenishment notifications. Preparing the land? Well that's building a desirable brand through authenticity, values and social proof. Having the tastiest produce? That's research and development, product and customer experience.

Research by Bain & Company shows that the average time to break even on a new customer is 12 months for e-commerce companies, owing to high acquisition costs. They also found that on average, the customer's average order value increases over time, being 40 per cent higher on their fifth purchase and 80 per cent larger on their tenth purchase (Baveja et al, 2000). So, it's not just customer acquisition that is essential for surviving (and thriving), but retention, too. It's not just the plants we already have, either – it's the seeds they spread. The longer you retain customers, the more time they have to advocate your brand. Which is no revelation. But what might be, is that customers who are acquired via these referrals actually spend more than the original customer who referred them to your brand in the first place. In some industries such as electronics and apparel, customers who are referred to you spend around 50 per cent more than the original customer (Baveja et al,

2000). The e-commerce brand can become very plump and content (profitable) thanks to the 'agriculture of e-commerce' that is retention.

Fundamental e-commerce retention metrics

The first step to knowing how you're performing is to benchmark your data. Without some kind of reference point, you'll get lost in either complacency because you don't know how much better you could be doing, or alternatively in chasing potentially unattainable goals, spending too much time, money and effort trying to improve a metric that you may well have squeezed enough juice out of already. Meaning your resources would be better spent elsewhere in the growth stack, to create a symbiotic relationship with other nodes in your growth network. Fundamental retention-related metrics are the customer retention rate, churn rate, lifetime value and net promoter score. **Customer retention rate** is the percentage of customers who remain with a business after a certain time period. At the time of writing in 2022, average retention rates for e-commerce verticals range from 20.9 per cent (tea) to 33 per cent (high-performance sports clothing) (Rentech Digital, 2022). The average retention rate for e-commerce businesses is 30 per cent (Omniconvert, 2019). **Customer churn** is the opposite of retention and is the percentage of customers lost over a certain time period. The average churn rate for subscription e-commerce is between 9 and 13 per cent over a 24-month period (Recurly, 2019). **Customer lifetime value** is the amount of money a business can expect to earn from a customer throughout their relationship. The average customer lifetime value for direct-to-consumer e-commerce companies is $168, but ranges from $55 for tea, to $477 (CBD oil) (Teneva, 2018). Lastly, **net promoter score** is a measure of how likely customers are to promote a brand and has an average score of 39 for internet shopping (Netpromoter, 2022).

Marketing leaders generally report spending a lot more time and effort monitoring acquisition metrics like conversion rate and customer acquisition cost, as well as average order value. While the majority of marketing leaders reported measuring conversion rate and average order value (80 per cent and 64 per cent respectively), slightly less than half reported monitoring customer satisfaction, and around one-third monitor customer retention rate and customer lifetime value (Omniconvert, 2019). Only one-quarter of marketing leaders reported measuring net promoter score, a metric with a philosophy strongly founded in customer-centricity

(Omniconvert, 2019). While these numbers are bound to fluctuate over time, the main takeaway is that more brands focus on monitoring acquisition-related metrics than retention-related metrics. At least at the time of writing in 2022 – hopefully that changes in no small part due to this book. **My advice to e-commerce brands?** What gets measured gets managed. A customer-centric e-commerce company should be monitoring all key metrics attentively to have a 360-degree view of the environment, including key satisfaction and retention metrics. Without it, you can't build a truly symbiotic cross-functional growth environment.

When it comes to retention and churn, it's important to understand what counts as retained and what counts as churned. This will help you make data-driven decisions and optimize your data strategy. For subscription businesses, churn is typically measured monthly, while for e-commerce stores, it may be measured on longer timeframes. Your product and average purchase frequency can give you hints on the best timeframes to measure. A mattress store that sells only mattresses will have a very long time between purchases. A company selling consumables like chocolate will, if it's good, have much higher purchase frequency. Measuring on a longer time period can help smooth out 'cliffs' where disinterested customers drop off early and definitively. Before calculating retention, it's important to understand the average value when calculating metrics like the average time between orders. This will help you avoid confusion. In general, measuring on a longer time period (for example six months) will help smooth out cliffs where disinterested customers drop off early and definitively, but interested customers trickle back in over a few months. Data from Rentech Digital (2022) shows that many e-commerce verticals have an average time between orders of between 71 days (high-performance sports clothing) and 132 days (tea). For a low purchase frequency brand, building out your product assortment can be a great way to increase purchase frequency. Add in both new lines to give consumers more products to purchase, and also higher-frequency items to bring in steady cash flow for your brand.

As a note, it's important to know the difference between mean and median when calculating statistics because they can give different results. The mean is the sum of all values divided by the number of observations, while the median is the middle value in the dataset. The mean can be heavily influenced by very small or very large values, while the median is not. When measuring the average time between purchases, it's helpful to use the median rather than the mean.

Other key metrics

Meticulously measuring, tracking and optimizing your retention metrics is essential for building a sustainable and highly profitable brand. A 5 per cent increase in customer loyalty can increase profits by between 25 and 95 per cent (Bain & Company, 2006), making it a key area of focus for businesses. By understanding and improving your retention metrics, you can not only retain more customers but also drive increased profits for your brand. With that in mind, here are some key metrics that you should be tracking:

- Repeat purchase ratio: the percentage of people who come back to buy from you. Calculated by dividing the number of customers who have purchased more than once by the total number of customers.

- Customer acquisition cost (CAC): the cost to get a customer 'in the door' divided by the conversion rate for getting them to become a customer. Can be calculated for each individual channel to find the most cost-effective acquisition sources.

- Customer lifetime value (CLV) to CAC ratio: the ratio of CLV to CAC, which should be considered when determining business strategy. A ratio of 3 to 1 or 4 to 1 is common, but it can vary based on the nature of the business and business strategy.

- Time to recover CAC: the amount of time it takes to recover the cost of acquiring a customer. Calculated by dividing CAC by the average order value.

- Average order value (AOV): the average amount of money spent per purchase. Calculated by dividing the total revenue by the number of orders.

- Cart abandonment rate: the percentage of shoppers who add items to their cart but do not complete the purchase. Calculated by dividing the number of abandoned carts by the number of completed purchases.

- Customer churn rate: the percentage of customers who stop doing business with a company. Calculated by dividing the number of customers at the beginning of a period by the number of customers at the end of the period, minus one.

- Net promoter score (NPS): a measure of customer satisfaction. Calculated by subtracting the percentage of detractors (unhappy customers) from the percentage of promoters (happy customers). A score of 0–6 indicates a detractor, 7–8 a passive and 9–10 a promoter (usually). Bain & Company places the customer lifetime value (CLV) of promoters at anywhere from 6 to 14 times greater than the CLV of detractors (Bain & Company, 2015)

For a full guide on how to calculate each of these key metrics and strategize with them in mind, head to 2xecommerce.com/book/chapter7.

Improving retention and CLV

Improving customer retention and customer lifetime value (CLV) doesn't have to be difficult or expensive. It begins with a good customer experience, and there are many things that you can implement right now. Factors that influence brand loyalty include efficiency, convenience and friendly and knowledgeable service. E-commerce brands can use up-to-date technology, easy mobile experiences and automation to deliver these. Accurate sizing guides, consistent photography and customer reviews can all improve customer experience for apparel retailers – none of these are high-tech or difficult to implement. In addition, transparent sizing information and product descriptions can reduce customer complaints and returns.

To get a little more high-tech, virtual try-on technology for apparel retailers, or even augmented reality for things like furniture stores, will go a long way to improving customer experience. The same goes for customer service. While not technically a high-tech solution, implementing effective customer-centric service in today's multichannel e-commerce environment definitely requires integrated and advanced technological solutions. About 80 per cent of customers say they would leave a brand after two bad customer experiences (Emplifi, 2022a). And for those that actually do leave, poor customer experience is the culprit in approximately two-thirds of cases.

When it comes to customer service, the essential ingredients are having the right touchpoints, fast response times and, of course, being able to solve the customer's problem. Preferred touchpoints include self-service options, social media, email and live chat. Telephones are also popular among consumers (Emplifi, 2022a). Customers expect your customer service agents to have all the necessary information about their previous purchases, which means a customer data platform or customer relationship management system integrated with your customer support software is essential. When it comes to response times, they vary by platform. But an overwhelming majority of customers expect a response within one day. If they're engaging with you on social media, then approximately half expect you to respond within one hour (Emplifi, 2022b).

The takeaway: customers want support from your brand when, where and how they want it. Your customer service is your first and last line of defence when it comes to customer retention.

Turning customer returns into a revenue-generating opportunity

The title of this section might seem counterintuitive, but you can turn your customer returns process into revenue opportunities. That's not to say you'll always come out with a positive net revenue. However, you can minimize your losses through intelligent process design and data-driven strategies. As an e-commerce store, it is easy to feel like you've lost when you get a return, like your product has failed, or you've failed the customer as a brand. It feels like a breakup. But a customer return is just another step in the customer journey, and another opportunity to use customer-centricity to turn your returns process into a retention opportunity. In episode #244 I chatted with Joe Vancena, who at the time of writing in 2022 was the product marketing manager at Loop Returns, a customer returns and retention optimization tool for retailers (Crook, 2021). He provided some great tips for optimizing your refunds and returns process. I went and did some digging too and found some incredible and counter-intuitive statistics on refunds and returns.

This may surprise you, but customers who make a refund or return request are actually more likely to come back (McEachern, 2021). Yes, that's right – refunds and returns can actually increase your repeat purchase rate. Research by Loop Returns found that exchanges increase the repeat purchase rate by one-third, and refunds (yes, even refunds) increase it by over 25 per cent (McEachern, 2021). In fact, the worst case for your business is a customer simply keeping a product they don't want (McEachern, 2021).

Making returns more than just a refund platform

INCENTIVES
Leading with incentives tells your customer that you're customer-centric, and that you're investing in them and in your relationship with them. It doesn't have to be anything complicated; simply offer a discount during the

returns process if the customer goes back to the store and buys again. For example, if something is just the wrong size, or the colour was a little bit off, then the customer isn't a high-churn probability. These problems are easily solvable. Responses like these are telling you 'I wish I could keep going, and how can I?' says Joe Vancena of Loop (2X eCommerce, 2020).

Consider what a customer is thinking when it comes to a 'colour wasn't what I expected' return. Are they saying, 'I don't want this product' or are they saying, 'I do still like it, but it's not perfect. I wouldn't have paid this much for the product if I knew it would be like this'? In the latter case, a discount on a next product, a store credit or even a shipping credit might be enough to tip the balance back in favour of your product and your brand. The main thing is to have an offer besides a return.

Optimizing your returns systems

To optimize your returns systems, there are some simple steps that you can take:

- **Make your returns policy easy to understand** and set expectations early. Make it legal jargon-free and set expectations early. Joe Vancena of Loop suggests that almost two-thirds of your customers may be checking your returns policy before they buy.

- **Connect with customers through human support staff.** Joe Vancena suggests that you connect your customer with a human as early as possible. Ideally your customer support staff have enough authority to resolve any issues for your customer in a timely manner.

- **Offer self-service options for returns.** Empower your consumers to take control of the returns process and ensure the process is efficient. Ninety-two per cent of customers say they will shop with a brand again if the returns process is efficient (Saleh, 2022).

- **You MUST offer a refund,** but you might not want to make it FREE. Loop cites one client who, after only two months of charging a shipping fee, saw exchange requests grow by just over 25 per cent, and refund requests dropping by almost one-third (McEachern, 2021). Test results for your own brand.

- **Consider offering free alternatives to refunds,** such as store credit or exchanges. An optimal returns policy doesn't box your customer in to any one option, it gives them choice to choose their returns journey.

Ideally the alternative is free for the customer – something like a store credit, exchange or a discount on their next order.

- **Use customer feedback to improve products and customer experience.** A refund request is about as good an indication as there is that your brand has let a customer down. But when life gives you lemons, you've got to make lemonade. Use it as an opportunity to gather valuable customer feedback and let your customer be heard.

- **Communicate feedback to all stakeholders.** Everyone should be aware of trends in customer feedback. That means communicating back to the product, operations and marketing teams so that any changes that need to be made can be fed through the entire cross-functional e-commerce growth stack.

By making returns a positive experience, you can increase customer retention and revenue.

Loyalty programmes

Look around you today, search for any product you can think of, and one thing you will notice is that you have a whole lot of choice. Almost too much. With so much to choose from, consumers are able to brand switch in an instant, without much thought. So, in this world of choice it is customer loyalty that gives you a real sustainable competitive advantage.

Loyalty programmes have good buy-in from consumers; in the retail space approximately three-quarters of consumers are part of at least one loyalty programme (Barton et al, 2018). But that doesn't mean they're a surefire way to succeed. Many consumers say they're more likely to react negatively to a company's attempt to earn their loyalty, because while they value access to exclusive offers, they also appreciate personalization, innovative experiences and brands that support causes, and they want your attempts to win their loyalty to reflect that (Wollan et al, 2017). So, does this mean that loyalty programmes are out? No. It just means that brands need to rethink the way they do them. You guessed it, they need to be more customer-centric. If your brand isn't on point with personalized marketing, communicating values and supporting causes, and through experiential marketing (like the Naked Wines events loved by many wine enthusiasts around the world) your loyalty programme isn't going to hit the mark (Naked Wines, 2022; Campbell, 2015).

Great examples of on-point loyalty programmes include The North Face and NikePlus. The North Face, for example, rewards loyal customers with actual experiences that fit with their lifestyles, values and interests – like mountain climbing with well-known athletes in that niche (The North Face, 2022). How's that for combining influencer marketing and customer loyalty programmes! Nike, on the other hand, adds a level of gamification to their loyalty programme, enabling customers to rack up loyalty points based on fitness achievements, which is a surefire way to get customers hooked into engaging with the brand (Williams, 2018) – much in the same way that web and mobile applications use gamification in the form of points, rewards and leadership systems to keep you coming back.

A tip to optimize your cross-functional growth stack: when you're designing your loyalty programme, go beyond simply rewarding purchases. What other behaviours do you want to reward? What else brings value to your brand? For example, things like brand advocacy should be rewarded, too. One company doing just that is Tarte, a skincare and cosmetics brand rewarding customers for posting video tutorials and selfies online (Purohit, 2020). At the time of writing in 2022, their programme is undergoing a makeover (pardon the pun) so we don't know what to expect in the future. But the main takeaway is not the brand, it is the principle. Always strategize with the entire cross-functional e-commerce growth stack in mind, and in this case, reward your consumers for the full suite of actions that benefit your company, not just direct purchases.

Making success a habit

Building habits into your brand and product can increase customer lifetime value, as well as revenue predictability and word of mouth. According to John Gourville, a professor of marketing at Harvard Business School, a competitor would have to be nine times better to take away your customers if you have built strong habits (Gourville, 2006 in Eyal, 2013). However, to integrate your product or solution into this framework, to become the *behaviour*, takes time and targeted strategic effort.

So, what is a habit? Well, according to cognitive psychologists (and I guess they're the people to listen to when it comes to these kinds of things), a habit is an *automatic* behaviour triggered by situational cues (Wood and Rünger, 2016).

Cue -> [something triggers inside the black box that is your brain] -> *Behaviour*

In this section I will show you how to leverage consumer psychology throughout your cross-functional value chain to create strong habit loops in your consumers.

Building the habit

Cues or triggers are the first step in the habit-forming (and activation) process. First you need to create associations between your product and satisfying user needs. Then you need to implement external cues to trigger certain behaviours. Habits often need reminding. If you've ever tried to make a change in your personal life, you know how hard it can be to stay motivated, but sometimes you really do just forget. That's because old habits take over, and without realizing we default back to our past selves.

There are two general types of triggers: external and internal. **External triggers** are typically visual and audio-visual cues; they could be notifications, 'click here' call-to-action buttons, advertisements at specific times that trigger an action – for example a Black Friday ad reminding your customers to shop for the holidays early and save. Advertising is such an important external trigger that increases its potency with frequency; that is why UK readers will be much too aware of the annoying but hugely successful TV ad for GoCompare that features Wynne Evans, the Welsh tenor who plays Gio Compario, GoCompare's longtime mascot. Triggers could also come in the form of using influencers your customers know, love and trust to remind them about using your products with regular cadence.

Internal triggers are emotions, feelings and needs. The idea is that external triggers create a cascading effect to reinvigorate internal triggers. Internal triggers nudge consumers to scratch a certain itch, and it is through associations they have built around how to scratch that itch, that they form an action plan to achieve that. Once established, this action plan becomes automatic, and the customer acts it out without really thinking about it. Ever found yourself opening an app on your phone and then wondering how exactly you got there? Almost like you did it subconsciously? Instagram or TikTok perhaps? That's the power of habit. Other internal triggers include the need for human connection which drives people to social media platforms and online communities.

Nir Eyal is the author of *Hooked: How to build habit-forming products* and cherished guest #24 on the 2X eCommerce podcast (at the time of writing, we have recorded over 450 episodes, so Nir was a guest of mine in the very early days of my podcasting journey). He mentions IKEA – which sells everything from entire kitchens (something not frequently purchased) to pens and other stationery (frequently purchased) to food from their restaurant (a super high replenishment rate – you get hungry many many many times a day). By satisfying various customer needs – experiential needs, utility needs, convenience needs and even satisfying their hunger cravings – IKEA give consumers everything they need to stay engaged with the brand (*frequency*) on multiple different timeframes in multiple ways.

With the right mix of demand generation, cues and habit forming you will create customers who regularly engage with your brand and purchase from you. For a consumer to take some kind of action, you typically need them to have two things: the motivation to take the action and, importantly, the ability to do so.

Motivation is created via your marketing efforts, through communicating *the experience of pleasure* thanks to using your product, or *the avoidance of pain*. Any number of psychological needs can be satisfied with consumer products, from hunger to prestige and status needs. Get deep into your target market's psychology. For example, the humble magnesium bath has more to offer than simply relaxation – it means better sleep and less pain, it means more energy throughout the day and being able to step straight into home life with family of an evening without breaking stride. It means having the energy to play with your children, read them a book and help them with their homework. It means not missing the most important moments in their lives because you were tired, exhausted even after work. It means more social connection and experiences, and not letting half your life 'outside of work' fade away because you don't have the energy. It's much more than just feeling relaxed.

Ability means that your product is *easy to purchase and use*, your brand is *easy to engage with online* and you have all the materials needed to fill any knowledge gaps. It means establishing communities that teach one another, for example a strong online community of makeup enthusiasts showing one another how to best use your products. It means the process doesn't take a long time or consume a lot of mental or physical effort.

Reward schedules

Variety is the spice of life, they say. And people's love of variable rewards shows it might just be true. The spice in this case is the hit of dopamine our brains get when we anticipate a reward. Wait, when we anticipate one? Not when we get one? That's right. Dopamine is not about pleasure, it is about the anticipation of pleasure, as Robert Sapolsky, professor of biology and neurology at Stanford University says: 'It's about the pursuit of happiness' (Sapolsky, 2011). Dopamine is essential for goal-directed behaviour.

Why variable? Why not just have the same reward each time? When a behaviour is rewarded consistently, it is called continuous reward. It's good for training new behaviour, but maybe your pet gets bored of the same old reward and progress starts to slip away. That's because the best way to maintain a behaviour is to use intermittent reward.

Intermittent reward can be broken down into four types – each of these might give you ideas for your brand (Grieve and Lowe-Calverly, 2016). They are:

- Fixed ratio rewards: for example, for every $1 spent you get one loyalty point.

- Fixed interval rewards: for every hour of work you do, you get paid your hourly salary.

- Variable ratio rewards: you're rewarded with loyalty discounts but the number of purchases you need to make before your next reward isn't known. But one day you buy something, and you're rewarded with a bonus. Potentially the rewards also differ each time.

- Variable interval rewards: you never know when a reward is going to come but you get rewards from time to time that are independent of your action. Perhaps by being a member of a community you get rewarded even if you're not engaged with it.

Using variable rewards turns off the brain's critical reasoning and judgment faculties. It also activates the regions in the brain responsible for desire (Sapolsky, 2011 in Eyal, 2013). But it's not just discounts and monetary rewards that do this. Social rewards do it too, as well as gaining a sense of mastery over a subject (Eyal, 2013). Think about platforms where users up-vote one another and how you can work that into your communities, and websites such as Masterclass.com that allow users to feel a sense of mastery over a topic. At the time of writing in 2022 you can learn the power of personal branding from Kris Jenner, how to elevate your singing and stage presence from Beyoncé, how to cook with Gordon Ramsay – the possibilities are endless (MasterClass, 2022).

Some real-world examples of habit-forming in commerce

Nir Eyal in his book *Hooked* provides an example of customer-centric behaviour that builds trust with consumers and creates habits. Amazon began advertising competitors' products on their marketplace, which may seem like a strange tactic on the face of it. Were they doing it for the ad revenue? Did they think the ad revenue would make up for any losses in sales? Maybe. But that wasn't the most powerful reason for doing so (if it was a reason at all). It satisfied customers' desire for competitive price information and made Amazon the default solution for all purchasing needs. This is an example of rewarding customers with added utility. Think about how you can reward your customers in unique ways to grow your brand, but keep in mind that what works for a marketplace may not work for a single brand.

Giving customers the chance to contribute to your brand in the form of a community can also help build habits. IKEA makes customers build their own furniture, which may not please everyone but brings a sense of pride and accomplishment. Enabling customers to build their own community, contribute to it and shape it can have a similar effect. Members become emotionally invested and develop unique connections within the community, leading to a sense of investment and pride in their reputation (Eyal, 2013; Zhang et al. 2013; West, 2020). If you have been to IKEA, you will also notice the restaurant placed strategically in the store. This is a win-win for habit and commitment building because we eat a lot more often than we buy furniture, and food is a much-needed reward that satisfies a crucial pain point – hunger.

Subscribe and save programmes are another common commerce feature that you will see. They're also a great way to systemize the principle of 'make buying a habit'. The more you can smooth the repurchase process, such that a customer literally doesn't have to think about making an additional purchase, the better. Convenience is top of mind for consumers – 97 per cent of them have backed out of a purchase because it was inconvenient for them, according to research by the National Retail Foundation (NRF) (2020). Convenience even ranked slightly higher than the brand's values for consumers in terms of importance. Eighty-three percent say that convenience in their shopping experiences is more important to them than it was five years ago (NRF, 2020). In fact, almost two-thirds of consumers across industries like personal care, electronics, pet supplies and clothing (all prime e-commerce industries) are willing to pay more for convenience (NRF, 2020).

Wrapping up

E-commerce brands and businesses rely heavily on customer retention for their success. By understanding their customers and their behaviour, e-commerce brands can create personalized experiences that will keep customers coming back for more. Using retention KPIs and implementing best practices can help e-commerce businesses measure and improve their retention efforts, leading to increased customer loyalty and sales. In the next chapter, we will move into audience and community building, which will serve as another crucial arrow in your quiver when it comes to engaging and retaining customers. Building a strong audience and community can help you retain customers by creating a sense of belonging and fostering loyalty. I will provide you with practical tips and best practices for implementing these strategies.

Lastly, don't let your e-commerce business miss out on the opportunity to improve its customer retention – access our expert-backed resources on customer retention KPIs and guides at 2xecommerce.com/book/chapter6 to start optimizing your retention strategy today.

References

2X eCommerce (2020) S05 EP20, Transforming product returns to a retention profit center, https://2xecommerce.com/podcast/244/ (archived at https://perma.cc/4WTX-6FJ5)

Bain & Company (2006) Retaining customers is the real challenge, 20 Jan, www.bain.com/insights/retaining-customers-is-the-real-challenge/ (archived at https://perma.cc/RAK4-9HBQ)

Bain & Company (2015) Are you experienced? 8 Apr, www.bain.com/insights/are-you-experienced-infographic/ (archived at https://perma.cc/3RT4-6N7B)

Barton, R, Quiring, K and Theofilou, B (2018) The Power of Brand Purpose, *Accenture*, 5 Dec, www.accenture.com/gb-en/insights/strategy/brand-purpose (archived at https://perma.cc/2XFK-CRL3)

Baveja, S, Rastogi, S, Zook, C, Hancock, RS and Chu, J (2000) The value of online customer loyalty and how you can capture it, *Bain*, 1 Apr, www.bain.com/insights/the-value-of-online-customer-loyalty-and-how-you-can-capture-it/ (archived at https://perma.cc/6R2R-HTZX)

Britannica (2019) Origins of agriculture – earliest beginnings, *Encyclopædia Britannica*, www.britannica.com/topic/agriculture/Earliest-beginnings (archived at https://perma.cc/G4RN-P6JV)

Britannica (2022) Levant – meaning & facts, *Encyclopedia Britannica*, www.britannica.com/place/Levant (archived at https://perma.cc/W9M7-ACDB)

Campbell, K (2015) How Naked Wines acquires and retains customers, 2X eCommerce, 19 Jun, https://2xecommerce.com/nakedwines-marketing/#16 (archived at https://perma.cc/T24F-35S5)

Crook, J (2021) Loop Returns locks in $65 million Series B led by CRV, *TechCrunch*, 21 Jul, https://techcrunch.com/2021/07/21/loop-returns-locks-in-65-million-series-b-led-by-crv/ (archived at https://perma.cc/NQ2P-E3CY)

Emplifi (2022a) 7 fascinating facts every customer service team must know today, https://go.emplifi.io/rs/284-ENW-442/images/Emplifi_Report_Consumer_Expectations_Customer_Service_EN.pdf (archived at https://perma.cc/CZ9B-XFWY)

Emplifi (2022b) 11 key things consumers expect from their brand experiences today, https://go.emplifi.io/rs/284-ENW-442/images/Emplifi_Report_Consumer_Expectations_US_UK_EN.pdf (archived at https://perma.cc/DZF2-MSA2)

Eyal, N (2013) *Hooked: How to build habit-forming products*, Portfolio, London

Grieve, R and Lowe-Calverley, E (2016) The power of rewards and why we seek them out, *The Conversation*, 25 Jul, https://theconversation.com/the-power-of-rewards-and-why-we-seek-them-out-62691 (archived at https://perma.cc/8AHP-P7T7)

MasterClass (2022) MasterClass online classes, www.masterclass.com/ (archived at https://perma.cc/6464-FGCT)

McEachern, A (2021) Why refunds can lead to repeat purchases, *Loop*, 16 Jun, www.loopreturns.com/blog/customers-repeat-puchase-when-they-refund/ (archived at https://perma.cc/SB8S-5LZC)

Naked Wines (2022) The Naked Tasting Tour, www.nakedwines.com/tastings (archived at https://perma.cc/TPM5-2489)

Netpromoter (2022) Comparing your net promoter score, www.netpromoter.com/compare/ (archived at https://perma.cc/J7K3-UYVN)

NRF (National Retail Federation) (2020) Consumer View Winter 2020, 14 Jan, https://nrf.com/research/consumer-view-winter-2020 (archived at https://perma.cc/3SVE-GQUP)

Omniconvert (2019) How to drive growth with e-commerce customer retention rate optimization, *Omniconvert E-commerce Growth Blog*, www.omniconvert.com/blog/ecommerce-customer-retention-rate-optimization/ (archived at https://perma.cc/FR9K-HXWU)

Purohit, N (2020) Reimagining customer loyalty through value-driven strategies, Adobe Blog, https://blog.adobe.com/en/publish/2020/06/23/reimagining-customer-loyalty-through-value-driven-strategies (archived at https://perma.cc/C3FX-AEKA)

Recurly (2019) Benchmarks for subscription e-commerce, *Recurly Research*, https://recurly.com/research/benchmarks-for-subscription-ecommerce/ (archived at https://perma.cc/KJ5T-7SKH)

Rentech Digital (2022) What is the average retention rate for a new e-commerce business? 27 Jan, https://rentechdigital.com/swipecart/blog/t/what-is-the-average-retention-rate-for-a-new-ecommerce-business (archived at https://perma.cc/X9JD-5GKF)

Saleh, K (2022) E-commerce product return rate – statistics and trends, *Invesp*, 16 May, www.invespcro.com/blog/ecommerce-product-return-rate-statistics/ (archived at https://perma.cc/53TH-B3TB)

Sapolsky (2011) Fora.tv. Dopamine Jackpot! Sapolsky on the Science of Pleasure, *YouTube*, 3 Mar, www.youtube.com/watch?v=axrywDP9Ii0 (archived at https://perma.cc/WJ94-Z2MJ)

Teneva, D (2018) Customer lifetime value in ecommerce, Metrilo Blog, www.metrilo.com/blog/customer-lifetime-value (archived at https://perma.cc/6S9A-YKX8)

The North Face (2022) The North Face XPLR Pass Loyalty Program, www.thenorthface.com/en-us/xplrpass (archived at https://perma.cc/F6MF-ZRWZ)

West, C (2020) What is a brand community and how to build a successful one, *Sprout Social*, https://sproutsocial.com/insights/brand-community/ (archived at https://perma.cc/9MPE-58UJ)

Williams, R (2018) NikePlus app woos mobile users with free music and training, *Marketing Dive*, 6 Feb, www.marketingdive.com/news/nikeplus-app-woos-mobile-users-with-free-music-and-training/516407/ (archived at https://perma.cc/VZD5-6FGW)

Wollan, R, Davis, P, De Angelis, F and Quiring, K (2017) Seeing beyond the loyalty illusion: it's time you invest more wisely, *Accenture*, www.invest-data.com/eWebEditor/uploadfile/20170302105231182267540.pdf (archived at https://perma.cc/S7MB-YWPV)

Wood, W and Rünger, D (2016) Psychology of Habit, *Annual Review of Psychology*, 67 (1), pp 289–314, doi:10.1146/annurev-psych-122414-033417 (archived at https://perma.cc/Q55K-7ULJ)

Zhang, N, Zhou, Z, Su, C and Zhou, N (2013) How do different types of community commitment influence brand commitment? The mediation of brand attachment, *Cyberpsychology, Behavior, and Social Networking*, 16 (11), pp 836–42, doi:10.1089/cyber.2012.0456 (archived at https://perma.cc/W8TZ-2NR7)

Further reading

Accenture (2018) Making it personal: why brands must move from communication to conversation for greater personalization, *Pulse Check 2018*, www.accenture.com/_acnmedia/PDF-77/Accenture-Pulse-Survey.pdf (archived at https://perma.cc/9YEL-NQ6A)

Baird, CH and Parasnis, G (2011) From social media to social customer relationship management, *Strategy & Leadership*, 39 (5), pp 30–37

Fechner, G T (1966) trans Adler, H R, *Elements of psychophysics* Volume 1, eds Howes, D H and Boring, E G, Holt, Rinehart and Winston, New York, NY

Gourville, JT (2006) Eager sellers and stony buyers: understanding the psychology of new-product adoption ^ R0606F, *HBR Store*, 1 Jun, https://store.hbr.org/product/eager-sellers-and-stony-buyers-understanding-the-psychology-of-new-product-adoption/r0606f?sku=R0606F-PDF-ENG (archived at https://perma.cc/7KZA-K8DV)

Harvard Business Review (2011) *Harvard Business Review on Increasing Customer Loyalty*, Harvard Business Review Press, MA

Keating, G (2021) Announcing Twilio Segment's the State of Personalization 2021 Report, *Twilio*, 2 Jun, www.twilio.com/blog/announcing-the-state-of-personalization-2021 (archived at https://perma.cc/GY83-7KDT)

MacKenzie, I, Meyer, C and Noble, S (2013) How retailers can keep up with consumers, *McKinsey & Company*, 1 Oct, www.McKinsey.com/industries/retail/our-insights/how-retailers-can-keep-up-with-consumers (archived at https://perma.cc/5CMA-6974)

Puthiyamadam, T and Reyes, J (2018) Experience is everything: here's how to get it right, *PwC*, www.pwc.de/de/consulting/pwc-consumer-intelligence-series-customer-exp (archived at https://perma.cc/S4VF-G6CU)

Ravishankar, S (2021) 6 ways to customer retention without giving discounts this holiday season with AI, *Vue.ai*, 5 Nov, https://vue.ai/blog/ai-in-retail/customer-retention/ (archived at https://perma.cc/89JP-XCZN)

Reichheld, FF and Schefter, P (2000) The economics of e-loyalty, *HBS Working Knowledge*, 10 Jul, https://hbswk.hbs.edu/archive/the-economics-of-e-loyalty#life-cycle (archived at https://perma.cc/QUP9-HL95)

Tarnowska, K, Ras, ZW and Daniel, L (2019) Customer loyalty improvement, *Studies in Big Data*, pp 7–11, doi:10.1007/978-3-030-13438-9_2 (archived at https://perma.cc/VKK6-PDB4)

Unicef (nd) Confirmation emails: missed connections, https://offers.unific.com/hubfs/Unific%20-%20ToF%20Offers/%5BeBook%5D%20Missed%20Connections%20(6.22.17)/missed-connections_confirmation-emails_unific.pdf (archived at https://perma.cc/7RG6-GN7H)

8

Audience and community building: why high-growth e-commerce brands are publishers

In the last chapter, I hinted that we would be covering community building and the fundamental sociological realities that e-commerce brands can leverage to create long-term sustainable brand growth. Here is where we dive deeper into how creating sociological and psychological connections can ensure the long-term success of your brand, and propel you toward building a long-lasting impact in your vertical. In this chapter you will learn how our human history informs e-commerce strategy and how to bring these lessons from the plains of Africa and the steppes of Asia into the modern digital commerce arena.

Building tribes

What is a tribe?

Tribes are the fundamental underpinning of the e-commerce journey that takes consumers from viewer to follower, to subscriber, to customer and finally to advocate. Here, Ralph Linton (an American anthropologist mostly remembered for his texts *The Study of Man* (1936) and *The Tree of Culture* (1955)) presents an apt description of a tribe. He says that a tribe is a group of bands who occupy a common territory and have a feeling of unity, which they derive from shared culture, interests and frequent contact in a community environment. Much like we see in our modern e-commerce tribes of today!

In the next section, I will show you how the forming of tribes and communities, and a shared language within them, developed when Homo sapiens were very much primitive, is a trait, or perhaps *the* trait that we have to thank for us being here today. You will find it is a function of our advanced human development and ability to connect in unique ways, namely through language. Of course, you will also find how you as a marketer or e-commerce brand can build and engage with your tribe to drive results for your brand.

Sociological underpinnings

Just like when your parents and caregivers had to teach you to cooperate in childhood, humans throughout history had to learn how to get along. Now, you could say we still aren't great at this; it only takes a glance around to see our shortcomings as humankind. But we've come a long, long way from where we were.

In his book, *Sapiens*, Yuval Noah Harari, renowned author and history professor, attributes the success of Homo sapiens (us), in comparison to other groups such as the 'strong, brainy and cold-proof' Neanderthals, to our ability to cooperate flexibly in large groups. Harari says that one essential ingredient to this was a unique shared language (Harari, 2015, 2022). The systems of cooperation and reciprocity that we developed long ago gave us a competitive advantage in our wild and harsh environment, where it wasn't only the lions and tigers we had to watch out for but other tribes, too. Groups that could cooperate better thrived, outcompeted and outlived those that could not.

Today in the e-commerce world it is no different. It is communication that sets us apart, and if you want to compete, you have to get pro-social, develop a shared language of hashtags and insider lingo, and rally your community behind a cause. And you must do all of it better than your competition.

Harari compares us to other cooperative groups like ants and bees, which cooperate well, but rigidly, and only with close family members (kin). In fact, ants' cooperation rules are so simple that if one ant starts walking in a circle it can turn the entire group into a walking death spiral that never ends. That is, all the other ants start walking in circles too, and they end up following one another until their little legs can't carry them any more (Leonard, 2022). Humans on the other hand cooperate well outside of their direct kin relationships, and often in dynamic and charitable ways. In fact, people with more friends engage in more volunteering and more charitable giving, highlighting the connection between how developed our community instincts are and the size of our communities. Keep that in mind when building your e-commerce communities – the path to community growth is through charity (satisfying your customers' needs through customer-centricity) and connection.

Today, we are hardwired for cooperation. As infants, we can already show empathy toward those in distress, and in adulthood, we routinely and inspiringly cooperate to reach hard-to-reach goals and help others in their most dire times of need (Knafo et al, 2008).

One could also say that we are expert community builders. In fact, we even create official societies that seek to uphold our cooperative ideals around the world, ideals of charity, reciprocity and cooperation. Furthermore, we have implemented a rule of law to formalize the upholding of these ideals in a way that leverages another psychological principle that has been with us since our primitive days as hunter-gatherers: that we seek reward and avoid punishment (Kim et al, 2006). It is the formalization of these ideals that gave us even more incentive toward pro-social behaviour, and those that did it well thrived in our new environment constructed of ideals based on cooperation and community. Those that couldn't get along suffered, so we further intensified the filtering for the most pro-social among us (Boyd and Richerson, 2009).

Why all this talk of ideals? I'm glad you asked. Because your communities are about more than just products, as you will learn in this chapter. They are about values and ideals, or what Yuval Noah Harari might call *shared myths*. And these are powerful tools to bond your community with. Later in this chapter you will learn the power of story and narrative in attracting and connecting your community.

So what does this all mean for the e-commerce brand?

By this stage in the book, assuming you haven't just skipped straight to this section, you've heard me say multiple times now that one subtle but powerful difference between communities and how most brands view a gathering of people, has an incredibly profound effect on the results that your e-commerce brand can expect to get. That is the difference between an *audience* and a *community*.

Community building fuels your brand's growth by putting the customer first. As Forbes Council member Himanshu Bisht (2021) says, by providing your community with the right context, support and guidance, they begin to naturally start and lead the conversation, flourish together and transform themselves together. All this creates a foundation for your brand to grow with minimal effort (Bisht, 2021). I myself have made my bread and butter building a community through my 2X eCommerce podcast, now with over 400 episodes (at the time of writing in 2022) and counting, where my guests and I deliver value for e-commerce brands worldwide, by providing expert insights into all of the most critical aspects of the cross-functional growth stack for e-commerce brands. In this chapter, I will show you how you can build your own tribe, too.

The importance of building tribes

As Evolutionary Psychologist Benjamin Crosier, co-author of *Wired to Connect*, says, humans are a social species with an innate desire to communicate and connect with one another (Haseltine, 2015). Connection calms our nervous system, makes us feel safe and lets us know we are not alone in this world (Grande, 2018). And connect we will, under any circumstance and by any means possible. This alone should be enough to highlight the importance of communities for e-commerce brands. As far as customer needs go, the need for connection is one of the most fundamental and basic of all, second only to sustenance. Building tribes is the only way we can ensure consistency in our connection. A sense of continuity in our daily social life and stability in the satisfaction of our need to connect. Tribes, communities, are what hold us together emotionally and physically.

For the e-commerce brand, a customer community allows you to obtain feedback on ideas and new products, increase your product awareness within your target audience, provide value to your customers that goes beyond any product or service, differentiate from your competition based on emotion and connection and, importantly, provide support to your tribe when they need it.

Are your brand's social media accounts 'communities'?

Are your brand's social media accounts 'communities'? The short answer is yes and no. While they are platforms that allow followers to gather and interact, having a following on social media does not necessarily mean you have a community. Audiences on social media gather based on shared interests to consume content and sometimes interact with it, but a community's main activity is interaction and connection. When an audience begins to engage with one another on an ongoing basis, then a community exists, says Nicole Saunders,

Senior Manager of Communities at Zendesk (Gomez, 2020). But, social media environments are becoming increasingly pay-to-play, and the sheer amount of content being posted daily leads to significant competition. This makes it difficult to truly connect with users organically. However, a well-executed organic strategy can set the stage for staying top-of-mind with your community and serve as the foundation for your paid strategy. That being said, on platforms like Facebook, potentially only 1 in 20 followers see your posts (Sehl, 2021). This highlights the importance of real communities on owned platforms for e-commerce brands to see a return on investment from their customer-centric marketing efforts in the form of customer engagement and interaction.

So, what are the main (even if subtle) differences between a social media platform and a community? Social media platforms are for everyone, bringing together different tribes that may or may not intersect. It is like a town centre where everyone gathers for trade or to strike up a conversation. However, social media does not typically satisfy users' needs for engagement and connection. It also covers a broad range of topics, similar to a city mall that sells everything. Like a town centre, it can become noisy and overcrowded, especially when a tribe gathers for a protest. Social media is also highly competitive, with millions of people vying for attention in the marketplace of ideas. In contrast, communities are focused on connection and engagement. Real engagement, not just fleeting interactions and likes, but interactions that last days, weeks or longer. **For this reason, communities are more satisfying for consumers as they fulfil their belonging and self-esteem needs.** Belonging needs include friendship, family and a sense of connection, while self-esteem needs include confidence, achievement, respect from others and the need to be a unique individual (Maslow, 1943). When managing your community, consider how you can fulfil these needs in unique ways that other brands may not, for example by promoting members of your community and their stories on your brand platform, or by promoting values that they hold dear. **Communities are also focused on a single topic, such as makeup or sports,** rather than being a large department store with a variety of products and services. Communities are often on owned platforms, giving the brand more control and the ability to create a unique experience. They also tend to be smaller, creating a sense of exclusivity and intimacy. In summary, while social media platforms allow for gathering and interaction, they do not necessarily constitute a community. Real communities, often on owned platforms, provide a space for e-commerce brands to foster engagement and connection with their customers and are focused on one specific topic rather than simply being a forum for discussion of many topics that also happens to discuss a specific topic related to your brand.

Communities as research tools

Conducting customer research is an essential part of any successful e-commerce business. By understanding your customers and their behaviour, you can create personalized experiences that will keep them coming back for more.

Your online communities are the ideal go-to source to find out answers to a brand's most pressing questions, such as:

- Do they like your product?
- Do they think there is any scope for improvement?
- How can you serve them better?
- How has the overall experience with your product and brand been?
- Will they recommend your product to their tribe?
- What should we build next?

As your community is the most customer-centric touchpoint for your business, integrating it into the rest of the cross-functional e-commerce growth stack is essential. At least half of marketers say they get valuable insights for product development from their communities and that their community has improved their decision making (Reslinger, 2015). Nurture your community and the discussion within and you will create a rich mine full of growth-stack optimizing gold. You will be able to inform communication plans for your marketing team, create reports for your market research stakeholders and enlighten product development and R&D teams on what is happening on the ground with your consumers' ever-evolving wants.

Take, for example, skincare and beauty products brand Glossier, who tap into their community for new product suggestions through their editorial arm (their blog) *Into the Gloss* (Karpis, 2018). Or LEGO, who hold contests for their brand community, 'LEGO Ideas', to incentivize them to come up with new product ideas (Brandalf, 2022). Not only does it show their consumers that they and their opinions are valued, but also ensures that through customer-centricity they create exactly the products their consumers are looking for, potentially making the difference between losing or making millions of dollars.

Building communities

The main things that your customers, or potential customers, are looking for from a community are fulfilment, socialization and to express themselves creatively or authentically (Ind et al, 2013). It is your job as a brand, and the leader of your tribe, to set the stage for these needs to be fulfilled; but how? In this section, I show you what goes into building a successful community, and how customer-centricity is key.

The first steps to building a community start with identifying who you want to be around you. Because not everyone will be a perfect fit. This is your target market and is discovered through copious amounts of marketing research and well-thought-out strategy. Because targeting anyone and everyone for a community isn't an option. Your tribe has specific needs and interests, and creating the ideal community or tribe for them means creating it just for them, not everyone else. Then you need to lead that tribe. You need to lead by example, sure, but you need to give your tribe a powerful story to relate to, and a compelling idea or narrative to follow, one that will orient them, guide them and lead them. Once you've gathered your tribe and given them a strong leader and a compelling vision to follow, you need to care for your tribe, to uncover and take care of their needs. To create a safe place where they can express themselves without fear of embarrassment. In the following sections, I show you the specific aspects that go into building a community, and why they are so important for you as an e-commerce brand. Let's break down the key aspects of community building for you...

Identify who you want around you

The success of any community relies on two key factors: understanding who your tribe is and knowing what they want. Building communities is not about casting the widest net possible and capturing anyone and everyone. This is not a sound strategy, even if community acquisition were free. Instead, it is important to maintain relevance and quality within your community to keep your tribe, the people who genuinely connect with you and value you, coming back again and again. This means defining the specific demographics and psychographics that you want to target. For e-commerce brands, this may involve identifying multiple demographics and psychographics. For example, Naked Wines offers experiential benefits that appeal to sensory individuals, community and connection for those seeking socialization, and knowledge and mastery for those who want to learn more about wine and food pairings. This means developing different messaging for each demographic and using it to inform how you build your community and platform. For example, users who value knowledge and mastery may appreciate a learning environment with greater options and gamification, similar to platforms like Duolingo. By understanding and targeting your tribe, you can build a successful and engaging community.

Be a leader

As Seth Godin says in his book *Tribes: We need you to lead us* (2014), a tribe is a group of people who are connected to one another, to an idea or shared vision, and to a leader. When it comes to your brand community, you are the leader that your tribe is looking to follow. As a community manager, it is your job to lead, and your members expect you to do as much. But that doesn't mean control or corral. In fact, it means to lead by example, and that example should be strongly founded in your brand values and the kind of community your customers want to see. Pay attention here, because I didn't say 'the kind of community that you want to see', I said the kind of community that your *customers* want to see. Get this right and community growth is a matter of 'build it and they will come' (with the help of a little awareness marketing, of course!). Become a chief facilitator and chief 'lead by example'. The more your brand lives and breathes its brand values, the easier this will be as a community manager.

Story and narrative matters

In the context of tribal communities, having an enemy can solidify the bonds among allies and provide a clear target for their energies. It can also fulfil higher-order needs like self-actualization and the desire to fight for something bigger than oneself. As Freud famously said, 'a family (tribe) that has outside enemies will be better able to maintain harmonious relationships within its own unit' (Moses, 1995). Studies have even shown that people are more likely to bond over a shared dislike than over a shared liking of a third party (Bosson et al, 2006). The participants in this study themselves thought that shared liking would be more effective in fostering connection, unaware of the hold that the power of a shared enemy had on their psyche and the way they bonded in tribes and communities (Bosson et al, 2006). Therefore, it is important for tribes to know not only who they are fighting for, but also who they are fighting against. However, brands should be cautious about making a competitor the enemy and instead focus on values and higher-order ideals to win the hearts and minds of all consumers, including their own community.

It's well established that tribes often come into conflict with other tribes over resources and ideas. This dynamic is also present in the world of e-commerce, where consumers engage in battles of ideas and values every day. These values and ideas are important to consumers, whether it be the environment, animal rights, mental health advocacy or the pursuit of healthier food. By incorporating these values into your brand narrative, you can strengthen the bond of your community. In fact, these values are so powerful that failing to engage with them can lead to the formation of an anti-community around your brand. For example, almost half of millennials have stopped purchasing from certain brands due to environmental and ethical concerns (Deloitte, 2020).

Kelley Higney, the founder of Bug Bite Thing, the best-selling insect bite relief product on Amazon with over 45,000 reviews, recommends creating a social mission for your company that is synergistic with your brand's values. Make a commitment to raising awareness across all your platforms so that customers can see that you are serious about your mission and that it comes from a place of authenticity (Fast Company, 2021). One example of this is Patagonia, an outdoor clothing brand that is committed to minimizing its environmental impact and even refused to participate in Black Friday sales, instead donating the $10 million earned on that day to environmental charities (B&T Magazine, 2020; Nair, 2021). This commitment to a narrative and the authenticity of that commitment is undeniable. As Simon Sinek, author of *Start With Why: How great leaders inspire everyone to take action*, says, 'People don't buy what you do; they buy why you do it. And what you do simply proves what you believe' (Kurichenko, nd). Like Patagonia, find a cause to stand up for and integrate it so deeply into your brand and product that they become a natural extension of that cause.

Know your customers' needs

Your customers only have so much time in a day, so the fact that they are willing to invest their time in your community shows how much they value your brand and what you offer within the community. Focus on meeting your customers' needs to keep them coming back and show your appreciation for their loyalty. Avoid the temptation to treat your community like an audience once it reaches a certain size. Maintain the authentic connection that you started with.

But how do you know what your customers want and need in a dynamic market? By building a community, you gain access to a powerful research tool for e-commerce brands. Use surveys and other research methods to gather valuable insights from your community, and remember to reward your customers for participating. Rewards don't have to be financial; meeting the needs of your community members can be a reward in itself, and it aligns with the platform's ethos. Treat your community differently from other channels and adjust your marketing tactics accordingly. For example, if your customers are focused on fitness, like Gymshark's consumers, educational content and support from influencers will be important to them. That's exactly what Gymshark does through their Gymshark Central blog and influencer platform (Gymshark, 2022a, 2022b), meeting the needs of their consumers by providing them with valuable information and support.

The more value your consumers perceive in what you offer, the more they will identify with your brand (Dholakia et al, 2004). This identification provides a unique identity for your consumers and can make them active community members and brand advocates.

Measuring with social monitoring and uncovering with social listening

Social listening and social monitoring are two powerful tactics that let you stay on top of what people think and feel about your brand and industry. With social media monitoring, you can track brand mentions, relevant hashtags and competitor mentions, and even conduct A/B testing to refine your tactics and maximize reach and engagement. But social monitoring is mainly about raw numbers; it doesn't give you deep insights into sentiment. That's where social listening comes in!

Social listening is all about understanding the general mood behind the data. It lets you dig into the online mood of your brand and competitors and gain insights into how to improve and deliver for your customers. These advanced tactics provide rich insights and enable you to engage with your consumers in real time, promoting your brand values and building a connection with your audience.

But nothing beats asking your target markets directly. If you already have a large base of your target market, don't be shy, just ask them! Refer to Chapter 5 on customer data for tips on how to integrate customer feedback into your e-commerce growth strategy.

Make your customers the stars of the show

I ask you to think back to our section on influence, from Chapter 6, 'Customer acquisition', because you will need to map these two concepts together. Recall that people like to be complimented (no surprises there) and that by satisfying this need for them, you build influence. But how do you do that as a brand?

You showcase your community members, you share and promote their unique perspectives, you give them a voice (or more precisely a microphone) and allow them to be heard through your platform in a way they wouldn't be able to do by themselves. You give them honest and sincere appreciation, and show genuine interest in them as they do you. Show your customers that you think they are important. As William James, an early American philosopher and psychologist is quoted as saying, 'The deepest principle in human nature is the craving to be appreciated' (Goodreads, 2022). If you are reading this, don't take the people in your life for granted; reach out and tell them how much you appreciate them. If you're a brand, let your customers and especially your community know. Reach out to them collectively, and start putting them front and centre. Somebody who has been rewarded in front of their community will feel more attracted to that community (Chavis and McMillan, 1986).

Captivate, don't just communicate: get your customers hooked

Create consistency

Consistency sets the foundation for habitual engagement. If your community members are going weeks without notifications from your brand community, they are going to forget about you. That doesn't mean spamming people with content, it means actively engaging in direct conversations with your consumers. Real conversations, not just an obligatory reply here and there that adds nothing to the depth of the conversation. This is because it's not just a matter of frequency of engagement, but quality, too. As a brand, you need to be adding value for your consumers, and surface-level engagement just doesn't cut it. After all, the greater the level of personal interaction, the higher the likelihood that people will become close (Chavis and McMillan, 1986).

If you will recall back to Chapter 6 where we covered the core fundamentals of influence, I will now introduce to you the *mere exposure effect* – this states that the simple act of building familiarity makes people like you more and, of course, makes customers like brands more (Schmidt and Eisend, 2015). It stems from a study in 1968 by Robert Zajonc, an esteemed professor of psychology at the University of Michigan. Zajonc initially showed that people began to feel a greater affinity toward nonsense words (think of a jumble of letters that looks like a word but isn't really one) that they had more exposure to (Zajonc, 1968). Since then, the effect has been shown to extend to other domains, such as marketing and advertising, creating greater affinity for your ad campaigns and brand. For example, Anthony Grimes, a senior lecturer in marketing at the University of Sheffield, shows in his research that repeated exposure to your brand, even if people don't engage with it, fosters familiarity and liking (Grimes, 2011; Grimes and Kitchen, 2007).

Events

The original communities that we came to love and find solace in were not the online digital communities that are common today. They were very much seen, heard and felt. They were in-person communities and real-life events. The internet is certainly a wonderful tool for connecting people, especially for niche interest groups who may never have found their tribe without it, but even pure-play e-commerce brands need to have an in-person (omnichannel) events strategy.

Events satisfy more than just social needs. Humans have a rich and extensive set of wants, needs and desires that they like to be fulfilled. Your consumers want to be part of something bigger than themselves, they want the latest from the experts, and they want a story to tell their friends and family. Being able to satisfy these for your customers will open a special place in their hearts and minds just for you, that your competitors can't touch. In short, they will get your customers deeply integrated into your brand environment, and effectively *hooked* on you. And you on them, too, of course, because that is what building relationships is all about.

The Naked Wines community and events masterclass

Let us take Naked Wines as an example of community success – a 100 per cent digital brand with a vision to disrupt the wine industry for the benefit of customers, winemakers and their people (Naked Wines, 2020). If that doesn't sound like a tribe then I don't know what does. Naked Wines is built around enjoying the sensory pleasures of good wine, whether it be alone or (often) in good company, and serves as a perfect example of both online and real-life community engagement. When it comes to real-life events, they solidify connections through the *Naked Tasting Tour* where wine lovers gather to try new wines and meet the very people who made them. No doubt they bring along a friend or two as well, and thus the community grows.

But they double this up with a strong online community platform, designed specifically to the needs of not only Naked Wines but, most importantly, the needs of their consumers. Their community dashboard is a masterclass in community engagement. Post a comment about wine and you *will* hear back from the maker themselves. It doesn't matter whether it is praise, criticism or just a comment on the tasting notes – consumers are able to engage directly with their winemakers and reliably receive an answer.

Not only that (I did say they were a masterclass in community building, right?) but they have a groups section with segmented groups for consumers of any interest – whether you're a Naked Newbie and need to be guided into the community by Naked's staff and most experienced Angels, want to share what you are drinking tonight or want to learn how to pair food and wine, Naked Wines has it all. Through these groups and communities, consumers satisfy not only their connection needs, but their need for learning and mastery as they build their knowledge and competence in the wine world, and build the confidence to then go out into new tribes and communities and advocate for the brand through its ideals and values and the knowledge instilled in them.

The Naked Wines community enabled the company's list of producers to balloon based on word of mouth alone. Not only that, but on the consumer side, they at least at one point had a waiting list to become an 'Angel' – which is their term for a customer who invests into their wine fund each month, that they can then use to purchase wines from producers within the Naked Wines network (McKenna, 2014). But there's more than just company growth; just as any real community comes to the rescue in times of need when one of their tribe is having it tough, the Naked Wines community is no different. When winemaker Katie Jones had her entire first vintage ruined by vandals, and her business was on the line, 2,500 of Naked Wines' finest Angels came to the rescue, pre-ordering a whopping 30,000 bottles in just two days, saving Katie's business, and keeping her part of the Naked Wines community (Rampen, 2017). Communities are much more than just key performance metrics, they are thriving, living and loving tribes that take care of one another in wholesome and inspiring ways. It is through this sense of community that Naked Wines continues to grow, counting almost a million community members as of 2021, a 25 per cent increase on the previous year (Clark, 2021). Nick Devlin, group chief executive at Naked Wines, attributes this growth to focusing on the customer experience for their members (being customer-centric and focusing on consumers' needs, as you have now heard me say many times throughout this book), as well as creating a tribe by connecting consumers and the world's best winemakers together on one shared platform (Clark, 2021).

Your brand as a publisher

Publishing frequently and on a large scale is essential for building a strong community around your brand. By providing enough content for your consumers to engage with, you can create a brand that they feel close to and want to be a part of. Some communities are so strong that you need to purchase the product first to really become a part of them. Tesla and Harley-Davidson are good examples of this. Every product has a customer persona or personas that are attracted to it for a particular reason and likely share other interests. For example, if you sell electric cars, your customer groups might be environmentally conscious consumers or tech enthusiasts. You need to become a quality publisher and thought leader in this space, naturally. The same goes for any vertical. Overall, publishing frequently and on a large scale, across multiple channels and with a diverse range of content is essential for building and maintaining a strong community around your brand. By providing engaging content and meeting the needs of your community members, you can create a brand that they are excited to be a part of and keep them coming back for more. The future will show the power of publishing as major YouTube and TikTok brands leverage their audiences and take over direct-to-consumer spaces thanks to their large and loyal networks. Existing direct-to-consumer brands need to move now to get ahead of this wave.

In conclusion, building an audience and community for your e-commerce brand is essential for achieving long-term growth and success. By engaging with your customers and providing them with value, you can create a loyal community that will help promote your brand and drive sales. To learn more about how to build an audience and community for your brand, check out the guides and resources available on the 2X eCommerce website: 2xecommerce.com/book/chapter7. These resources will provide you with practical tips and strategies for creating a thriving community around your brand. Next up, in the following chapter, we will explore the importance of lifecycle marketing for e-commerce brands. Lifecycle marketing is all about engaging with consumers in the right way throughout all stages and touchpoints of their journey with your brand. By understanding the needs and preferences of your customers at each stage of their lifecycle, you can create personalized and relevant experiences that will drive customer loyalty and retention. Don't miss out on this crucial guide to lifecycle marketing and how it can help your brand succeed. Continue reading to learn more.

References

B&T Magazine (2020) Patagonia says no to Black Friday, Cyber Monday: 'Buy Less, Demand More', *B&T*, www.bandt.com.au/patagonia-says-no-to-black-friday-cyber-monday-buy-less-demand-more/ (archived at https://perma.cc/ZE33-KY5J)

Bisht, H (2021) Council Post: How to build 'online tribes' through community-based marketing, *Forbes*, 31 Mar, www.forbes.com/sites/forbescommunicationscouncil/2021/03/31/how-to-build-online-tribes-through-community-based-marketing/?sh=5074ed5c5942 (archived at https://perma.cc/UG6V-MBFB)

Bosson, JK, Johnson, AB, Niederhoffer, K and Swann, WB (2006) Interpersonal chemistry through negativity: bonding by sharing negative attitudes about others, *Personal Relationships*, 13 (2), pp 135–50, doi:10.1111/j.1475-6811.2006.00109.x (archived at https://perma.cc/XVC7-KGTJ)

Boyd, R and Richerson, PJ (2009) Culture and the evolution of human cooperation, *Philosophical Transactions of the Royal Society B: Biological Sciences*, 364 (1533), pp 3281–88, doi:10.1098/rstb.2009.0134 (archived at https://perma.cc/BP5N-N4ET)

Brandalf (2022) 7 powerful benefits of brand communities that increase profit, 7 May, https://brandalfblog.com/7-benefits-of-brand-communities/ (archived at https://perma.cc/GW8H-47GQ)

Chavis, DM, Hogge, JH, McMillan, DW and Wandersman, A (1986) Sense of community through Brunswik's lens: a first look, *Journal of Community Psychology*, 14 (1), pp 24–40

Clark, HS (2021) Naked Wines shares plunge after wine availability falls below targets, *The Independent*, 18 Nov, https://sg.finance.yahoo.com/news/naked-wines-shares-plunge-wine-131651850.html (archived at https://perma.cc/CBK6-CGET)

Deloitte (2022) Shifting sands: how consumers are embracing sustainability, *Deloitte*, www2.deloitte.com/uk/en/pages/consumer-business/articles/sustainable-consumer.html (archived at https://perma.cc/Y2SQ-Y2LZ)

Dholakia, UM, Bagozzi, RP and Pearo, LK (2004) A social influence model of consumer participation in network- and small-group-based virtual communities, *International Journal of Research in Marketing*, 21 (3), pp 241–63, doi:10.1016/j.ijresmar.2003.12.004 (archived at https://perma.cc/5HSU-6VCW)

Fast Company (2021) 16 ways to build a strong community around your brand, 6 Aug, www.fastcompany.com/90644446/16-ways-to-build-a-strong-community-around-your-brand (archived at https://perma.cc/G4BH-4LB9)

Godin, S (2014) *Tribes: We need you to lead us*, Piatkus Books, London

Gomez, V (2021) Customer community: Definition, benefits, and tips for building your own, Zendesk Blog, www.zendesk.co.uk/blog/benefits-building-customer-community/ (archived at https://perma.cc/LD8V-3675)

Goodreads (2022) William James Quotes (author of *The Varieties of Religious Experience*), www.goodreads.com/author/quotes/15865.William_James (archived at https://perma.cc/LD8V-3675)

Grande, D (2018) The neuroscience of feeling safe and connected, *Psychology Today*, 24 Sep, www.psychologytoday.com/us/blog/in-it-together/201809/the-neuroscience-feeling-safe-and-connected (archived at https://perma.cc/TM4U-D52V)

Grimes, A (2011) Examining the mere exposure effect in a marketing context. pp 500–05, https://hull-repository.worktribe.com/output/4211545/examining-the-mere-exposure-effect-in-a-marketing-context (archived at https://perma.cc/S3G4-MJR7)

Grimes, A and Kitchen, PJ (2007) Researching mere exposure effects to advertising: theoretical foundations and methodological implications, *International Journal of Market Research*, 49 (2), pp 191–219, doi:10.1177/147078530704900205 (archived at https://perma.cc/3WEF-JWDP)

Gymshark (2022a) 4 Chocolate Recipes To Indulge In This World Chocolate Day https://central.gymshark.com/article/4-chocolate-recipes-to-indulge-in-this-world-chocolate-day (archived at https://perma.cc/U273-JRJS)

Gymshark (2022b) The Benefits Of Weightlifting Gloves, Wrist Wraps And Lifting https://central.gymshark.com/article/the-benefits-of-lifting-gloves-wrist-wraps-and-lifting-straps-and-when-you (archived at https://perma.cc/J7MD-C5HR)

Harari, YN (2015) *Sapiens: A brief history of humankind*, Harper, New York, NY

Harari, YN (2022) www.ynharari.com/ (archived at https://perma.cc/UWH4-F6GN)

Haseltine, E (2015) The urge to connect, *Psychology Today*, 19 Mar, www.psychologytoday.com/us/blog/long-fuse-big-bang/201503/the-urge-connect (archived at https://perma.cc/5GN7-REBV)

Ind, N, Iglesias, O and Schultz, M (2013) Building brands together: emergence and outcomes of co-creation, *California Management Review*, 55 (3), pp 5–26, doi:10.1525/cmr.2013.55.3.5 (archived at https://perma.cc/6FRC-DJ9H)

Karpis, P (2018) Why building community is critical to your brand's success, *Forbes*, 29 Nov, www.forbes.com/sites/paulinaguditch/2018/11/29/why-building-community-is-critical-to-your-brands-success/?sh=7360e5193458 (archived at https://perma.cc/UMJ4-U6BV)

Kim, H, Shimojo, S and O'Doherty, JP (2006) Is avoiding an aversive outcome rewarding? Neural substrates of avoidance learning in the human brain, *PLoS Biology*, 4 (8), p e233, doi:10.1371/journal.pbio.0040233 (archived at https://perma.cc/K45K-WZY6)

Knafo, A, Zahn-Waxler, C, Van Hulle, C, Robinson, JAL and Rhee, SH (2008) The developmental origins of a disposition toward empathy: genetic and environmental contributions, *Emotion*, 8 (6), pp 737–52, https://doi.org/10.1037/a0014179 (archived at https://perma.cc/N4M3-BP9V)

Kurichenko, V (nd) Consumers do not buy what you do, they buy why you do it, *Publicist*, www.publicist.co/the-spin/the-inside-scoop/consumers-do-not-buy-what-you-do-they-buy-why-you-do-it (archived at https://perma.cc/VNB2-ME3V)

Leonard, D (2022) The truth behind the phenomenon of the ant death spiral, *Grunge*, 8 Apr, www.grunge.com/826574/the-truth-behind-the-phenomenon-of-the-ant-death-spiral/ (archived at https://perma.cc/6HB7-QZ7M)

Linton, R (1936) *The Study of Man*, Internet Archive, Appleton Century Crofts, Inc, https://archive.org/details/studyofman031904mbp/page/14/mode/2up (archived at https://perma.cc/L4NH-HR9L)

Linton, R (1955) *The Tree of Culture*, Knopf, New York, NY

Maslow, A (1943) A Theory of Human Motivation, *Psychological Review*, 50 (4)

McKenna, G (2014) Naked Wines looks to recruit 25,000 more angels by year-end, *Harpers*, https://harpers.co.uk/news/fullstory.php/aid/16181/Naked_Wines_looks_to_recruit_25,000_more_angels_by_year-end.html (archived at https://perma.cc/RL7T-M5GF)

Moses, R (1995) The perception of the enemy: A psychological view, *PIJ*, https://pij.org/articles/603/the-perception-of-the-enemy-a-psychological-view (archived at https://perma.cc/DZ3G-QBVE)

Nair, D (2021) US retailer Patagonia donates $10m from Black Friday sales to protect environment, *The National*, 6 Dec, www.thenationalnews.com/business/energy/2021/12/06/us-retailer-patagonia-donates-10m-from-black-friday-sales-to-protect-environment/ (archived at https://perma.cc/89NJ-DKRK)

Naked Wines (2020) Delivering growth, opportunity accelerated: Naked Wines plc Annual Report and Accounts 2020, p 132, https://s3-eu-west-1.amazonaws.com/business-radar-reports-storage/42e2d126-b9a9-475c-8dbc-9ceba3f2b75e.pdf (archived at https://perma.cc/9ST5-BM58)

Rampen, C (2017) Making mutual commerce work at Naked Wines, *Medium*, 12 Jun, https://medium.com/@claire.rampen/making-mutual-commerce-work-at-naked-wines-9ed88ee809aa (archived at https://perma.cc/8WWC-LKH8)

Reslinger, M (2015) 10 brand community statistics that every marketer should know, *Potion*, 1 Oct, https://potion.social/en/blog/10-amazing-brand-community-statistics/# (archived at https://perma.cc/TP5L-GC3R)

Schmidt, S and Eisend, M (2015) Advertising repetition: a meta-analysis on effective frequency in advertising, *Journal of Advertising*, 44 (4), pp 415–28, doi:10.1080/00913367.2015.1018460 (archived at https://perma.cc/5L3F-ACKJ).

Sehl, K (2021) Organic reach is in decline—here's what you can do about it, *Hootsuite*, 24 Aug, https://blog.hootsuite.com/organic-reach-declining/ (archived at https://perma.cc/4RD8-BNCV)

Zajonc, RB (1968) Attitudinal effects of mere exposure, *Journal of Personality and Social Psychology*, 9 (2), pp 1–27, doi:10.1037/h0025848 (archived at https://perma.cc/35K8-LY7N)

Further reading

Baer, J (2012) 53 percent of Americans who follow brands in social are more loyal to those brands, *Convince & Convert*, www.convinceandconvert.com/social-media/53-percent-of-americans-who-follow-brands-in-social-are-more-loyal-to-those-brands/ (archived at https://perma.cc/8HQC-QLY6)

Bartels, J (nd) How Gymshark sold 90% of their product on the 1st day of their Canadian pop-up, *Uppercase*, http://uppercasehq.com/blog/how-gymshark-sold-through-90-percent-off-their-product (archived at https://perma.cc/R3XH-TKMF)

Burton, C (2022) 7 steps to building an online community (with examples), *THINKIFIC*, 17 Jun, www.thinkific.com/blog/how-to-build-an-online-community/ (archived at https://perma.cc/U48V-32DZ)

Chavis, DM, Hogge, JH, McMillan, DW and Wandersman, A (1986) Sense of community through Brunswik's lens: a first look, *Journal of Community Psychology*, 14 (1), pp 24–40

Fuchs, C and Schreier, M (2010) Customer empowerment in new product development, *Journal of Product Innovation Management*, 28 (1), pp 17–32, doi:10.1111/j.1540-5885.2010.00778.x (archived at https://perma.cc/FRG5-Z43M)

Gomez, V (2020) Customer community: definition, benefits, and tips for building your own, *Zendesk Blog*, 24 Feb, www.zendesk.nl/blog/benefits-building-customer-community/ (archived at https://perma.cc/E6HN-5PHZ)

Hristova, K (2020) How Gymshark disrupted the fitness industry, *CEO Today*, 28 Aug, www.ceotodaymagazine.com/2020/08/how-gymshark-disrupted-the-fitness-industry/ (archived at https://perma.cc/ZL35-ACKP)

Ind, N, Iglesias, O and Schultz, M (2013) Building brands together: emergence and outcomes of co-creation, *California Management Review*, 55 (3), pp 5–26, doi:10.1525/cmr.2013.55.3.5 (archived at https://perma.cc/NGZ4-TF28)

Islam, J, Rahman, Z, and Hollebeek, L (2018) Consumer engagement in online brand communities: a solicitation of congruity theory, *Internet Research*, 28 (1), pp 23–45, doi: 10.1108/intr-09-2016-0279 (archived at https://perma.cc/P6Z5-82H5)

Muniz, AM and O'Guinn, TC (2001) Brand Community, *Journal of Consumer Research*, 27 (4), pp 412–32, doi.org/10.1086/319618 (archived at https://perma.cc/MF8R-BTVB)

Wright, S (2019) *Community Psychology: Psychological sense of community: Theory of McMillan & Chavis*, Wright-house, http://wwwwright-housecom/psychology/sense-of-communityhtml

Zak, PJ (2014) Why your brain loves good storytelling, *Harvard Business Review*, 28 Oct, https://hbr.org/2014/10/why-your-brain-loves-good-storytelling (archived at https://perma.cc/7WF7-D9KT)

9

Lifecycle marketing and personalized experiences

Introduction to lifecycle messaging

Think of your customers as adventurers on what should be a journey that delights. Just like adventurers need different things at different stages of their expedition, your customers also have different needs and preferences at different stages of their relationship with your brand. Lifecycle marketing is all about providing the right support and guidance to your customers at each stage of their journey with your brand. By understanding and addressing their needs at each stage, you can create a seamless and satisfying experience and build long-term loyalty and retention. In this chapter, we will explore the different stages of the customer lifecycle and how to effectively engage with your customers at each stage.

Lifecycle marketing is about attracting customers into your orbit and keeping them there. It sounds a lot simpler than it is, because in reality, it involves all the moving parts of the cross-functional e-commerce growth stack, delicately balanced and finely tuned, to attract and keep your customers within your brand orbit harmoniously. Too much promotion and you could send them spinning out. Too little emphasis on customer care and they'll drift away. Not communicating your brand values and personality might have them forgetting why they even came in the first place. Too many messages and they might feel so overwhelmed that they self-combust, taking with them all their potential lifetime value. But done right, your gravitational pull will create a wonderful and diverse ecosystem of consumers, all orbiting your brand, and even recruiting new customers for you through advocacy and referrals. In this chapter, I show you how to use messaging as the medium that attracts customers into your orbit and achieve a delicately balanced holistic messaging strategy necessary to keep them there for many months and years to come.

Customer data: the foundation of customer-centric messaging

Personalization is crucial to any customer-centric messaging strategy. To achieve this, you need first-party data. Customers often willingly provide this data if they trust that they will receive a personalized shopping experience in return. Over 75 per cent of customers are willing to provide their first-party data if they know that it will result in a personalized experience (Accenture, 2018). In fact, over half of customers say they are more likely to make repeat purchases after a brand provides them with a personalized shopping experience (Keating, 2021). First-party data allows you to create personalized marketing experiences from the first purchase and beyond. This leads to better conversions, higher average order values and improved retention. Brands providing personalized experiences see revenue increases of 6–10 per cent and grow two to three times faster than those that don't (Abraham et al, 2017).

As you know by now, unless you have skipped ahead to this section, customer data is more than just name and email. As you will learn in this chapter, proper segmentation using methods such as recency, frequency and monetary value (RFM) analysis allow you to tailor your entire messaging strategy to very specific customer segments.

Messaging tips

Before we begin getting into the details of segmentation and messaging tactics, I want to take a moment to orient you toward the right ways of thinking when it comes to your messaging strategy. Enticing your customers to be part of your brand experience and community is about much more than discounts and bonus offers.

Taking a page from Huggies' customer-centric marketing playbook is also a good idea. Kimberly-Clark, the company that owns Huggies, says their purpose for the brand is to 'navigate the unknowns of babyhood' (Cornfield, 2021). 'Selling nappies' isn't mentioned here – the brand's strategy is based on what their customers need and want, with the nappies simply being part of that. This approach allows you to move beyond simple promotion and connect with consumers through helpful informational content, such as tutorials, blog posts and videos.

You also need to think long term. Nothing will nosedive your messaging strategy like burning your list with way too much communication because you want to maximize short-term revenues. The reality is, for a sustainable strategy, you will be messaging your consumers over a long time period. Three to six months or more should be your minimum outlook on a complete messaging strategy.

Additionally, Jess Chan, founder and CEO of Longplay, a fast-growing retention and lifecycle marketing agency, offers insights into how her team kicks off a brand's messaging strategy. It all starts by answering questions such as what customers need to know about you before they make a purchase (think values, founder stories, tutorial videos, social proof), your approach to discounting (including how often and at what level), setting your tone of voice and deciding on key business goals to build a three- to six-month messaging campaign targeting these goals (2X eCommerce, 2022).

Defining the customer journey

Your brand's specific customer journey will depend on your product mix, as well as how many stages you decide to split your customer journey into. But typically, your customers will follow these main stages: awareness; engagement and consideration; conversion; and retention and repurchase. That doesn't mean the journey will be linear – in many cases, your customer will oscillate between different stages in the journey, progressing very close to purchase and then abandoning the cart at the last minute, and going back to the engagement stage for some time. Other customers will complete a purchase, or even several, and then fade away and disengage from your brand. In which case you need to have systems in place in the form of automated messaging sequences to re-engage them and bring them back to converting. Let's break down each stage.

Awareness

Bringing your ideal customers to the awareness stage will require a combination of tactics outlined in the previous chapters of this book including treating your brand like a publisher and content creator, influencer marketing and more. As soon as you have their awareness, you want to funnel them toward some kind of commitment to your brand, be it a first purchase or a newsletter sign-up. Once you have them hooked into the funnel, your task is to bring them deeper and deeper into your brand's orbit using a series of messaging funnels and tactics.

FIGURE 9.1 The customer journey

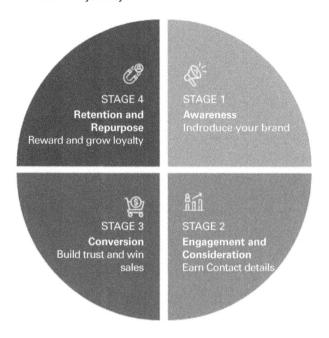

At the awareness stage, your customer is likely engaging with one of several touchpoints, including your social media and your website. So how do these touchpoints fall into your messaging strategy? When it comes to your website, you want to have multiple avenues for capturing your customer's email and phone number. Common touchpoints to achieve this include banners, lead magnets, pop-ups and of course at checkout with a pre-unchecked opt-in for email and SMS subscribe. When it comes to your social media, you need to be promoting your messaging funnels to your audience and offering incentives for joining your lists. Discounts, free shipping and being the first to know about new products are all ways you can entice your consumers. Don't just tell them about it either – show them too. Create specific marketing creative showing your SMS list in action, complete with two-way messaging if you can – show your consumers how they could be engaging with your brand all via mobile through text message, to get product recommendations, chat with support about orders and more.

Engagement and consideration

When it comes to the engagement stage, this is where your messaging comes into play via automated SMS and email series and campaigns. This stage is where you get to begin putting into action much of what you have learnt from this book so far. Sprinkle social proof throughout your messaging in the form of testimonials and star ratings, add authenticity with user-generated content features, express your brand values through founder stories, satisfy your consumers' informational needs through blog posts or instructional videos so they feel comfortable that they will be able to use your product. To do this, you will need to set up not only campaigns but also automated messaging flows, such as a welcome series, to nurture your consumers to purchase. Now is the time to focus on further segmentation opportunities through fun engagement tactics such as quizzes, or through keyword opt-ins (the kind where you text a keyword to a phone number to indicate your interest in receiving marketing messages about a specific topic) that allow your customers to customize the kind of messaging they receive from you to suit their interests.

Conversion

All the hard work that you have done to push your (potential) customer into your funnel and nurture them shouldn't go to waste. To push through to conversion, use incentives such as discounts or time-sensitive sales. When it comes to time-sensitive actions that users should take, SMS is the perfect medium because their phones are usually right with them, so they're less likely to miss the notification, in comparison to email. That being said, don't over-promote – make sure you're delivering value via your SMS channel too in the form of fun interactive quizzes and two-way chat with live customer support.

As I mentioned earlier, three to six months is a good timeframe on which to base your campaign strategy – rather than three to six weeks. As Scott Flear, founder of Rugby Warfare, says, many people are slow buyers and take three to six months to decide to buy something (Harper, 2021). So don't rush things, take your time with your customers, and certainly don't burn them out with a flurry of emails because you're desperate to see them convert.

Retention and repurchase

Retention is where it really gets exciting for your messaging strategy. Available at your disposal are a series of powerful automated messaging sequences such as your post-purchase series, up-sell and cross-sell opportunities (enhanced by your customer data and personalized marketing platforms to send specific personalized recommendations to each consumer) and more. Not to mention the ability to take advantage of transactional emails and SMS, which enjoy high open and engagement rates.

Order confirmation emails are crucial, not only because they show your customer everything is moving behind the scenes with their order. Research by Unific shows that order confirmation emails are by far your best chance to get your customers' attention. Order confirmation emails get an almost seven times higher open rate and almost double the viewing time (Green, 2022; Kurt 2022).

Retention is also the stage at which customer service will really come into play. Your customer will turn to you for shipping updates, product queries and returns or refunds just to name a few. The importance of this touchpoint cannot be understated given that 90 per cent of consumers say that customer support influenced their choice of brand, and which brands they remained loyal to (Microsoft, 2020). To advertise the quality of your customer support as a selling point, show off the personality of your AI-enhanced customer service bot or your live chat with support via text message. Post screenshots and videos of these channels to your social media through owned or UGC accounts. This way customers can see what it is like to engage with your brand throughout the entire customer journey, even before they have made their purchase.

Don't forget about customer data and a 360-degree view of the customer. Eliminate the need for your customers to repeat themselves and smooth the entire process for your customer. You could go further, as Bell Canada did, by anticipating possible downstream issues that the customer may not have even been aware of yet. In doing this, Bell Canada could get in front of the problem and smooth the entire process for their customers. They found that 22 per cent of calls involve downstream issues, and that by anticipating their customers' needs in advance they could significantly improve the customer service experience (Dixon et al, 2010).

RFM analysis

Recency, frequency, monetary (monetary value) (RFM) analysis is a key way to group your consumers into unique segments, enabling your brand to create targeted campaign and automation actions aimed at maximizing your brand's revenues. RFM analysis is founded on the core principle of 'pay attention to what people do, not what they say', and enables brands to segment consumers on key behaviours that are simple to track and don't require overly complicated first-party data collection. All you need to know is when they purchase and how much they spend. From these three simple metrics you can create many different segments, enabling your brand to completely personalize the entire marketing experience for consumers based on their RFM characteristics.

Recency means how recently has your customer purchased. What your store considers recent will depend on your brand and product mix. However, as a general rule, anything less than four months is recent for many industries, and anything longer than that would be considered not recent, out to about 12 months, beyond which you may well consider a customer as churned. **Frequency** is typically measured in purchases per year – but for a brand that expects much more frequent purchases, they may measure on a shorter timeframe. For most brands, three purchases a year is a good benchmark for a frequent purchaser.

Monetary value is generally measured in relation to your average order value – if a customer has an average purchase value above your brand's average order value for all customers, then you may consider placing them into a 'high value' category.

From an RFM analysis, you will be able to segment your core audience into groups like 'high frequency and recent', 'recent but not frequent' and 'lapsed (not recent) but frequent'. Each of these will have specific marketing goals attached. As an example, your recent and high-frequency consumers can be split further into high and low monetary value groups. The high-value group will be your VIPs who you can treat with exclusive perks and prompt with opportunities to advocate for your brand. The low-value consumers, on the other hand, you will be able to tempt with volume discounts and cross-sells to try to increase their average order value and bring them into the VIP category. Whereas a segment like 'lapsed (not recent) but frequent' is ripe for your win-back flows that try to bring the customer back into the brand orbit and get them purchasing again. Other groups like 'lapsed (not recent) and not frequent' should generally be avoided; you don't

FIGURE 9.2 Customer grouping with RFM analysis

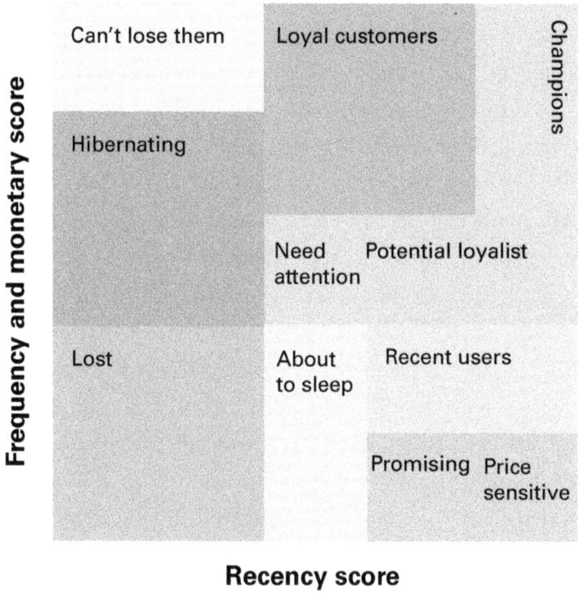

want to send these consumers a lot of campaigns because they have not shown interest in engaging with your brand.

By segmenting into groups based on, essentially, how much commitment a consumer has shown to your brand, you can then target your messaging strategies accordingly, including message types and frequency. Klaviyo suggests that brands earn three times more revenue per recipient when sending to targeted segments, versus sending indiscriminately (Klaviyo, 2022).

A primer on your tools of the trade

Email and SMS are essential tools for e-commerce marketers looking to engage consumers throughout the customer journey. While email has long been the go-to option for many brands, the shift to mobile has seen SMS emerge as a popular and profitable messaging channel. Marketers are increasing their use of SMS in campaigns and automations, with sends rising over 3.5 times from 2019 to 2020 (Omnisend, 2020).

When it comes to email and SMS, marketers have two main tactics at their disposal: campaigns and automations. Campaigns are one-off sends, such as a promotional offer or weekly newsletter. Automations, on the other hand, are either one-off emails or sequences triggered by specific user actions, such as a purchase. Automation sequences only need to be created once and are sent on demand when triggered.

Automated email series made up just 1.8 per cent of email sends in 2020, but accounted for almost 30 per cent of revenues (Omnisend, 2020). Open rates for automated email series should range from 25 per cent for lapsed purchaser or customer winback series to nearly 38 per cent for product abandonment emails (Omnisend, 2020). Transactional emails, like your post-purchase emails, tend to perform better than other emails, with high open rates, click-through rates and even conversion rates (approximately 56, 27 and 9.5 per cent respectively) (Omnisend, 2020).

SMS is a relatively new channel for e-commerce marketers, but it's quickly gaining popularity. In fact, the volume of SMS messages sent as part of campaigns and automations rose over 3.5 times from 2019 to 2020 (Omnisend, 2020). Consumers also prefer SMS for certain types of communications, such as loyalty programmes, coupons and promo codes, and post-transactional events like order confirmations and delivery reminders (Textlocal, 2017). Overall, SMS can be a valuable addition to your messaging strategy, providing a more personal touch and allowing you to reach consumers in a way that they prefer. By incorporating SMS into your omnichannel strategy, you can improve your customer-centric approach and drive better results. A combination of both email and SMS is advisable, with SMS for things like the most important or urgent engagements and interactive personalized quizzes.

If you're new to SMS and unsure of how to manage it, Alex Beller, co-founder and president of text messaging specialists Postscript, suggests that you can reuse a lot of your existing email and social media content (2X eCommerce, 2020). However, you will still need to set a specific tone of voice for SMS to match the energy that consumers expect from the platform. You should aim for approximately 80 per cent of your messaging to be automated sequences or transactional events, and only 20 per cent to be campaign messages. But how many messages should you send in total each month? Industry guidelines suggest between two and six messages is a good target (Vagaro, 2019). If you're just starting out on your SMS marketing journey, start with shipping and fulfilment first to establish SMS as a source of helpful information from your brand, with some added personality, of course, and then think about things like upsells and reorders.

Due to the nature of the channel (mobile-first, more interactive, two-way messaging capabilities), SMS presents unique opportunities for e-commerce brands. One campaign type particularly suited to SMS is the **reply-to-buy campaign** – quite simply, customers are prompted to order an item purely via text message. As an example, leading health brand 310 Nutrition stepped into the SMS marketing arena with this strategy and were able to generate an additional \$400,000 in revenue per month, which equated to a 59X ROI, and \$2.65 earnings per message (EPM) (Postscript, 2022). Keep in mind though that an approach like this, in order to scale, requires that you integrate with your entire cross-functional growth stack. 310 Nutrition, for example, utilized multiple aspects of their growth stack to achieve this success, including Shopify, Gorgias (customer service), ReCharge (subscriptions) and CartHook (post-purchase offers platform). Other creative uses of SMS that Postscript have seen from brands include running book clubs purely via the channel, sending scannable gift cards and even sending plant watering reminders to customers, says Alex Beller in the 2X eCommerce podcast #257 (2X eCommerce, 2020).

When it comes to SMS, compliance is key. To get a compliant list of phone numbers, you will need to get explicit permission for marketing, which you may not have gotten through your checkout when your SMS goals were purely for transactional (not campaign) purposes. So, you will want to begin building your compliant and marketable email list. A few ways you can do this include desktop pop-ups, leveraging your existing email list by offering them an incentive for signing up for SMS marketing as well, and especially using mobile pop-ups because the mobile browser and SMS marketing combination is a logical perfect match. Everything you do from gathering your list to engaging with it must be compliant. In the United States, you have things like the Telephone Consumer Protection Act (TCPA) to abide by. The consequences of non-compliance can be up to \$500 per message sent and \$1,500 for willful violations, at least in the United States, so for a campaign where 100,000 SMS messages are sent it can easily cost a brand millions of dollars (DNC, 2022).

To get our full guide for creating a compliant SMS list, benchmarking your SMS strategy, full guides with examples for the top email and SMS automations you need to be using, and implement other email and SMS best practices for your brand, head to https://2xecommerce.com/book/chapter9.

Automated messaging essentials

- Welcome series: automated messages sent to new users to introduce the brand and offer incentives.

- Browse abandonment: messages triggered when a customer has been browsing but hasn't completed checkout, containing reminders and cross-sell opportunities.

- Abandoned cart: automated messages sent when a customer has added items to their cart but hasn't completed checkout, with the goal of converting the abandoned cart into a purchase.

- Post-purchase: messages sent to thank customers and ask for feedback, as well as to up-sell or cross-sell complementary products and provide customer support.

- Win-back: messages sent to customers who haven't made a purchase in a while to re-engage them and remind them of the brand. Can include special discounts or promotions, new product highlights and helpful content.

- Birthday/anniversary: messages sent to customers on their birthday or other special occasions, such as the anniversary of their first purchase. Can include personalized offers or discounts to celebrate the occasion.

- Quizzes: using quizzes as a way to gather customer data and incentivize phone number collection by sending quiz results to mobile phones. Can be used to grow the SMS list and start SMS conversations with customers.

For a full guide on what you need to include in these various messaging flows, complete with examples and wisdom from unicorn brand builders, head to 2X eCommerce to access our guides and resources. Take control of your messaging strategy today at 2xecommerce.com/book/chapter9.

For a little bit of strategy around your automations and messaging roll-out, if you're just getting started because many of your transactional emails like your order confirmation and shipping confirmation are already set up, email marketing expert Chase Dimond suggests that you focus on your campaigns and automations like abandoned cart series before you worry about your transactional emails. You can listen to all the email marketing wisdom Chase has to offer in 2X eCommerce podcast #277 (2X eCommerce, 2021b). That being said, the default transactional emails will need some work to bring them up to standard in terms of your brand image and brand tone of voice, so once you have your automated messaging sequences set up, come back to give your transactional emails some love.

Other channels

Before you begin utilizing all the channels available to you, think about what your brand can feasibly do well, with frequency and consistency. Is it one channel or two channels? Also consider where your customers actually are, too. If your customers aren't on WhatsApp, then even if another brand is getting great results from that channel, it might not be for you.

Push notifications

At 2X eCommerce, we sat down to discuss all things push notifications with Josh Wetzel, chief revenue officer at OneSignal, a leading customer engagement platform for messaging channels like SMS, push notifications and email. In 2X eCommerce podcast #259 Josh tells us that while brands might be tempted to use this channel frequently, it really should be treated much like email or SMS – more than one push notification a day is probably too much (2X eCommerce, 2021a). Push notifications can be effective, with conversion rates of almost 30 per cent (Omnisend, 2020). However, they should be used carefully, as consumers may be turned off by too many notifications. Push notifications are preferred for price alerts, quantity updates and restock reminders, but overdoing promotions or cart abandonments can be detrimental. Opt-in rates for push notifications are generally 5–15 per cent, with higher rates on mobile (Android) devices. Desktop opt-in rates are lower, at 3–15 per cent, but these users tend to be more loyal and engaged, making them a profitable audience. Some retailers see 12 per cent of revenue generated through push notifications. Benchmarking for push notifications should be around a 50 per cent view rate, a 3 per cent click-through rate and a 28 per cent conversion rate for those who clicked (Omnisend, 2020)

Direct mail

While we've focused heavily on digital channels here in this chapter, the physical world isn't dead. Physical communication, such as direct mail, can be integrated with digital strategies to enhance its effectiveness. For example, a direct mail campaign can include a QR code that incentivizes potential customers to join an SMS list. Direct mail can also be effective in reaching specific customer segments, such as older demographics who may not use digital channels as much, or those who have not engaged with your email list in a long time. Although direct mail is more expensive than email or SMS, it can still have good response rates and a high return on investment. A 2018 study showed that direct mail had response rates of 9 per cent compared to 1 per cent for digital channels such as email and social media (ANA, 2018 in De Caprio, 2021). Return on investment for direct mail is also high, with an estimated 112 per cent ROI (ANA, 2022), potentially even higher than the ROI for SMS and email, which in one study came in at 102 per cent and 93 per cent respectively. However, direct mail should not be overused and should be targeted to the right customer segments.

Identifying areas for improvement in your messaging

As an e-commerce brand, there are six main problems that you might face when implementing your messaging strategy. In this section I will give you some tips to orient yourself in the right direction to solve these problems. The truth is, all brands will deal with these, no matter their size or experience – it's just a part of testing and trialling new campaigns and strategies. So don't feel disheartened if you come up against them – we all do from time to time. Here are the six most common hurdles you may need to overcome in your messaging strategy and how to tackle them:

1 **Low open rates:**
   - Ask yourself if you are sending to the right audience.
   - Use segmentation to create more relevant content at more suitable frequencies.
   - Use AI tools or A/B testing to improve your subject lines.

2 **Low click-through rates:**
   - Use segmentation to send the right content to the right segments.
   - Review your goals and customer-centric approach.
   - Improve your call to action to have one clear goal for each email.

3 **Low conversion rate:**
   - Make sure your website and offer are congruent with the email campaign.
   - Create dedicated landing pages or revamp the homepage to align with your messaging.

4 **High unsubscribe rate:**

- – Reduce the number of emails or SMS sent to unengaged customers.
- – Use the RFM analysis to create segments most responsive to your brand and messaging.

5 **High spam rate:**

- – Ensure that your email includes an unsubscribe link or button.
- – Avoid using spammy subject lines and image-only emails.
- – Review your sending practices and avoid using spam trigger words.

6 **Low ROI:**

- – Review your segmentation, content and targeting.
- – Focus on providing value to your subscribers to increase engagement and conversions.
- – Use A/B testing to optimize your messaging and improve ROI.

Wrapping up

In conclusion, lifecycle marketing is a powerful strategy that can help e-commerce brands build strong, long-lasting relationships with their customers. By sending relevant and personalized messages at the right time, brands can engage their customers and improve their overall experience. If you want to learn more about how to build a complete messaging strategy and avoid common mistakes, be sure to visit our website at 2xecommerce.com/book/chapter9, where you will find a wealth of resources and information to help you succeed. Thanks for reading, and happy marketing!

Stay tuned for the next chapter where I will be discussing how to build a strong brand and culture for growth. By reading this chapter, you can expect to learn the importance of defining your brand's mission and values, and how to align your messaging with these to create a cohesive and authentic brand experience. You will also gain valuable insights and strategies for building a positive company culture that can help drive growth and success for your business.

CTA for tools

If you're ready to take your lifecycle marketing to the next level, be sure to visit my website at 2xecommerce.com/book/chapter9, where you can download a variety of materials and guides to help you build a complete and effective messaging strategy. From templates and checklists to in-depth guides and tutorials, you'll find everything you need to succeed with lifecycle marketing. Visit my website today and start building your complete messaging strategy.

References

2X eCommerce (2020) S05 EP33, Getting personal with customers using SMS marketing, https://2xecommerce.com/podcast/ep257/ (archived at https://perma.cc/6GE7-BN7W)

2X eCommerce (2021a) S05 EP35, Leveraging personalized push notifications in ecommerce, https://2xecommerce.com/podcast/ep259/ (archived at https://perma.cc/HWW3-F363)

2X eCommerce (2021b) S06 EP03, Email marketing insights from a $50M ecommerce email marketer, https://2xecommerce.com/podcast/ep277/ (archived at https://perma.cc/A5UH-2QCE)

2X eCommerce (2022) S07 EP23, How to play the long game with life cycle marketing – Jess Chan, Longplay Brands, https://2xecommerce.com/podcast/ep366/ (archived at https://perma.cc/9MHA-N52A)

Abraham, M, Mitchelmore, S, Collins, S, Maness, J, Kistulinec, M, Khondabandeh, S, Hoeing, D and Visser, J (2017) Profiting from personalization, *BCG*, 8 May, www.bcg.com/publications/2017/retail-marketing-sales-profiting-personalization (archived at https://perma.cc/R72D-R7WB)

Accenture (2018) Widening gap between consumer expectations and reality in personalization signals warning for brands, *Accenture Interactive Research Finds,* https://newsroom.accenture.com/news/widening-gap-between-consumer-expectations-and-reality-in-personalization-signals-warning-for-brands-accenture-interactive-research-finds.htm (archived at https://perma.cc/L2HT-G88A)

ANA (2022) New ANA study shows marketers still favor email for direct ads, 24 Jan, www.ana.net/content/show/id/71311#:~:text=The%20study%2C%20Response%20Rate%20Report (archived at https://perma.cc/Y9E2-GMA8)

Cornfield, G (2021) Recognizing your customer's purpose is key to growth, *Harvard Business Review*, 20 May, https://hbr.org/2021/05/whats-your-customers-purpose (archived at https://perma.cc/3UPC-QY2A)

De Caprio, M (2021) How to wisely test out direct mail retargeting in 2021, SG360, 26 Jan, https://sg360.com/how-to-wisely-test-direct-mail-retargeting-2021/ (archived at https://perma.cc/397F-XE7W)

Dixon, M, Freeman, K and Toman, N (2010) Stop trying to delight your customers, *Harvard Business Review*, Jul–Aug, https://hbr.org/2010/07/stop-trying-to-delight-your-customers (archived at https://perma.cc/6XFB-MSQM)

DNC (2022) Contact Center Compliance, What is the penalty for violating the TCPA?, www.dnc.com/faq/what-penalty-violating-tcpa# (archived at https://perma.cc/HB72-JD9X)

Green, G (2022) CTR & open rates for order confirmation emails, www.unific.com/blog/ctr-open-rates-order-confirmation-emails (archived at https://perma.cc/9534-PZFJ)

Keating, G (2021) Announcing Twilio Segment's The State of Personalization 2021 Report, *Twilio Segment*, www.twilio.com/blog/announcing-the-state-of-personalization-2021 (archived at https://perma.cc/53JA-HHMK)

Klaviyo (2022) Getting started with segments, https://help.klaviyo.com/hc/en-us/articles/115005237908-Getting-started-with-segments (archived at https://perma.cc/E7P2-MZKD)

Kurt, D (2022) Why transactional emails are a missed marketing opportunity, www.unific.com/blog/transactional-emails-missed-opportunity (archived at https://perma.cc/554M-9EJP)

Microsoft (2020) Global State of Customer Service | Microsoft Dynamics 365, https://info.microsoft.com/ww-thankyou-global-state-of-customer-service.html?lcid=en (archived at https://perma.cc/TLH2-2MJB)

Omnisend (2020) 2020 Ecommerce Statistics Report: Email, SMS & push messaging insights for 2021, www.omnisend.com/resources/reports/ecommerce-statistics-report-2021/ (archived at https://perma.cc/8395-NPW3)

Osman, M (2021) Customer Lifecycle: All about the 5 stages of the ecommerce customer lifecycle, *Klaviyo*, 23 Mar, www.klaviyo.com/blog/customer-lifecycle-marketing-ecommerce (archived at https://perma.cc/6DZ4-WVU9)

Postscript (2022) 8 Ecommerce Brands Using SMS Marketing to Grow Fast, https://postscript.io/guide-sms-for-ecommerce-examples (archived at https://perma.cc/FE8W-FQGM)

Textlocal (2017) Free SMS Marketing Statistics 2017 – Complete State of SMS, https://www.textlocal.com/the-state-of-sms-2017 (archived at https://perma.cc/BZ2M-TFXF)

Vagaro (2019) Top 10 Text Marketing Best Practices, https://blog.vagaro.com/pro/top-10-text-marketing-best-practices-your-business-needs/ (archived at https://perma.cc/TMX2-NE5D)

Further reading

CodeBreaker (2018) Consumer mobile engagement research results: shoppers share their preferences for receiving mobile coupons, messages and offers, https://codebroker.com/resources2/doc/CodeBroker_Consumer_Mobile_Engagement_Research_Results.pdf#page=10 (archived at https://perma.cc/CU4F-JAUB)

Community (2022) Long codes vs short codes: understanding the different types of SMS numbers, *Community*, 2 May, www.community.com/post/long-codes-vs-short-codes-understanding-the-different-types-of-sms-numbers (archived at https://perma.cc/MW97-R79R)

Damen, A (2022) Direct mail for retail is alive and well: how these 5 retailers use direct mail to increase sales, *Shopify*, 24 May, www.shopify.com/au/retail/direct-mail-retail (archived at https://perma.cc/NF9U-KQTR)

Gray, D (2020) 10 amazing abandoned cart and browse email examples, *Freshrelevance*, 5 Aug, www.freshrelevance.com/blog/browse-abandonment-email-examples (archived at https://perma.cc/22V3-8MST)

Klaviyo (2021) Abandoned Cart: Ecommerce Industry Benchmark Report, www.klaviyo.com/marketing-resources/abandoned-cart-benchmarks (archived at https://perma.cc/F9L9-2R6G)

McGreevy, A (2022) Use email marketing as a retention strategy to keep customers loyal to your brand, *Klaviyo Blog*, 10 Feb, www.klaviyo.com/blog/retention-marketing-strategies-brands (archived at https://perma.cc/L7EV-U3KR)

Patel, N (2022) How to use Facebook Messenger to sell more e-commerce products, https://neilpatel.com/blog/facebook-messenger-to-sell-products/ (archived at https://perma.cc/A4RQ-PHXZ)

Phaneuf, A (2022) Ecommerce statistics: industry benchmarks & growth, *Insider Intelligence*, 8 Jan, www.insiderintelligence.com/insights/ecommerce-industry-statistics/ (archived at https://perma.cc/D7WX-6ZTB)

Postscript (2022) Guide to SMS for ecommerce in 2022: resources, checklists, and examples; the rise of SMS marketing in ecommerce, https://postscript.io/guide-sms-for-ecommerce (archived at https://perma.cc/UCC3-BLK8)

Puckett, T (2021) 5 text messages to trigger customer conversion, *Hawke Media*, 4 Jun, https://hawkemedia.com/insights/sms-to-trigger-customer-conversion/ (archived at https://perma.cc/ZY2Q-ECBJ)

Salecycle (2021) Cart abandonment conversion rate by sector, www.salecycle.com/wp-content/uploads/2019/05/copy-cart-abandonment-email-conversion-rates-2021.png (archived at https://perma.cc/8ZUP-28KZ)

Sara (2021) What is RFM analysis? How to use it for customer segmentation, *NotifyVisitors*, 27 Aug, www.notifyvisitors.com/blog/rfm-analysis/ (archived at https://perma.cc/74T6-X4NV)

Wright, C (2022) SMS marketing compliance overview, *Postscript*, 17 Jun, https://help.postscript.io/hc/en-us/articles/1260804685749-SMS-Marketing-Compliance-Overview-Guide#Complaince-Language-Requirements (archived at https://perma.cc/J4JJ-RABC)

10

Search engine marketing

Why SEM?

The cross-functional e-commerce growth stack is like a puzzle. Each piece represents a different aspect of the overall strategy, from marketing and sales to product development and customer service. When put together, these pieces form a cohesive and effective plan that can drive growth and success for your online store. One of the key, crucial even, pieces in your growth stack when it comes to being discovered and giving your brand the opportunity to both generate demand and capture demand generated through other channels, is the search engine and its two key growth tools, 'search engine optimization' and 'paid search' marketing.

Search engine marketing (SEM) increases a brand's visibility in search engine results pages (SERPs) through two methods: search engine optimization (SEO) to get your content to rank organically (without having to pay for ads) and pay-per-click (PPC) campaigns. PPC advertising differs from other forms of advertising because it only charges when someone clicks a campaign. PPC campaigns typically appear at the top, bottom and right-hand side of search engines, and may make up the majority of 'above the fold' screen space (Safire, 2006). SEM is important for e-commerce brands because it serves as a hunting ground for bringing in new customers. But it requires knowledge of where to show up and what will get customers to click, which is exactly what you will learn in this chapter.

SEO is the process of improving a website's ranking on search engines by making it more relevant and popular. Privacy laws, such as the General Data Protection Regulation (GDPR) in Europe and the California Consumer Privacy Act (CCPA) in California, make targeted digital advertising more challenging (Wolford, 2022). Not to mention changes by companies like Apple that make consumer data harder to come by. Brands can improve their SEO performance by understanding how to capture or generate demand by being top of page for key search queries, optimizing content for algorithms and following best practices that I will outline in this chapter.

Paid search campaigns, also known as pay-per-click (PPC) campaigns, allow businesses to bid on keywords and gain more control over their search ranking. The first page of search results is a valuable space for businesses. However, three-quarters of users do not click past the first page when searching, and SEO does not always guarantee a first-page ranking (La Barbera, 2022). Due to high competition, organic efforts are simply unlikely to reach these top positions in today's search environment. Paid search is often necessary to reach the top three links, which receive the majority of clicks – or at least on the first page, which most users do not go past, preferring to launch new queries rather than scan the depths of search engine results (Dean, 2022). Whereas SEO is a slow-burn strategy that takes time to realize results, paid search is immediate and scalable. When it comes to the hunting ground, SEO as a weapon of choice is like a net; it takes a long time to weave it together and build the connections necessary to capture the incoming traffic. Paid search, on the other hand, is like a spear; it is very straightforward and targeted. It doesn't take as long to build as a large net does, but once the spear is thrown, you have to keep making more. Unlike a net which will sit and capture demand for months and years to come, with some maintenance. Due to the cross-functional nature of e-commerce, it's not one or the other, SEO or paid, but how to bring together both strategies in symbiotic harmony. In this chapter, you'll learn how.

Popular search engines and key platforms for paid search

Most likely, you're already familiar with several search engines on the market. Google, the search engine founded in 1996 which has placed its founders amongst the top 10 richest people in the world, is the household name for most, so much so that 'googling' has taken over our lexicon as a term for searching for something on the internet (Law, 2022). You've probably even said something along the lines of 'just google it' or 'I'll google it'. Let's look at just a few of the options on the search engine market today:

- Google: most popular search engine, with approximately 80 per cent of all search traffic on the internet (Law, 2022).

- Bing: second most popular search engine, with a market share of between 3 and 8 per cent of global search traffic; popular in the United States with approximately 15–30 per cent of the desktop market share (Comscore, 2019; Statcounter, 2022).

- Baidu: less than 5 per cent market share globally, but the most popular search engine in China, with over 80 per cent market share locally (MarketMeChina, 2022; Law, 2022; Statista, 2022).

I mention this not so much to talk about the specific differences, market share or growth. I mention this to highlight the fact that even with these stark differences, each platform has its own specific advantages. This will always be the case, no matter who the market leader is. Baidu dominates the Chinese market, making it a good idea to include it in a search engine strategy when targeting that market. In the United States, Bing and Google are the biggest search engines, with 66 billion and 62 million users respectively. Advertising on Bing has been shown to increase branded Google searches, highlighting yet again the cross-functional opportunities in eCommerce (Irvine, 2021a, 2021b). As an example of a platform-specific advantage, Bing typically has less competition for keywords, meaning a lower cost per click. By some estimates, Bing is one-third of the cost of Google in terms of cost per click (Vasu, 2017; Spinutech, 2017). This may of course change – but the reason I mention this is that you should always be looking for opportunities like this rather than only looking at gross search traffic numbers.

The fundamentals of SEO

Creating good SEO-optimized content with the right information architecture in place is no easy task. But it is the price of entry when it comes to getting access to the hunting ground that is search engine results pages (SERPs). And if done well, it pays off. On average, over half of web traffic is driven by organic search results (Brightedge, 2022a).

When creating content, remember to focus on providing value to your audience. Your content strategy should flow from this mindset, and SEO tactics can help your content appear in front of interested and useful readers. The earlier chapters in this book can serve as a guide for creating content that customers want to see, such as user-generated content and edutainment. Keep in mind that SEO is a slow-burn strategy and it may take time to build up search engine credibility and appear on the first pages of search engine results. You may not see results for several months to a year. Investing in SEO may not be the right choice for some e-commerce brands due to budget constraints and slow results. The first stage of starting SEO should always begin with an analysis of how it fits into your overall growth strategy and goals. Getting fast ROI from paid search might be a better short-term tactic.

Competitor analysis

Tools like Semrush have features that enable you to find competitors and then split them into groups based specifically on their online presence metrics. This is a critical step in your SEO process. Getting granular will help you define who you need to be competing with online, as well as who you can actually possibly compete with. As an example, competing on the same keywords as a company with a large audience and a high growth rate will be difficult. In addition to audience size and growth there is 'domain authority'. Domain authority is a prediction of how likely a domain is to rank in SERPs. It's not a Google ranking factor in and of itself, but it does predict how likely a brand will land in the search engine results (Moz, 2022). A site with high authority is going to be hard to compete with, so choose competitors and keywords wisely and in line with your current authority and growth stage.

Keywords

Once you have defined who your competitors are, the first thing you should look at is the keywords that they are getting visibility on. Try to identify keywords that your competitors are only just beating you on (Slegg, 2022). These will be a great place to start as you don't have too much ground to gain to take out the top spot. Beyond that, Semrush CSO and CDO Eugene Levin, who sat down with me in episode #245 of the 2X eCommerce podcast to discuss all things SEM, suggests finding keywords that are a little less competitive than those your competitors are using, but that still have lots of search volume (2X eCommerce, 2020). Long-tail keywords are much closer to a customer's purchase intent than generic short-term keywords, which means they typically convert better, so these could be a good place to start (2X eCommerce, 2020). The majority of search traffic consists of long-tail keywords (Wordstream, 2022).

FIGURE 10.1 Short-tail, mid-tail and long-tail keywords and search volume

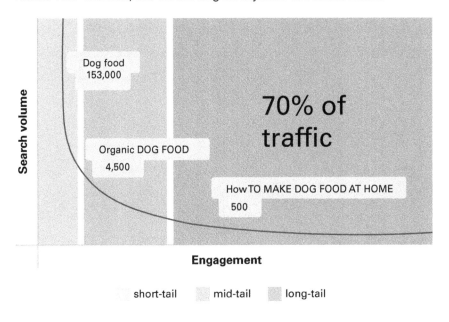

FIGURE 10.2 Search intent demonstrates the purpose of search queries

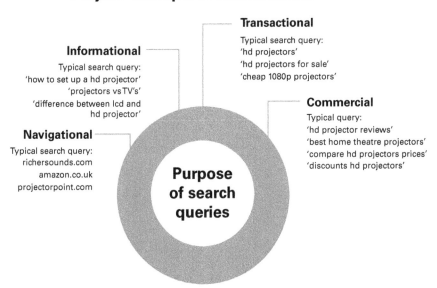

FIGURE 10.3 Bottom-of-funnel search intent types: transactional and navigational

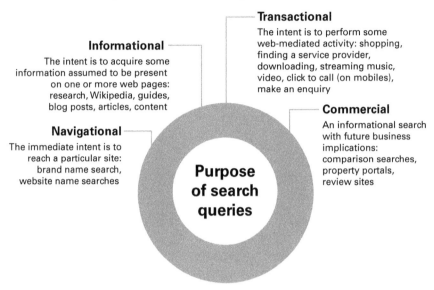

All keywords are not equal search intent

Informational
The intent is to acquire some information assumed to be present on one or more web pages: research, Wikipedia, guides, blog posts, articles, content

Transactional
The intent is to perform some web-mediated activity: shopping, finding a service provider, downloading, streaming music, video, click to call (on mobiles), make an enquiry

Navigational
The immediate intent is to reach a particular site: brand name search, website name searches

Commercial
An informational search with future business implications: comparison searches, property portals, review sites

Purpose of search queries

SOURCE IBM Research, A taxonomy of web search. Via www.cis.upenn.edu/~nenkova/Courses/cis430/p3-broder.pdf

What kind of content do search engines (and consumers) prefer?

The thing about winning at search is that you need to please both the algorithm and the consumer. What pleases the consumer will typically please the algorithm too, because it will result in things like longer dwell time, as well as more shares and backlinks. But then there is the technical SEO aspect, which really is about pleasing the algorithm so that it can better serve the customer. All in all though, customer-centricity, again, is the aim of the game. Let's dive into how to improve your search results.

Dwell time is simply the amount of time a searcher spends on a page after clicking through to it from the search results before they return to the search engine results page. It's an important ranking signal for search engine performance, not to mention a great indicator of how well you are doing to satisfy your readers' needs when it comes to the kind of content you are producing (Backlinko, 2022).

Bounce rate is when someone clicks on a link to your site and then hits the back button to go right back to where they came from without clicking on anything on your page. You might think that it's because the content either wasn't what they were looking for, or your site took too long to load and they got impatient. But whether the reader spends one second or one hour on your page, so long as they clicked back to the search results without clicking anything on your page, it's counted as a bounce. That's why bounce rate is typically not as strong an indicator of your content performance as dwell time is. The bounce rate doesn't care how long the reader spent on your site. Dwell time, on the other hand, does.

To find out exactly what customers and search engines like to see, Semrush (a leading search engine marketing tool) crunched the numbers on over a million blog articles. They analysed things like word count, headlines and subheadings, structure and visual content (images and videos) (Semrush, 2020; Petrova, 2021).

When it comes to length, that is, word count, long reads are clear high performers. Semrush found that articles with over 7,000 words get almost four times the amount of traffic as shorter articles of between 900–1,200 words (which is about the average length of a blog post). Not everyone is going to have the time to go through an entire 7,000 words, so include a mix of content lengths to keep all your consumers engaged. Content at anywhere from 1,000 to 5,000 words performs well, too (Petrova, 2021).

FIGURE 10.4 Content-length and organic search engine traffic [Semrush]

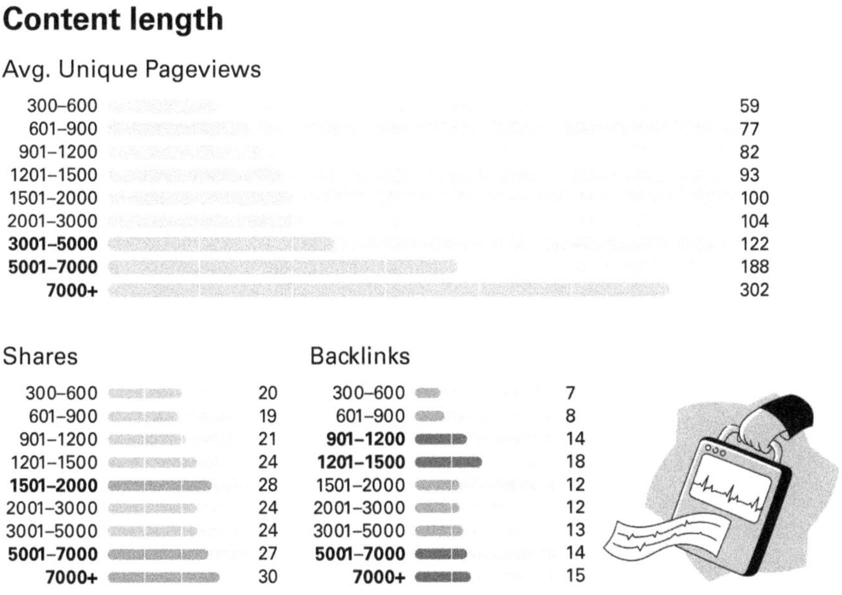

Content length

Avg. Unique Pageviews

300–600	59
601–900	77
901–1200	82
1201–1500	93
1501–2000	100
2001–3000	104
3001–5000	122
5001–7000	188
7000+	302

Shares

300–600	20
601–900	19
901–1200	21
1201–1500	24
1501–2000	28
2001–3000	24
3001–5000	24
5001–7000	27
7000+	30

Backlinks

300–600	7
601–900	8
901–1200	14
1201–1500	18
1501–2000	12
2001–3000	12
3001–5000	13
5001–7000	14
7000+	15

Getting into the finer details of what to actually include within your content, Semrush has some more tips:

- Use lists, like this bullet point list right here. Including a list every 500 words or so is advisable. Such posts get approximately 70 per cent more traffic than posts without lists.
- Use images. Text-only posts get half as much traffic as posts with at least one image. Not to mention that posts with images are more likely to be shared and backlinked to.
- Use video. Posts containing videos get up to 60 per cent more unique page views (Petrova, 2021). Additionally, people spend about 1.4 times longer on pages with video than on pages without (Fishman, 2022). For the e-commerce brand, integrating video throughout your growth stack could be as simple as featuring your UGC or video testimonials on-site, embedding your tutorial or educational videos on a page or showing off your latest behind-the-scenes from a photoshoot. The opportunities for content creation using video are almost endless.

Linking it all together

Links are essential to the functioning of the internet. Optimizing your SEO means building an external network of links to your website and complementing that with a comprehensive internal network to guide your customers and search engine algorithms to the content you want them to see most. Your linking strategy should include both backlinks and internal links. Backlinks are links from external domains and can be earned through useful and informative content or through tools like outreach and services like Help A Reporter Out. Internal links are within your own domain and incentivize users to stay on your website by providing connections to relevant content.

Marieke Van de Rakt, co-founder and CMO of Yoast, one of the most well-known SEO platforms in the world, sat down with me for episode #360 of the 2X eCommerce podcast to talk all things SEO (2X eCommerce, 2022). Marieke says that you need to look at your internal linking structure regularly. Look at where your internal linking is pointing – do you have lots of links pointing to places that aren't so relevant anymore? Like to a 2015 report on search engine usage statistics when you could instead be linking to the latest version from those older blog posts?

Marieke says, 'It's not very sexy to talk about site maintenance, but it is really important to get that part of your site done' (2X eCommerce, 2022). But it's not just about cramming links everywhere; you should link from lots of less important articles to the few pages that are most important to you. This way, search engines (and customers) will find their way to your most important pages with greater frequency, which will boost their ranking (2X eCommerce, 2022).

Technical SEO

Tools in your technical SEO arsenal include XML sitemaps, navigation schemas and breadcrumbs. There's no need to be intimidated by the word 'technical'; this chapter will give you everything you need to start optimizing your own SEO, and all the tools you need to direct a freelancer or agency and tell them what it is you want to focus on. I spent many of my early years in the trenches of SEO and even wrote my diploma thesis on the topic – rest assured, you're in good hands.

XML sitemaps for SEO

An XML sitemap is a list of URLs that serves as a map of your site for search engine crawlers. It tells the search engine how often your website pages are updated, when they were last updated and the priority of pages. Not having a sitemap can make it difficult for a search engine to know what is important on your site and may lead to the search engine thinking you have duplicate content, which will hurt your rankings. If you're going the DIY route, using a service like Screaming Frog is relatively simple and will help you create an XML sitemap for your website. Feel free to engage an SEO professional to help, just make sure you get this item ticked off.

Redirecting and fixing broken links

A redirect is when you send people who clicked on a link to a location other than the link they clicked on. Before we start discussing redirects, you'll need to know some status code basics. You've likely seen website status codes before – I think everybody has come across a 404 error. If you have a lot of 404 errors, then you have a few options. First, you can create a user-friendly 404 page with links to other website pages and added brand personality. Alternatively, you can permanently redirect (a 301 redirect) to another page on your website. This way, your 404 is put to good use, and your crawling budget isn't spent on dead ends.

When it comes to redirects, you'll need to know what a 301 and a 302 are – but it's quite simple. A 301 is a permanent redirect, and it passes on 90 per cent (or more) of the original page's authority. A 302 on the other hand is a temporary redirect – it tells the search engine that you'll be restoring the original page soon. The main thing is to not leave a 302 redirect up for long – if you don't want to have a page on your site anymore, use a 301 redirect.

Markup schemas

Schema markup helps search engines create rich snippets from your data, which is the result that shows in the SERP. Search engines like Google are really good at recognizing text on a page, but not so good at knowing what that text is about – it recognizes the text, but it doesn't know what is what. An example would be specific product attributes and time-limited special offers or price drops. So you need to create schemas to help it know what is the size, what is the product name, what is the product description, what is a review and things like that. This will help your brand show the most relevant information to searchers and boost your click-through rates (2X eCommerce, 2022).

Schema markup looks like Figure 10.5, and is not seen by the searcher, only by the search engine crawler and algorithm.

This gives search engines all the structured data they need to create a rich snippet, which is what users see. With rich snippets you can mark up things like your product review ratings via the *Review Schema*, and price information and stock availability using the *Product Schema*. This means that things like your average star reviews, their corresponding rating (i.e. 4.5/5 stars) and product prices, as well as whether an item is in stock or not, will show directly in the search engine. Without marking this up, you lose out on the ability to showcase valuable social proof and useful information to internet users.

On top of this you have the navigation schema. With the navigation schema, you get the opportunity to add to the weight of your search results and take up a lot more search real estate with links to your different

FIGURE 10.5 Schema markup example for 'Product'

```
<script type="application/ld+json">
{
  "@context": "https://schema.org",
  "@type": "Product",
  "aggregateRating": {
    "@type": "AggregateRating",
    "ratingValue": "3.5",
    "reviewCount": "11"
  },
  "description": "0.7 cubic feet countertop microwave. Has six preset cooking categories and co
  "name": "Kenmore White 17\" Microwave",
  "image": "kenmore-microwave-17in.jpg",
  "offers": {
    "@type": "Offer",
    "availability": "https://schema.org/InStock",
    "price": "55.00",
    "priceCurrency": "USD"
```

categories or important pages. But there is no guarantee that search engines will show this information. If you search for a known retail brand with an extensive product catalogue size on Google, you'll even notice a search bar is added to the result. However, this won't show all the time, even if the rest of the navigation schema does.

Other schemas you can use include the organization schema to show things like your contact details, your 'about us' page or your legal information such as terms and conditions. Recall from Chapter 7 that approximately two-thirds of your customers are checking your returns and exchanges information before they purchase. Well, adding a link to your refunds and exchanges page via your rich snippet might be a good idea.

Breadcrumbs

A breadcrumb is basically the path of links that you took to get to where you are now. As an example, if you first clicked the 'lighting' category on your favourite home interior website and then 'table lamps', your breadcrumb would look like YourBrand.com > Lighting > Table Lamps. So, you can see your breadcrumbs are related to your taxonomy and site structure. Why is this important? Because by using breadcrumbs in your schema, search engines can then pull through your category information and information architecture to search results. Not only does it make for a better-looking search result, but it also adds more context and weight to your listing – enabling you to convey more information in less space. Some schema tactics will even enable you to take up more space in your search listings, which pushes competitors further down the page.

Measuring your SEO performance

Naturally, you are going to want to measure and track your SEO efforts so that you can report back to key stakeholders with real concrete proof that your work is driving measurable business impact. With that in mind, I have put together some top-line key metrics to communicate to your data and marketing teams.

SERP visibility

This is how many people see your website in the search results. This metric gives you an overall bird's-eye view of your SEM efforts.

Position tracking

To maximize your chances of being seen and drive SERP visibility, you will want to improve your ranking position. The majority of clicks are for the first three results on the first page of search results. Basically, the higher up, the better.

Click-through rate

This is, quite simply, how many people actually click through to your website out of all the people that saw your search engine result. If this is low, then you might have problems with your organic keywords, ad targeting or copy. Improving your search engine ranking will also improve this metric. As I said, most people click one of the first three results – in fact, over a quarter click the first result alone (Beus, 2020).

Traffic analysis

Obviously, it's important to know how much visibility you are getting and how many people are clicking through to your website. But where are they coming from? Traffic analysis will show you a breakdown of your traffic sources by referring domain, as well as direct search, organic search and paid advertising.

Website authority

This is typically measured on a logarithmic scale from 1–100, with a higher number meaning a better ranking. Improving your domain authority will have a ripple effect across all of your other SEO efforts.

Backlinks

Track the number of backlinks you are getting and also pay attention to the authority of the domains that are referring to your site. You want to opt for a balance of quality authoritative backlinks, without trying to maximize quantity through poor-quality domain referrals (referrals from low-authority domains).

Page speed

A website that takes too long to load is costing you big time. If your website takes 10 seconds to load, it doubles your bounce rate (Google, 2017). Page speed is typically measured from 0–100. A score of 90+ is considered good; anything less than that and you have work to do (Varagouli, 2020).

Paid search

Having been introduced in 1998, paid search has become a popular and necessary tool in the cross-functional e-commerce growth stack (Laffey, 2007). Pay-per-click campaigns that charge brands based on clicks, not impressions, are a cost-effective way for e-commerce brands to bring in new customers to their funnel. Given that there are estimated to be over 200 ranking factors of organic content, paid content is a simple way to ensure your brand stays front and centre (Brooks, 2018). To illustrate this for you, I did a search of my own for vegan protein powder. I estimate that 25 per cent of the page was taken up by shopping ads (the kind that showcase product images), the next 25 per cent of the screen was taken up by search ads (text-based ads) and only then, after that, would a user reach real organic results. Simply, paid is taking up an ever-increasing amount of space on our screens, and it's essential for your brand to have a paid strategy in place (Brightedge, 2022b).

Paid search isn't just about advertising your brand though – you need the content to back it up. Your advertising needs to be both customer-centric and congruent with what the consumer will see when they click through to your page. Always remember that when your users come to a search engine, they are not looking for ads, they are looking for information. Three-quarters of users say that paid search has helped them find the information they were looking for online (Kemper, 2018).

Brand name vs non-brand name search

Brand name searches refer to when a user searches for a specific brand name or a variant of it, such as the brand name plus a product or service offered by the brand. Non-brand name searches on the other hand refer to when a user searches for a product or service without mentioning a specific brand.

Branded search is an indication of how well your demand-generation activities are performing. It shows that consumers are being reached by your content, and that your content is persuading them to seek out your brand directly. Brand name searches are also often simple navigational searches, meaning customers are essentially using the search engine as if it were the search function on your site's homepage. For this reason, the top result gets almost two-thirds of the clicks (Dean, 2022). To increase brand name search, build awareness at the top of the funnel through your content and marketing strategy, user-generated content and influencer marketing, and continue to generate demand using the tactics you have learned and will learn in this book.

But I want to add some nuance to your branded search understanding that is often missed when discussing this topic. Branded search for a retailer and branded search for a manufacturer are two very different things. Branded search for a retailer, like 'Amazon', or even 'Apple AirPods Amazon' is very much a navigational search. The customer knows exactly which retailer they want to go to. But consider, for example, the customer searches for Apple AirPods – that is a branded search, sure, but Apple AirPods are available from a variety of online stores, not just the Apple store. When it comes to search, navigational intent is highest for Brand.com-type searches, followed by 'brand' searches, then 'brand product' searches. So, not all branded search is created equal.

Some branded search results with no ads interfering will yield the brands a topmost result. Not to mention that the 'people also ask' section could also feature the brand up to four more times below the main sitelinks results.

This enables brands to take up a huge amount of screen real estate; but to really capitalize on this, brands need to generate the awareness necessary for a consumer to even make this search in the first place. Recall earlier in this chapter under our section on technical SEO where I showed you how you can give your brand the best chance of having these extra links show up.

Do you need to pay for branded search ads?

Whether you need to pay for your branded search terms or not depends on how much competition there is. If you can still maintain a high SERP position based on your organic authority alone, then maybe you can afford to reduce your budget on branded terms. If, however, you can't compete with your competitors on organic alone (and it only takes a few of your competitors to bid on your branded terms to make this very difficult) then chances are it will be beneficial to your brand to bid on your branded terms. Greg Swan of performance marketing firm Tinuiti, which has managed over $3 billion in paid media, provides one example of a retailer who tested turning off their branded search campaigns. They lost an estimated $40,000 in only two weeks and were forced to turn their brand search campaigns back on again. They thought that they would continue to rank and that their brand search campaigns were just dead ad spend (many retailers are at least tempted to turn off their branded campaigns to see if they can save on ad spend). The result, though, was lost revenue opportunities that outweighed any money saved by not paying for clicks from their paid campaigns (Swan, 2018). My recommendation is to create a separate brand name PPC account in order to silo non-brand campaigns and understand your ads' true performance. With this set-up, you are also able to understand branded performance a lot better as an entire account will deliver clean data to your team for analysis.

Bonus tip: trademark your brand. If you trademark your brand, it can prevent competitors from using your brand name in their ad copy. Although they can still bid on your brand name as a keyword, their copy cannot contain your brand name at all. This can serve as a shield when facing other brands in the search engine arena.

Non-brand search, the battle arena

Non-branded search is where you really go up against your competitors in the battle arena. For a D2C mattress brand like Purple, non-branded search can be especially competitive as 'many brand' retailers and marketplaces are able to surface a lot more results for a mattress-related query than a single-brand mattress website with only a handful of products. When it comes to non-brand search, you should expect a higher cost per conversion because these keywords are super competitive, and a lower conversion rate (because as I mentioned before, a brand name search is often the 'closer' search, in that it is what customers search for when they are ready to buy). Non-brand search, on the other hand, is the 'discovery' search. You'll have more customers entering the top of your funnel from these searches.

Consider for example a comparison between branded and non-branded search for mattresses. You've already read about branded search above – now for a non-branded example. In this search, I wanted to find myself a Purple mattress. If you didn't know, Purple is not the colour of mattress I required, it is, rather, a popular direct-to-consumer brand in the space. The result might shock you – Purple mattresses weren't featured on the first page at all (that you will have to take my word for as I can't include the screenshot here). The first page, rather, was dominated by ads, mostly from big box multiple-brand retailers. None of them were advertising a Purple-branded mattress. For direct-to-consumer brands whose competitors' products are sold through large multi-brand retailers, like those sites selling a plethora of mattress and bedding products, the search space is particularly challenging.

Sitelink extensions in search

As we discussed in the branded and non-branded search sections, some websites display additional links below their search results. These links are called site links and they serve to aid in navigational search and provide a smoother customer journey for search users. If you're not sure what these look like, head to any search engine, type in a query for your favourite product and look around the webpage for any sub links underneath the main site link in the search results. If you find one, that's a site link. Site links not only enable you to link to specific pages of your site (for example, double mattresses), but you can also use them to communicate the additional benefits of your product offering, like a 180-day money-back guarantee or having financing available.

These extra links can actually take up a lot of screen real estate, pushing any other results much further down the page. This is because in some cases, they are displayed vertically rather than horizontally. For a brand, that means any competing retailers would be pushed down the page, giving you more opportunity to capture the sale. Sitelink extensions are a great way to build out your search engine real estate.

Shopping in the search engine

Search has gone visual. With the advent of tools like Google shopping, which allow brands to present item tiles in the search environment, complete with images, search began to present new opportunities to brands and new experiences for consumers. But there are some nuances to the Google shopping platform that the e-commerce brand needs to be aware of. First, you cannot bid on keywords for Google shopping, but you can use negative keywords (Modena, 2022). Instead of bidding on keywords, you set your bids on product groups – which are sometimes called buckets. You can group by brand, product type or even performance. When it comes to improving your campaigns, it's important to follow some best practices. One key practice is to group your bids in a way that allows you to identify trends while still being effective with your bidding. Additionally, it's essential to keep in mind that different platforms may have different bid costs, so you shouldn't simply copy over your bids from one campaign to another. Instead, gather data specific to each platform and use that to make informed decisions about your bidding. Another best practice is to use custom tags to separate out your best-performing products, but it's important to gather enough data first before assuming that what sells well in one campaign will also sell well in another. By analysing shopping-specific data and separating out your winners, you can optimize your campaigns for success. These best practices can help you get the most out of your campaigns and improve your overall performance.

Key paid search metrics

How should you go about measuring the effectiveness of your paid search campaigns? Well, it depends… In this section, I will explain how you can (and should) take a nuanced approach to campaign measurement for your e-commerce brand depending on campaign goals. The two main metrics you will be using are Return On Ad Spend (ROAS) and Cost Per Acquisition (CPA) (otherwise known as Customer Acquisition Cost (CAC).

Return on ad spend (ROAS) measures the profitability of a campaign by dividing the revenue generated by the amount spent on advertising. The result is expressed as a percentage. If the ROAS is above 100 per cent, the campaign has generated more revenue than it cost to run. If it is less than 100 per cent, the campaign has cost more money than it has made.

Cost per acquisition (CPA) tells you the cost to acquire a customer. This metric is useful for determining the long-term profitability of a campaign if you know the customer lifetime value (CLV) and the CPA. ROAS is useful for comparing campaigns against each other, while CPA is more useful for understanding the overall performance of a campaign within the context of your e-commerce growth strategy.

Hiring a paid search agency

When hiring an agency for your paid strategy or SEO, it is important to have a clear understanding of your goals and how the agency will help you achieve them. Good communication and chemistry between your brand and the agency are also key. It is also important to evaluate the agency's processes and systems, as well as to clearly define roles and responsibilities. Definitely consider an agency's portfolio and track record of results. But be aware that bigger is not always better, and a smaller agency may be able to give you a more personalized service. In any case, make sure the agency has a regular reporting cadence of two weeks, and consider whether they work with any of your competitors, which could affect the results you get. You'll find the SEO and SEM industry full of specialists of all colours and stripes. A niche specialist at a large agency may be able to provide more in-depth insights into your industry, but a generalist agency can also be a good starting point for your SEM development. Keep in mind though that a larger brand with a larger ad budget may require a partner with the experience and systems in place to manage larger ad spends. If this sounds like you, you will benefit from working with an established, larger agency.

Hiring in-house

We've covered what to look for in an agency, but what about your internal hires? Regardless of whether you're working with an agency, or have built out your own internal team, you're going to need someone who has oversight of your campaigns and over the people doing the actual work. This person should have both the bird's-eye view of everything that is going on in your organization, and the SEM expertise to set a strategy with that in mind. In short, you need someone who speaks the language of SEM and can also keep their finger on the pulse of your organization. In addition to a head of marketing, you will likely need a head of search. The fact is, SEO or SEM agencies don't have the resources to keep their fingers on the pulse of your organization and its entire marketing strategy. Don't let your search engine marketing be a black box because you don't have a go-between that can relay information to your SEM agency and back from your SEM agency to your key stakeholders like your marketing team. This person will be all over the difference between ROAS and CPA and when you might prefer to use one over the other for your North Star goal depending on whether the campaign is acquisition- or conversion-focused, and they will be invaluable to your team.

Wrapping up

In conclusion, search engine marketing (SEO and SEM) is a crucial component of any e-commerce brand's growth strategy. By optimizing your website for search engines and implementing targeted paid campaigns, you can drive relevant traffic to your site and increase conversions. While the process can be complex and time-consuming, the rewards are well worth it. In the next chapter, we will dive into the world of paid social media, where you can leverage the lessons learned in this chapter to stand out from the competition and drive even more growth for your e-commerce brand!

With the right tools and guidance, you can avoid the pitfalls and mishaps that can hurt your search engine rankings and results. We've put together a wealth of resources and frameworks that can help your business succeed in the world of SEO and SEM. Get access at 2xecommerce.com/book/chapter10.

References

2X eCommerce (2020) S05 EP21, The vital role of competitor and keyword research in DTC ecommerce, https://2xecommerce.com/podcast/245/ (archived at https://perma.cc/5AJV-CX5T)
2X eCommerce (2022) S07 EP17, Yoast SEO is taking on SEO on Shopify, https://2xecommerce.com/podcast/ep360/ (archived at https://perma.cc/6Z4L-LEW3)

Backlinko (2022) Dwell Time and SEO: The Complete Guide, https://backlinko.com/hub/seo/dwell-time (archived at https://perma.cc/456T-BQ4E)

Beus, J (2020) Why (almost) everything you knew about Google CTR is no longer valid, SISTRIX, 14 Jul, www.sistrix.com/blog/why-almost-everything-you-knew-about-google-ctr-is-no-longer-valid/ (archived at https://perma.cc/BMF3-XZF9)

BrightEdge (2022a) Organic channel share expands to 53.3% of traffic, www.brightedge.com/resources/research-reports/channel_share (archived at https://perma.cc/5RJX-QHLC)

Brightedge (2022b) Organic search improves ability to map to consumer intent: Organic Search remains the dominant source of trackable web traffic and the largest digital channel, https://videos.brightedge.com/research-report/BrightEdge_ChannelReport2019_FINAL.pdf (archived at https://perma.cc/PT4Y-GDWT)

Brooks, M (2018) Branded vs non-branded search, *SEOteric*, 11 Oct, www.seoteric.com/branded-vs-non-branded-search/# (archived at https://perma.cc/QEL4-S8WX)

Comscore (2019) Comscore is a trusted currency for planning, transacting, and evaluating media across platforms, www.comscore.com/Products/Ratings-and-Planning?cs_edgescape_cc=US (archived at https://perma.cc/B6AP-P8VU)

Dean, B (2022) We analyzed 4 million google search results. Here's what we learned about organic CTR, *Backlinko*, 14 Oct, https://backlinko.com/google-ctr-stats (archived at https://perma.cc/7WYH-X24A)

Fishman, E (2022) How videos can boost the average time spent on your website, *Wistia*, 24 May, https://wistia.com/learn/marketing/video-time-on-page (archived at https://perma.cc/T5JX-CPD9)

Google (2017) Find out how you stack up to new industry benchmarks for mobile page speed, Feb, https://think.storage.googleapis.com/docs/mobile-page-speed-new-industry-benchmarks.pdf (archived at https://perma.cc/K3A3-U8XR)

Irvine, M (2021a) Want more brand searches on Google? Advertise on Bing or Facebook, *WordStream*, 23 Nov, www.wordstream.com/blog/ws/2017/03/13/cross-network-advertising-brand-search-lift (archived at https://perma.cc/SEM2-2YHB)

Irvine, M (2021b) Who uses Bing, anyway? 10 surprising ways you probably do, *wordStream*, 25 Nov, www.wordstream.com/blog/ws/2019/11/19/who-uses-bing-anyway# (archived at https://perma.cc/J9Z3-DYUJ)

Kemper, G (2018) Search engine marketing: why people click on paid search ads, Clutch, 13 Dec, https://clutch.co/seo-firms/resources/search-engine-marketing-why-people-click-paid-search-ads (archived at https://perma.cc/92ZL-H59P)

La Barbera, V (2022) 8 SEO stats that are hard to ignore, *imFORZA Blog*, www.imforza.com/blog/8-seo-stats-that-are-hard-to-ignore/ (archived at https://perma.cc/3DMH-C68N)

Laffey, D (2007) Paid search: the innovation that changed the Web, *Business Horizons*, 50, pp 211–18, doi: 10.1016/j.bushor.2006.09.003 (archived at https://perma.cc/K5NM-G8RF)

Law, TJ (2022) Meet the top 10 search engines in the world in 2022, *Oberlo*, 10 Apr, https://sg.oberlo.com/blog/top-search-engines-world (archived at https://perma.cc/45NS-WJP6)

MarketMeChina (2022) Baidu search engine market share in China Mar 2022, 4 Apr, www.marketmechina.com/baidu-search-engine-market-share-in-china-mar-2022/ (archived at https://perma.cc/LG4N-HK3W)

Modena, J (2022) Google shopping campaigns guide: best practices, tips & tricks, *WordStream*, 9 Aug, www.wordstream.com/blog/ws/2015/03/04/google-shopping-campaigns-tips-tricks# (archived at https://perma.cc/V7LS-2QBP)

Moz (2022) Domain Authority, https://moz.com/learn/seo/domain-authority (archived at https://perma.cc/8U4C-FNR5)

Petrova, A (2021) The anatomy of top performing articles: Successful vs invisible content – Semrush Study, *Semrish Blog*, 2 Feb, www.semrush.com/blog/anatomy-of-top-performing-articles/ (archived at https://perma.cc/75SV-KQYU)

Safire, W (2006) Blargon, *The New York Times Magazine*, 19 Feb, www.nytimes.com/2006/02/19/magazine/blargon.html (archived at https://perma.cc/865D-CA44)

Semrush (2020) The State of Content Marketing 2022 Global Report, www.semrush.com/state-of-content-marketing/?utm_source=anatomy-of-top-performing-articles&utm_medium=blog-post&utm_campaign=impacthero2 (archived at https://perma.cc/EH3Z-FW6K)

Slegg, J (2022) How to do an SEO competitive analysis, *Semrush Blog*, 10 Mar, www.semrush.com/blog/how-to-do-seo-competitive-analysis/ (archived at https://perma.cc/MF93-2Z6H)

Spinutech (2017) Let's talk about Bing Ads (or, Bing Ads vs Google AdWords), 3 May, www.spinutech.com/digital-marketing/paid-media/sem/google-adwords-vs-bing-ads/ (archived at https://perma.cc/FDE9-ED6S)

StatCounter (2022) Desktop search engine market share United States Of America, https://gs.statcounter.com/search-engine-market-share/desktop/united-states-of-america (archived at https://perma.cc/6TSN-6N67)

Statistica (2022) Worldwide desktop market share of leading search engines from January 2010 to July 2022, 27 Jul, www.statista.com/statistics/216573/worldwide-market-share-of-search-engines/ (archived at https://perma.cc/J9VF-YL2S)

Swan, G (2018) Why paid branded search matters (or how to lose $40k in two weeks), *Tinuiti*, 26 Jul, https://tinuiti.com/blog/paid-search/paid-branded-search/ (archived at https://perma.cc/UW5N-DVG7)

Varagouli, E (2020) How to measure SEO performance and results, *Semrush Blog*, 29 Oct, www.semrush.com/blog/seo-results/ (archived at https://perma.cc/BDR8-XKKS)

Vasu P (2017) 10 reasons to encourage you using Bing Ads in addition to AdWords, *Reportgarden*, 26 Sep, https://reportgarden.com/10-reasons-to-use-bing-ads/ (archived at https://perma.cc/ESF4-7ZZK)

Wolford, B (2022) What are the GDPR fines? *GDPR EU, Proton Technologies AG*, https://gdpr.eu/fines/ (archived at https://perma.cc/K4DM-CQPZ)

Wordstream (2022) Long-tail keywords: a better way to connect with customers, www.wordstream.com/long-tail-keywords (archived at https://perma.cc/TG8X-JTVM)

Further reading

Batista, H (2019) Empowering a new generation of SEOs with Python. Agile SEO by RankSense, 14 Mar, www.ranksense.com/empowering-a-new-generation-of-seos-with-python/ (archived at https://perma.cc/8ZRB-3BL5)

Bulygo, Z (nd) Learn paid search marketing and become a more effective online marketer with these 44 resources, Neil Patel, https://neilpatel.com/blog/44-paid-search-marketing-resources/ (archived at https://perma.cc/52WC-6E6C)

Davis, D (2021) Google's search quality raters guidelines: a guide for SEO beginners, *Search Engine Journal*, www.searchenginejournal.com/google-eat/quality-raters-guidelines/ (archived at https://perma.cc/9NJX-KVBU)

Dean, B (2022) The Backlinko SEO Blog by Brian Dean, *Backlinko*, https://backlinko.com/blog (archived at https://perma.cc/XGB7-FZZ6)

Hurley, S (2020) The ultimate guide to structured data for ecommerce websites, *NOVOS*, 21 Oct, https://thisisnovos.com/the-ultimate-guide-to-structured-data-for-ecommerce-websites/ (archived at https://perma.cc/P335-37LY)

Olennikova, J (2020) PPC Tools: 40 solutions for paid advertising pros, *Semrush*, www.semrush.com/blog/ppc-tools/ (archived at https://perma.cc/9R2T-RMN8)

Pavlik, V (2022) Top 8 SEO certifications (free & paid), *Semrush*, www.semrush.com/blog/seo-certification/, (archived at https://perma.cc/9VQP-ANY6)

Rodriguez, J (2018) Schema Markup for ecommerce: using structured data & rich snippets, *Shift4shop Blog*, https://blog.shift4shop.com/structured-data-for-ecommerce-schema.org-and-rich-snippets (archived at https://perma.cc/H5DP-GHSN)

Spinutech (2017) Let's talk about Bing Ads (or, Bing Ads vs Google AdWords), 3 May, www.spinutech.com/digital-marketing/paid-media/sem/google-adwords-vs-bing-ads/ (archived at https://perma.cc/FDE9-ED6S)

11

Paid social advertising

Why social?

Welcome to the chapter on paid social advertising for e-commerce. In this chapter, we will be exploring the role of paid media in driving social media traffic, engagement and conversions. We will be discussing the fundamental levels in social media that you should be amplifying though in-platform advertising, as well as how to double down on organic influencer marketing campaigns through whitelisting.

Whether you're new to paid social advertising or looking to improve your existing strategy, this chapter has something for everyone. So, let's dive in and learn more about how paid social advertising can drive growth for your e-commerce brand.

Social media itself, used as an organic tool, when done well, is a force multiplier for the rest of your cross-functional e-commerce growth stack. You're probably familiar with many force multipliers in everyday life; these make large tasks much easier, turning the little effort we put in into a lot of force and end result. Consider for example a fulcrum and lever, or even a hammer. In short, force multipliers provide us with a mechanical advantage. The equation for calculating mechanical advantage is output force (the load) divided by input force (your effort). Anything with a result greater than 1 is said to have a 'mechanical advantage'. But it's not actually so simple, because each method of force multiplication will have different levels of efficiency – not all energy that is put in comes out as the kind of energy or force that you would like it to. Some of it gets converted to things like thermal energy, sound and vibration. By building out your social media, you're crafting a lever that will enable you to exert effort and get a return.

The larger your audience, the better your mechanical advantage. The better your creative and your ad campaigns, the more efficient your force multiplier, and the greater the yield on every organic post and ad dollar that you put into your campaigns.

Why paid social?

Traditionally, there are three main types of promotional media for brands: earned, owned and paid. Earned is media that your brand earns in the form of shares and publicity through newspapers and online publications. Likes, shares, shoutouts and people talking about your brand on dark social channels – that's all earned media. Owned media is content that is created by your brand; things like your email newsletter, organic social media content and your company blog are all owned media. Paid media, on the other hand, is channels and advertising activity such as display ads, pay-per-click campaigns and if we are talking about real-world examples, activity like billboard or TV advertising. In the digital world, when most people think of paid media, they think of pay-per-click campaigns. But today there are many creative forms of paid advertising available to the e-commerce brand, like blending influencer marketing and paid campaigns together through activity like whitelisted campaigns (to be discussed) which allow brands take control of influencers' ad accounts.

Paid social media advertising has become essential to marketing strategies thanks to its ability to drive targeted traffic to websites and social media pages. It provides brands with much more control, not to mention measurability. Organic campaigns are long-term endeavours, can be difficult to measure and may not yield results on a timeline of even several months. Organic campaigns often provide clues to success, like shares and more, but conversions will come later. Paid campaigns, on the other hand, especially at the bottom of the funnel, provide marketers with the opportunity for control, immediate traffic and, most importantly, scalability.

But don't think that you can just buy your way to success with paid ads. You're only guaranteed one thing when you advertise, and that is reach. And while you may only pay per click, it's not about who has the biggest advertising budget. It's about who is creating content that resonates with their audience and drives engagement and demand. That takes skill; it takes a customer-centric e-commerce growth stack.

Problems with organic

One of the main problems with organic content on social media is the constantly changing algorithms used by platforms to rank and display content. These algorithms often prioritize visual content and it can be difficult for brands to keep up with. Additionally, even with a strong organic strategy, there is no guarantee that a significant portion of users will actually see the content, as organic reach on social media platforms has been declining for years. This means that e-commerce brands must consider paid advertising on social media in order to reach their target audience and drive conversions.

Decreasing attention spans and rising advertising costs

Advertising costs

Basically, there are two costs you are going to be concerned with when it comes to paid ads – cost per thousand (CPM, or cost per mille) and cost per click (CPC). These are always changing, and giving you an overview of the current costs in this book won't be overly helpful to you, so I won't do that. Instead, you should know that they have been increasing rapidly as brand competition heats up and social platforms seek to generate returns – in some cases rising 185 per cent year on year (Bannerboo, 2022; Marino, 2021; Codrington, 2022). So, you really need to be optimizing your campaigns for what matters: conversions. And that typically means a very targeted type of advertising, one that focuses on the product and the value proposition. That means brand story and brand values fall by the wayside when it comes to your ad campaigns. Not because they aren't important. It's simply because you need to hook your customers and push them to convert and that means getting straight to the point, as you will learn throughout this chapter. Later in this chapter, experts in paid ads and video, such as Moshe Saraf, will provide advice on how to construct effective campaigns within the constraints of a rowdy social media environment.

A word on attention spans

Human attention spans are shrinking at such a rapid rate that some are calling this, the era comprising the first one-fifth of the 21st century, the 'age of the goldfish' (eHotelier, 2020). Reports have come in, and they tell us that eight seconds is currently the average attention span (Stutsman, 2021). However, some research suggests that this may not be the case. The fact is that attention is very much task-dependent, and we do just fine paying attention when something either attracts our interest or demands it (Maybin, 2017). One professor of psychology and psychiatry at the University of Chicago, Edward Vogel, who has been measuring human attention spans for 20 years, says it has been remarkably stable in the time he has been measuring it, and throughout the decades (McGinty, 2017; University of Chicago, 2022). In fact, there is no real evidence it has changed since the 1800s!

So, it seems like this is a case of 'a lie gets halfway around the world before the truth has got its boots on' (ironically, I don't know who to attribute this quote to, as its origin seems to be an exemplary case of, well, this quote. It's often attributed to Mark Twain. And sometimes even to Winston Churchill. However, there's no evidence for either ever saying this) and so our attention spans may not be as fried as we have been led to believe (Coohill, 2020; Chokshi, 2017). Luckily, some researchers and journalists had attention spans long enough to uncover the truth!

So, what does that mean for your brand? It means that you can't blame poor ad performance on shrinking attention spans. Your task is to learn to attract and hold people's attention, and the only thing getting in the way of that is you and your ad creative. As copywriter and founder of ad agency Anomaly, Ernest Lupinacci, says, breakthrough advertising is only getting harder as the quantity of content approaches levels that are almost inexhaustible, not to mention it's all on demand (Kane, 2020). Consumers quite simply have content shock, and given that many brands opt for quantity over quality, they have every reason to be very selective about what is worth their time. As Apollo Robbins, pickpocket and illusionist, says, 'Attention is like water. It flows. It's liquid. You create channels to divert it, and you hope that it flows the right way' (Green, 2012). The attention is there; if it's not flowing your way, you're just not constructing the channels to divert it properly.

This means that in your ad creative, most often video, you have to get straight to value and show your customer why they are sticking around. If you do that, nobody in your marketing department will be lamenting short attention spans. Moshe Saraf, CEO of Pareto Solutions, a world-renowned performance marketing agency, who appeared on 2X eCommerce podcast #251, agrees. He says that brands spend too long talking about themselves rather than showing their consumer what they will get. Story makes you feel good; value makes you buy (2X eCommerce, 2020a).

The power of video

The power of video cannot be ignored. Research has shown that consumers are more likely to pay attention to video content than text-based content. This is because video consumption requires less cognitive effort and provides a more engaging and exciting experience than text-based content. This is especially true in the fast-paced world of social media, where a majority of consumers simply skim through blog posts or multitask while reading them. While this doesn't mean that you should stop creating blog content altogether, as it can still be a valuable medium, the data clearly shows that consumers are more engaged by video. While this may not excite your marketing team if you're not already established in video marketing, the fact remains that video is an essential part of your growth strategy. Over half of consumers say they want to see more video content from the brands they engage with. It's simple, really – customer-centricity is telling you exactly what you need to do to satisfy your customers. So, I've put together some ways that you can start delivering exactly the kind of content your consumers want to see, in the way they want to see it. Claudiu Cioba of Videowise, who appeared on 2X eCommerce episode #319 as part of our Commerce Accel event, says that the conversion rate of shoppers who have watched video is almost 18 per cent; in contrast, the average conversion rate for e-commerce stores is just under 3 per cent (2X eCommerce 2021; Saleh, 2020).

But the fact is, paying up for advertising on social platforms doesn't guarantee your brand success. Not only are you up against on-feed (and off-feed) distractions, you're also up against other brands. And ad spend has been steadily rising year on year for at least the past decade. In 2022, paid social ad spend surpassed $50 billion, and that was in the United States alone (Pavlovic, 2022). That's up from only $15 billion in 2016, so we've seen it triple in only six years. You can't rely on ad spend to carry your strategy. So as always, customer-centricity will set you apart and help you cut through what is a very rowdy and crowded social media environment.

Types of video

If you're not already using video content in your growth strategy, here are some ideas to get you started. Even if you are already using video, you may find some new ideas in this section.

User-generated content

User-generated content (UGC) is a highly effective type of content that can be shared on social media and used in paid ad campaigns. UGC is any original content produced by your customers specifically for your brand. You can see examples of user-generated content on the #shareacoke or #mycalvins hashtags. Unlike influencer posts, which are paid for, customers posting user-generated content do so out of their love for your brand. This connection with your customers, your community and your tribe is what gives user-generated content its power. As social media users become more savvy content creators, the quality of user-generated content available today is impressive. Not only can they create beautifully framed and edited photos, podcasts and videos, but they can also provide compelling testimonials and product reviews.

User-generated content gives your brand credibility and reach in a way that is seen as authentic. Consumers view UGC as a valuable informational signal, indicating the quality of your brand and product and signalling that they can trust you. A majority of consumers see UGC as the most authentic type of marketing content, more so than branded or influencer content. They are also more likely to click on UGC (DeGruttola, 2019). In fact, almost 80 per cent of consumers say that UGC is highly influential in their purchasing decisions, far more than branded or influencer content (13 and 18 per cent respectively). This extra influence is why UGC ads often have higher click-through and conversion rates and lower cost-per-click than branded content (Greenbaum, 2020; Dawson, 2022). This can be seen in your key metrics as a lower cost per acquisition and higher return on ad spend (Dawson, 2022). However, this does not mean that you should completely discard branded and influencer content. Your branded content is crucial for building your brand and cultural authority, as you learned in Chapter 9. Influencer content is also valuable for increasing your reach and building trust with your target audience. The key is to use a combination of different types of video content in your marketing strategy to maximize their impact.

Other types of video to include in your growth stack

PRODUCT AND EXPLAINER VIDEOS

Product videos are a great way to showcase your products and can even include a buy button to increase sales. Moshe Saraf of Pareto Solutions recommends focusing on your product and cutting out any fluff like metaphors or brand stories in your ads. Instead, focus on highlighting the value and performance of your product (2X eCommerce, 2020a). In the online world, customers can't touch or try your products before purchasing, so product videos are essential in replicating the in-store shopping experience as closely as possible. In fact, over half of consumers watch product videos while shopping in-store, showing that they also add value to the in-store experience (Kumar, 2019). To create effective product videos, show consumers what your product is capable of. For example, if the stretch in your chinos is a unique selling point, show the chinos being pulled and stretched in various ways. If you're selling an avocado slicer, show it slicing and dicing to demonstrate how well it solves the customer's problem. These types of videos can be the difference between a customer choosing your product or a competitor's. Many customers use product videos to help them decide between brands or products when they're unsure which to buy (Kumar, 2019). Investing in product videos can pay off in the long run, as 94 per cent of consumers have watched an explainer video to learn more about a product (Wyzowl, 2021). These videos can be a great addition to your product pages, especially if your product has unique features that customers need to know how to use.

SHOPPABLE VIDEO

Product and explainer videos help customers make decisions while also entertaining them (Ertekin, 2017). Shoppable videos add a commercial layer on top of these videos, or more explicitly conversion-focused videos. Brands that use shoppable videos see approximately 60 per cent higher conversions at a lower cost (Murray-Jones and Campbell, 2021). Your video should showcase your brand, product and call to action within the first few seconds (Murray-Jones and Campbell, 2021). Shoppable videos can be implemented as organic content or paid advertising on most top social media platforms, with the most popular platforms being Instagram and TikTok and even YouTube. This makes shoppable videos an effective tool for e-commerce brands looking to drive conversions and improve the customer journey.

Advanced video marketing tips

CAPTIONS AND SUBTITLES
Include captions in your videos because many consumers watch them with the sound off. This may be because they are in a public place or in the office.

You may have even noticed that it is sometimes more comfortable to watch videos with the sound off and read the captions instead. Over two-thirds of consumers watch videos with the sound off when in public; a quarter of users even watch videos with the sound off in private (McCue, 2019). Captions provide a more comfortable viewing experience for many and improve accessibility for those who are hard of hearing. When it comes to captioning your existing video (and any future videos) there are lots of great apps you can use to make this process simple. But when you do, you may still need to edit further, as these will likely caption word for word. Moshe Saraf of Pareto Solutions, who manages campaigns for some of the world's fastest-growing e-commerce brands, suggests using summary captions (rather than captioning every word) of approximately every four words at the most (2X eCommerce, 2020a).

Platforms

Platform breakdown

TABLE 11.1 Social platform breakdown

	TikTok	Facebook	Instagram	Pinterest
Main age group	18–24 years (40%). Females in this age group outnumber males 2.5 to 1	25–34 years	23–34 years and 18–24 both account for almost one-third of users each	50–64 (38%)
Monthly active users	1 billion and fast growing	2.9 billion	1.4 billion	459 million
Fun fact	TikTok users spend on average an hour each day on the platform	75% of monthly users are active daily	37% of Instagram users engage with influencers	82% of Pinterest users also use Instagram, presenting interesting cross-channel marketing opportunities for brands

SOURCES Influencer Marketing Hub (2022); Statista (2022, 2023a, 2023b, 2023c); Backlinko (2022); Hootsuite Blog (2023); Maci (2022); Meta (2021); Takumi (2022)

Influencer marketing in detail

Categories of influencer (influencer breakdown)

NANO INFLUENCERS

Nano influencers typically have between 1,000 and 5,000 followers. They can provide a good return on investment for brands with smaller budgets and are more relatable and authentic for consumers. However, they may not be the best choice for campaigns focused on brand awareness. One to five thousand might seem small when you compare it to someone like Huda Kattan (@hudabeauty) with over 50 million followers (Le Guyader, 2022). But I take you back to the Battle of Agincourt in October 1415, when Henry V was left with only 5,500 men and against the 20,000 strong French army (Powell-Smith, 2016). The result, an English victory in what was a decisive battle in the Hundred Years' War (Britannica, nd). When you're out on the social media battlefield, don't discount the effectiveness of a small group of 5,000–10,000. In many cases they can beat out much larger groups when it comes to return on investment for your brand. We've seen time and time again large brands using nano influencers to give themselves authenticity and credibility, and connect with their customers at a more niche, community level – as an example, Sperry with influencers like Michaela Bee (Grin, 2022).

MICRO INFLUENCERS

Micro influencers typically have between 5,000 and 20,000 followers. They engage more with their audience and are known in specific niches. However, they may not have a consistent brand image, requiring regular monitoring and guidance from brands. Micro influencers can provide high reach and help build brand awareness. Pay attention to your onboarding flow, though. I know plenty of micro influencers who have received brand guidelines books and suddenly felt overwhelmed, to the point that they didn't want to work with the brand anymore. So, having an onboarding flow that breaks everything down into manageable steps is a good way to keep your influencers engaged and, most importantly, on-brand.

MACRO INFLUENCERS

Macro influencers typically have 100,000 to 1 million followers. They have high reach and are effective for building brand awareness. They may be celebrities or other well-known individuals, but are often very expensive to work with and require a high level of effort to manage. One example of a macro influencer is Susie J Todd. Susie is proof that influencers aren't just about presenting idyllic lifestyles. At the time of writing in 2022, she has almost 1 million subscribers on YouTube, and one of her popular videos, with over 100,000 views, is her cleaning her house, and showing her subscribers her new pimple on her forehead (SusieJTodd, 2022). The video, as Todd explains in the description, is partially sponsored by Gymshark, a brand known for identifying unique influencer opportunities. Todd in this video is far from presenting idyllic landscape shots from a beach in Bali. My point is that just because an influencer has more than 100k followers, that doesn't mean they are any less authentic. In fact, as customers are demanding more and more authenticity from both brands and the people they follow online, authenticity is key for an influencer to build an audience and differentiate in the increasingly competitive influencer economy.

Influencer marketing can also be connected to paid social media through something called campaign whitelisting. This is when a brand gets access to an influencer's paid ads channels to promote to their audience. The ads are managed by the brand, but go out under the influencer's name. This provides the brand with more control and scalability for their influencer strategy. When you put effort into developing influencer relationships and creating content, campaign whitelisting can help you get the most out of it. It is a win-win situation, as the influencer and the brand both gain more reach and followers. Influencer content can also be used for your own paid campaigns, but make sure to not overwhelm the audience with sales messaging. Using influencer content for paid marketing should be planned from the start, rather than as an afterthought. If you simply repurpose the content, you will waste ad budget and not optimize your campaigns for the paid ads environment. Segment your campaigns accordingly and look for paid advertising opportunities for organic, user-generated and influencer content that performs well. Kelley Thornton, a marketing veteran in consumer goods, recommends long-term engagements with influencers instead of one-off engagements and working closely with influencers to tailor the content (2X eCommerce, 2020b). Many one-off engagements just aren't as effective as the compounding results that come from fewer long-term commitments.

Influencer marketing as a testing ground

One thing many brands do not utilize enough is influencer marketing as a testing ground for messaging and creative. When something comes from a small influencer, it is seen as more authentic and 'from the hip' than a polished brand campaign. This allows your brand to test new messaging without being closely tied to it. Influencers are present on every platform, providing an opportunity for your brand to test new platforms without incurring the expense of setting up an account and creating content. Use influencer marketing to assess the response from consumers, then boost the best-performing posts with a paid campaign and gather data on the performance. It's a great way to test out new messaging, new creatives and even new platforms.

Paying up: your paid strategy

Boost your top-performing organic content

Marketers say it takes on average two weeks to produce one piece of video content from start to finish (Alfred, 2022). Use data on likes, shares and comments to find your top performing organic content for boosting or repurposing as paid creative.

Expand the reach of your targeting

Creating custom lookalike audiences helps you reach an even wider audience beyond the people who already follow your brand or visit your website. Creating lookalike audiences broadens your reach by using information about your current audience. A lookalike audience is a group of potential customers who are likely to engage with your business because they're similar to your current customers. When it comes to bringing new people into your funnel, basing your targeted audiences off segments of your current audience is a great place to start. Additionally, you can segment further based on all the first- and third-party data that you have, and find lookalikes for specific segments of your consumer, like your VIPs for example.

But don't forget about your existing audience. Re-engage your existing audience to stay connected with them. Because this audience is already warm to your brand your focus will be on direct response ads. Direct response ads are intended to get people to take a specific action like clicking on your link or making a purchase, making them a great way to re-engage your existing customers. Not to mention to have all of your first-party customer data to use for segmentation and the delivery of the ideal ad creative.

Optimize with A/B testing

Now that you've created an ad campaign, it's important to run an ad test to determine the most effective ad type. Facebook's former vice president of core ads (and now vice president of Oculus at the time of writing in 2022), Mark Rabkin, recommends that brands, instead of testing their ads on a six-monthly cycle, test on a weekly cycle (Rabkin, 2017). Moshe Saraf recommends that a creative should be performing 20 per cent better than its previous iteration (2X eCommerce, 2020a). When it comes to iterating and improving, Savannah Sanchez, known as Social Savannah, a D2C marketing expert, who appeared on 2X eCommerce podcast #319 says to try and isolate as many variables as possible, and don't try to change too much. Identifying which variable is moving the needle can be the hardest part and if you change too much, it will be impossible to isolate what actually makes users click. Keep a document of everything you are testing (2X eCommerce, 2021).

Paid KPIs

Before diving into KPIs, it's important to understand how different platforms track conversions. For instance, Facebook will attribute any conversion to itself, even if there were other touchpoints in the customer's journey. While it's tempting to base ad-scaling decisions on Facebook attribution data alone, I recommend using a third-party attribution platform like Rockerbox or Hyros for omnichannel attribution capabilities. On the other hand, Google Analytics defaults to last click attribution, which means the last touchpoint before a purchase gets 100 per cent of the attribution. The problem with this is that it may not necessarily indicate what drives demand for a brand as these touchpoints may be navigational behaviours after a user has seen your marketing materials elsewhere.

Delivery within bid

Moshe Saraf of Pareto Solutions says that ads with a big delivery within bid are typically winners (2X eCommerce, 2020a). Monitor this.

Return on ad spend (ROAS)

It's important to consider sending educational content to potential customers before driving them directly to a product, as this approach may lead to a higher ROAS. A good benchmark for ROAS is between 2.5 and 5. However, it's important to note that Facebook ROAS has been declining in 2022 and is currently sitting around 1.5–3, so these numbers may change going forward. It's important to understand how different platforms track conversions, as Facebook will attribute any conversion to itself even if there were other touchpoints in the customer's journey. Using a third-party attribution platform like Rockerbox or Hyros for omnichannel attribution capabilities can provide a more accurate picture of conversion data. On the other hand, Google Analytics defaults to last click attribution, which may not necessarily indicate what drives demand for a brand.

Learn to spot creative fatigue

Moshe Saraf, again, in episode #319 of my 2X eCommerce podcast as part of our Commerce Accel event, says that likes and comments, in addition to being an indicator of what organic content is worth boosting, can also be a sign of creative fatigue. He adds that if you fear your ad performance issues are due to creative fatigue then they probably are.

Click through rate can also be an indicator of content fatigue for stable ad accounts. To avoid this, if you have money, then keep producing (and improving) content (2X eCommerce, 2021). Savannah Sanchez adds that there is no specific shelf life for your content; it could be several months, or it could be one day.

Measure results, not seconds

While time spent engaging with your content is important, it's results that matter. If you can drive purchases even with 10 seconds' view time, then you're achieving your brand's end goals.

Hiring

When hiring to build out your paid social advertising team, you need to integrate two schools of thought. You will most likely have a team of creatives focused on motion graphics, animators, video editing and design, who love making visually engaging content that often aligns with your core and visual brand identity.

Just like you have your brand tone and voice, they will need to have a set brand look and feel for your ads. In general, any design should be goal- and conversion-focused. But ads will really burn your money if your design elements aren't working in sync with your reach and conversion rate optimization goals. This, of course, will require a high-touch relationship with your ads team and your data team, as it is these teams that are testing and seeing results of the campaigns on the ground. Your creative team will need to have processes for testing improvements, like not changing too many elements at the same time, so that your ads and data teams can isolate the elements in your creatives that actually move the needle, and the elements or sections that do not.

Making too many changes at once in an ad creative that result in incremental improvement in conversion would not yield any insights because that actual impactful change or changes you made would have been buried in a sea of inconsequential adjustments. Often it's not the most beautiful content that converts the best. Hence, your ads and data teams need to be high touch with the content team. Your creative is more important than ever, so dedicate a lot more resources into creative testing, to learn and iterate as quickly as possible.

Data teams are essential for large ad accounts

Your ad teams are creative and analytical, and they can undoubtedly analyse one or a few ad accounts. But for large ad accounts, you need to involve a dedicated data team to get the insights you need. Regular excel-based ad account dashboards may not suffice as you scale up spend, targeting and creative promotion. You will no doubt need a workflow-driven media buying platform to streamline all aspects of your media buying.

Summary of key roles

To build your ad account dream team you are going to need a media buyer, ad manager, creative strategist, video specialist and dedicated data specialist, at minimum. Content creators and motion/graphic designers will handle the production of assets. Your brand owner or head of marketing will act as the conductor that gets the team playing in tune together with the rest of your cross-functional e-commerce growth stack.

Payment models

While many agencies work on a performance model, expecting your creatives to work on performance can be unfair, says Savannah Sanchez (Social Savannah). The fact is that due to the very nature of social media, some creatives might just not perform well. Of course, you want your creatives to be aligned with performance, but haggling your agency to work purely on performance will probably lead to a short-lived relationship. And if you believe in them as an agency, then there's no need to burn a potentially profitable relationship for both parties.

Wrapping up

To wrap up, paid social is a valuable layer in your e-commerce growth stack to reach and engage with potential customers. By optimizing your ad campaigns and targeting strategies, you can drive awareness (in the form of impressions and reach), traffic and sales. For more information and resources on paid social, visit our website and check out my recommended tooling stack for social media advertising and a hiring guide for finding the right social advertising agencies: 2xecommerce.com/book/chapter11.

In the next chapter, we will be discussing the importance of omnichannel retail for e-commerce brands. Stay tuned for more insights and tips on how to grow your business online.

References

2X eCommerce (2020a) S05 EP27, Scaling DTC Facebook ads with product centred video ad creatives, https://2xecommerce.com/podcast/251/ (archived at https://perma.cc/CZU6-RMCH)

2X eCommerce (2020b) S05 EP42, Scaling DTC mens grooming brand Tiege Hanley to 8-figures+ in 2 years, https://2xecommerce.com/podcast/ep265/ (archived at https://perma.cc/X6BB-LU9M)

2X eCommerce (2021) S06 EP45, Creative and creators, https://2xecommerce.com/podcast/ep319/ (archived at https://perma.cc/2R3Z-G2G4)

Alfred, L (2022) 50 Video Marketing Statistics to Inform Your 2022 Strategy [New Data], Hubspot, https://blog.hubspot.com/marketing/video-marketing-statistics#sm.0000h4rgwfoa1fouwqm23llpma557 (archived at https://perma.cc/N297-NAMT)

Backlinko (2022) How many people use Instagram? 95+ user statistics, https://backlinko.com/instagram-users (archived at https://perma.cc/K6GY-QAQH)

BannerBoo (2022) How much do Instagram ads cost in 2022? https://bannerboo.com/blog/how-much-do-instagram-ads-cost-in-2022/ (archived at https://perma.cc/7TY2-9U53)

Britannica (nd) Battle of Agincourt, *Britannica*, www.britannica.com/event/Battle-of-Agincourt (archived at https://perma.cc/Q9U4-KUZ2)

Chokshi, N (2017) That wasn't Mark Twain: how a misquotation is born, *The New York Times*, 26 Apr, www.nytimes.com/2017/04/26/books/famous-misquotations.html (archived at https://perma.cc/EY8F-S4P8)

Codrington, T (2022) The price of digital ads has skyrocketed – here's how to counteract it, *The Drum*, www.thedrum.com/opinion/2022/04/28/the-price-digital-ads-has-skyrocketed-here-s-how-counteract-it (archived at https://perma.cc/Y56H-B7BZ)

Coohill, Dr J (2020) Mark Twain: 'A lie can travel halfway around the world before the truth puts on its shoes' – Quote or no quote? *Professor Buzzkill History Podcast*, www.professorbuzzkill.com/twain-lie-travels/ (archived at https://perma.cc/838Z-4MVW)

Dawson, L (2022) User-generated content's important role in marketing, *3Q Digital*, www.3qdept.com/blog/user-generated-contents-important-role-in-marketing/ (archived at https://perma.cc/8XVW-XKMQ)

DeGruttola, M (2019) Stackla survey reveals disconnect between the content consumers want & what marketers deliver, *Stackla*, www.businesswire.com/news/home/20190220005302/en/Stackla-Survey-Reveals-Disconnect-Between-the-Content-Consumers-Want-What-Marketers-Deliver (archived at https://perma.cc/X9L9-LKCR)

eHotelier (2020) Learning in the age of the goldfish, https://insights.ehotelier.com/announcements/2020/11/30/learning-in-the-age-of-the-goldfish/# (archived at https://perma.cc/5W2D-MARE)

Ertekin, S (2017) Shoppable videos are in: how do consumers respond?, doi: 10.1007/978-3-319-45596-9_110, www.researchgate.net/publication/314276535_Shoppable_Videos_Are_In_How_Do_Consumers_Respond (archived at https://perma.cc/8G8A-CM4U)

Green, A (2012) A Pickpocket's Tale, *The New Yorker*, 30 Dec, www.newyorker.com/magazine/2013/01/07/a-pickpockets-tale (archived at https://perma.cc/T8L4-NJYG)

Greenbaum, T (2020) 7 user-generated content examples and why they work so well, *Bazaarvoice*, www.bazaarvoice.com/blog/7-ugc-examples/ (archived at https://perma.cc/X4VC-Q22L)

Grin (2022) Is going viral with nano influencers likely? The answer lives in brand love, https://grin.co/blog/go-viral-with-nano-influencers/ (archived at https://perma.cc/U96K-F3FR)

Hootsuite Blog (2023) 38 Pinterest stats that matter to marketers in 2023, https://blog.hootsuite.com/pinterest-statistics-for-business/ (archived at https://perma.cc/46EG-RTJ8)

Influencer Marketing Hub (2022) The State of Influencer Marketing 2022, https://influencermarketinghub.com/ebooks/Influencer_Marketing_Benchmark_Report_2022.pdf (archived at https://perma.cc/74HU-FMH9)

Kane, B (2020) *Hook Point: How to stand out in a 3-second world*, Waterside Production, California

Kumar, S (2019) 3 unexpected ways shoppers turn to video in the store aisle, *Think with Google*, www.thinkwithgoogle.com/marketing-strategies/video/in-store-video-shopping-behavior/ (archived at https://perma.cc/QW9J-HMK9)

Le Guyader, K (2022) Top 10 beauty influencers in 2022, *Influence4You*, https://blogen.influence4you.com/top-10-beauty-influencers/ (archived at https://perma.cc/MUZ4-RAF7)

Maci (2022) Tiktok facts, *Facts.net*, 2 Jun, https://facts.net/tiktok-facts/ (archived at https://perma.cc/KV84-8EXN)

Marino, K (2021) Higher prices, weaker targeting push companies to rethink digital ads, *Axios*, 7 Oct, www.axios.com/2021/10/07/higher-prices-weaker-targeting-push-companies-to-rethink-digital-ads (archived at https://perma.cc/AL62-RMFG)

Maybin, S (2017) Busting the attention span myth, BBC, www.bbc.co.uk/news/health-38896790 (archived at https://perma.cc/MKU5-HNVV)

McCue, TJ (2019) Verizon Media says 69 percent of consumers watching video with sound off, *Forbes*, 31 Jul, www.forbes.com/sites/tjmccue/2019/07/31/verizon-media-says-69-percent-of-consumers-watching-video-with-sound-off/?sh=117f7ca435d8 (archived at https://perma.cc/885X-975X)

McGinty, JC (2017) Is your attention span shorter than a goldfish's?, *The Wall Street Journal*, 17 Feb, www.wsj.com/articles/is-your-attention-span-shorter-than-a-goldfishs-1487340000 (archived at https://perma.cc/V3LG-2QKM)

Meta (2021) Meta Earnings Presentation Q4 2021, https://s21.q4cdn.com/399680738/files/doc_financials/2021/q4/Q4-2021_Earnings-Presentation-Final.pdf (archived at https://perma.cc/9L7F-QCFJ)

Murray-Jones, D and Campbell, K (2021) How shoppable video is shaping the future of retail, *Think with Google*, www.thinkwithgoogle.com/intl/en-gb/marketing-strategies/video/shoppable-video-youtube (archived at https://perma.cc/4GCS-SQWM)

Pavlovic, U (2022) The ultimate guide to paid social advertising, *Hunch*, 19 Oct, https://blog.hunchads.com/the-ultimate-guide-to-paid-social-advertising (archived at https://perma.cc/4EUF-PGJY)

Powell-Smith, M (2016) When David beat Goliath: 10 small armies that defeated large ones, *History Collection*, 5 Sep, https://historycollection.com/david-beat-goliath-10-small-armies-defeated-large-ones/ (archived at https://perma.cc/VZ9N-9UAN)

Rabkin, M (2017) New medium, new rules: Video advertising in the mobile age, Meta, www.facebook.com/business/news/new-medium-new-rules-video-advertising-in-the-mobile-age (archived at https://perma.cc/XZL3-UJHJ)

Saleh, K (2022) The average website conversion rate by industry (updated November), *Invesp Blog*, www.invespcro.com/blog/the-average-website-conversion-rate-by-industry/ (archived at https://perma.cc/2KLP-R37B)

Statista (2022) U.S. Pinterest reach by age 2021, www.statista.com/statistics/246183/share-of-us-internet-users-who-use-pinterest-by-age-group/ (archived at https://perma.cc/8NFN-R77Y)

Statista (2023a) U.S. Facebook demographics age 2023, www.statista.com/
statistics/187549/facebook-distribution-of-users-age-group-usa/ (archived at
https://perma.cc/K8XA-JUZR)

Statista (2023b) Global Instagram user age & gender distribution 2023,
www.statista.com/statistics/248769/age-distribution-of-worldwide-instagram-
users/ (archived at https://perma.cc/4RRF-DSPK)

Statista (2023c) Instagram: age distribution of global audiences 2023,
www.statista.com/statistics/325587/instagram-global-age-group/ (archived at
https://perma.cc/ZW4P-TRCB)

Stutsman, L (2021) You have eight seconds. Differentiate your business through the art
of storytelling, US Partner Community Blog – Microsoft, 15 Nov, www.microsoft.
com/en-us/us-partner-blog/2021/11/15/you-have-eight-seconds-differentiate-your-
business-through-the-art-of-storytelling/ (archived at https://perma.cc/YJ6K-RRLV)

SusieJTodd (2022) Productive days in my life | trying reformer pilates, living my
hot girl life, *YouTube*, 1 Aug, www.youtube.com/watch?v=tHU00VIZlB0
(archived at https://perma.cc/W89U-K6MZ)

Takumi (2022) Influencer marketing: 2022 trends and predictions, takumi.com/
insight/influencer-marketing-2022-trends-and-predictions (archived at https://
perma.cc/U7P2-AMVV)

University of Chicago (2022) Edward K Vogel, Department of Psychology, https://
psychology.uchicago.edu/directory/edward-k-vogel (archived at https://perma.
cc/W3SG-YKBV)

Wyzowl (2021) Report: State of Video Marketing 2021, www.wyzowl.com/
state-of-video-marketing-2021-report/ (archived at https://perma.cc/RV46-P7QQ)

Further reading

Facebook IQ (2016) Capturing attention in feed: the science behind effective video
creative, *Meta*, 20 Apr, www.facebook.com/business/news/insights/capturing-
attention-feed-video-creative (archived at https://perma.cc/9FQ8-6C28)

Harris, W (2021) The Facebook ROAS death spiral: fix it now — or lose your
Shopify store, *Elumynt*, https://elumynt.com/facebook-roas/ (archived at https://
perma.cc/PQ7Y-J6GJ)

Influencer Marketing Hub (2022) Complete guide To TikTok video ad formats
(with examples!) *Shuttlerock*, https://blog.shuttlerock.com/complete-guide-to-
tiktok-video-ad-formats#:~:text=In%2DFeed%20ads%20are%20up (archived
at https://perma.cc/Y9TF-UMTK)

Meta (nd) Meta blueprint: free online training for advertising on Facebook,
www.facebook.com/business/learn?ref=ens_rdr (archived at https://perma.cc/
G8EU-F9P2)

Williams, R (2017) Facebook: Why mobile video ads must work fast, *Marketing
Dive*, 30 Jun, www.marketingdive.com/news/facebook-why-mobile-video-ads-
must-work-fast/446217/ (archived at https://perma.cc/J2BB-9WBK)

12

Channel marketing

Your journey will start on a single channel

While most retailers start out as single-channel operators, as you begin to scale, channel expansion is something that needs to be on your roadmap. In fact, a brand should need a very good reason not to sell across multiple channels – utilizing multiple channels should be the default development strategy for an e-commerce brand. As the brand-building geniuses at 2PM, industry leaders at the intersection of commerce and media, say, it's extremely expensive for a brand to remain single-channel, as a pure-play direct-to-consumer operation – and a much rarer scenario than many marketers new to the scene would think (Smith et al, 2022).

There are many reasons why an e-commerce brand needs to build their channel strategy, not least expanded distribution, but also strategic considerations about channel dependency and brand longevity. Marketers are constantly being spun around by different channels and platforms with new rules, requirements and challenges. Take changes to Apple's iOS or Facebook's third-party cookies for example; any brand that is over-reliant on specific platforms and channels, be they marketing or distribution, is sitting on a single point of failure. This is why my focus is so strongly on e-commerce as a cross-functional growth stack. Not only is it more effective any time of the year, during times of boom or bust, you're perfectly positioned to limit losses, or capture extreme upsides. Today, brands are returning home to retailers to boost their distribution, brand equity and to find a safe haven from high acquisition costs. But the strongest argument for omnichannel retail is, as is usually the case, the simplest one, and to find it we come back to our first principle of customer-centricity. Being customer-centric is going where your customers are, the platforms that are the centre of their attention, and that their shopping experiences revolve around. Going where the customers are has been the traditional trade strategy for millennia. While Andrew Carnegie would say to put all your eggs in one basket and to watch it carefully, this most certainly does not apply to the modern e-commerce world (Moore, 2019).

Putting all your eggs in one basket and watching it carefully is a great approach to take when starting your brand – it enables you to focus. But that doesn't mean it's the best approach to take for seriously scaling your brand. To grow an e-commerce brand, you need to utilize a multitude of acquisition channels, to collect more eggs for your basket, and then use the full suite of customer experience and retention tactics at your disposal – all of them outlined here in this book – to nurture your customer base into a strong, healthy army of repeat purchasers and brand advocates. I will take a moment here in the introduction to align your new ways of thinking toward an omnichannel mindset, by highlighting the main growth levers that omnichannel retail opens up for your brand.

Omnichannel e-commerce creates symbiotic relationships between your different channels. In nature, a symbiotic relationship is one between two species. Most of the time, when people talk about symbiotic relationships, they have in mind 'mutualism', which is where both parties benefit. However, in nature, and in the e-commerce world, too, the reality is that this is not always the case. We also have parasitism (in the marketing world, this is often called cannibalism), where the success of one party, or channel, comes at the expense of another, and commensalism, in which case one party clearly benefits, while the other party is neither helped nor harmed (Osterloff, nd). It's important to keep this in mind, as your omnichannel strategy is just as likely to harm as it is to help if you don't formulate the right strategy first. But, done right, omnichannel e-commerce opens up a world of opportunity to create symbiotic relationships in your cross-functional growth stack. It's bi-directional, meaning that advancements in one area fuel advancements in the other – just as Hero Cosmetics achieved by feeding their Amazon insights into their other marketplaces, and eventually their marketplace insights into their own direct-to-consumer website strategy. Typically, for an increase in sales on the marketplace, retailers' own online stores experience an increase in sales (Maier and Wieringa, 2020). In fact, omnichannel customers shop 1.7 times more than single-channel customers (Burns and Harris, 2022). Omnichannel retail has been the cornerstone of development for hit (originally online-only) DTC brands like Warby Parker, Allbirds, Hero Cosmetics and more.

FIGURE 12.1 The case for omnichannel retail

Omnichannel approach to growth

+250%	73%	48%
Purchase frequency of an omnichannel brand vs single channel brand	Of shoppers use multiple channels for shopping	Of shoppers will share date for more personalized service (Deloitte)
+13%	**+287%**	**$600b**
Average order value of an omnichannel brand vs a single channel brand	Marketing campaigns funneled through 3+ channels vs a single channel deliver higher purchase rate	Going omnichannel is a $600 billion spending opportunity with millennials increasing spend.

SOURCE Omnisend (2019); Sopadjieva et al (2017); Simpson et al (2016); Vermut (2018)

We've even seeing DTC brands themselves becoming marketplaces, or layering in their own marketplace offerings to their growth stacks. One recent example (at the time of writing in 2022) of a brand turned marketplace is Victoria's Secret, the world's most famous lingerie label. They have opened their well-known brand platform as a marketplace for brands that align with their values of innovation and inclusivity (Howland, 2022). They join other retailers like Anthropologie, with their 'Curated by Anthropologie' marketplace offering and Urban Outfitters with UO MRKT, which connects consumers with culturally minded brands (Anthropologie, 2022; Urban Outfitters, 2022).

There are many marketplace platforms available to e-commerce retailers, including Amazon, eBay, Target Plus and Walmart.com. Some platforms are more accessible than others, with some such as Target Plus being strictly invite only. Each platform has its own unique features and advantages, and e-commerce retailers can choose the platforms that best fit their needs and target audience. Some key points to consider when choosing a marketplace platform include the platform's customer base, fees and support for sellers. However, as you probably already know, when it comes to your omnichannel strategy, you're not limited to broad category retailers like Amazon, Walmart or Target. In addition to these major platforms, there are also niche platforms like Tophatter, Farfetch, NewEgg and Boots. These present rich watering holes for brands with offerings in these niches. NewEgg, for example, did over $1.5 billion in sales in 2021, and is ranked #9 in the electronics and media market in the United States (eCommerce DB, 2022). In the health and beauty industry, brands seek out leading niche market-places like Boots.com (UK) for their network of over 2,000 stores, huge existing customer base and market share of over 40 per cent within its region and niche (Fresen, 2021).

Distribution – how to rapidly grow your company with minimal effort

Distribution is essential for rapid growth with minimal effort. Just as not all consumers use a single social media platform, they are also spread across various purchasing channels. They prefer to build customized shopping experiences by combining multiple channels into their customer journey. This is where consumer psychology comes into play in omnichannel retail. Customers have lives outside the digital world, and in-store experiences are important to them in their purchasing journeys. However, it's important to approach distribution as a marketing channel, not just a distribution chan-nel. This requires a strategic approach that aligns with your brand image, values and goals. Later in this chapter, I will provide examples of how some of the best up-and-coming brands, such as Hero Cosmetics and Tony's Chocolonely, have used their distribution channel strategy to build brand equity and communicate their brand values effectively.

Discovery

Marketplace platforms aren't simply used for purchase, they're also used in the research stages of the customer journey for product discovery. As an example, up to 70 per cent of searches in the United States begin on the Amazon platform – you almost can't afford not to be on the platform from a discovery perspective (Jungle Scout, 2021). The dynamic is similar on other marketplace platforms, too. Even if customers aren't buying on them, they are using them for discovery and may later purchase through your owned channels.

Consumer experience – building for your customers

From a customer experience perspective, in-store offers unique experiences that online platforms struggle to replicate. For example, shopping, trying on clothes and building occasions around shopping experiences like a morning coffee with friends and a stroll through the central shopping district. Online and offline experiences can coexist harmoniously to provide the most value and pleasure for customers. Many retailers recognize the power of omnichannel strategy and are preparing for the increasing demand for it. Customers want to be able to purchase what they want, where they want and when they want. This means that if they are shopping at Walmart, they want to be able to add your product to their basket as well. Companies like Target and Walmart are opening up their marketplaces to direct-to-consumer retailers to provide the product selection that customers are looking for.

However, while some retailers are focused on an 'endless aisle' strategy, Dean McElwee, director of international ecommerce strategy at The Stanley Black & Decker Company, shared a consumer behaviour reality check at our 2022 Commerce Accel conference. He said that while aisles can be endless from a digital and technological perspective, they rarely are from a consumer psychology perspective. Customers are not going to scroll forever. This has led to the emergence of niche marketplaces like Boots.com and DIY.com. These platforms, unlike broader marketplaces like Amazon, allow brands to differentiate themselves and offer unique experiences to customers. Niche marketplaces also allow brands to target specific customer segments and provide a more personalized experience. Additionally, they offer a level of trust and credibility that is difficult to achieve on broader marketplaces. Niche marketplaces can be a valuable addition to an omnichannel retail strategy.

Tapping into changing consumer behaviour

There are three broad behaviours that customers engage in when shopping in an omnichannel world. The most common is spreading their shopping across different channels depending on which suits them best at the time. The customer might interchange channels and use omnichannel as a way to shop around different brands or storefronts for the best deals. Then there is single-brand omnichannel shopping – this is the kind of shopping that you want your customers doing. They are brand-loyal, but they buy from you across multiple channels depending on what is convenient. As an example, if they know they only need to buy clothing today then they might shop directly from your owned website. However, if they need to purchase clothing, homeware and cleaning products, then they might shop from Amazon. The third typical behaviour that omnichannel shoppers engage in is researching a product via one channel, and then making the purchase via another

(PwC, 2011). The typical assumption is that they are researching online and then buying in-store, but it works both ways. Being across multiple channels enables you to benefit from channel opportunism, rather than trying to fight consumer preferences as a single-channel DTC brand.

Allocating your e-commerce assets like a hedge fund

But there is also a more practical reason for going omnichannel. It both gives you insurance and puts you in the position to capitalize on upside potential. Insurance comes from spreading your revenues across multiple platforms – in a world where you are beholden to the rules and limitations of each platform that you establish your brand on, you need a diversified portfolio of revenue streams to act as insurance against any platform changes that could negatively affect your brand. Not to mention that the chance to establish on another platform also puts you in a position to benefit from all the upside the platform itself experiences, all the work they do, and ad money they spend to bring customers to their platform. Although we can certainly hazard a guess, we don't know for sure which online marketplace will be the market leader in 10, 20 or 30 years from now. Amazon has huge market capital and is gaining steam in the United States at an unprecedented rate, counting itself as a touchpoint in a majority of customer journeys, accounting for a majority of spend, and also for a majority of the growth in the e-commerce marketplace industry – but, that doesn't mean the consumer love affair with Amazon is forever. Not to mention affinities for different marketplaces vary across continents. Why spend huge dollars establishing a presence in South America if you can tap into an existing marketplace that already has the exact customers you're seeking, ready and waiting to be introduced to your product. You could spend thousands on ads, or you could just broker a deal (or simply sign up for an account) with the marketplace. Imagine getting in early on the next niche or regional Amazon and benefiting not only from the platform's growth but your established SEO, reviews, feedback and more on the platform as a long-time reputable seller. For your brand to survive and thrive in the long term, you need to look at your channels the same way a hedge fund does their asset allocation. If a hedge fund was holding over 20 per cent of their investments in any one asset, they would view themselves as overweight and look to redistribute. Of course, you also need to be ready to cut your losers and reinvest in your winners, as Nike did with Amazon for example, pulling their range citing concerns about counterfeit products flooding the marketplace (Zimmerman, 2020). Omnichannel is certainly not without its drawbacks, though. You will face issues like long wait times for payment from third-party retailers, a lack of control over or access to your customer data, a lack of simple and clean access to your customer feedback (and the potential inability to even respond to it as a brand because it sits on a platform you do not own), not to mention being beholden to the contractual conditions of the platform owner. As always, do your due diligence.

In-store is the final frontier for the digital-first D2C player

As I mentioned in the introduction to this chapter, your customers have rich and intricate lives outside of the digital world, in offline environments that are primed to trigger strong emotional connections with your brand, and form unbreakable habits or simply irresistible moments of convenience as they go about their daily lives. Ignoring offline shopping experiences is sure to hamper the growth of your brand. Approximately one-third of customer

FIGURE 12.2 Omnichannel shoppers represent one in three journey types today

Breakdown of shopping journeys in apparel
% of shoppers

Purchased online — Digital only **27**

Omnichannel online purchase **20**

Purchased in store — In-store only **39**

Omnichannel in-store purchase **13**

Research and purchase in same channel

Research and purchase in different channels

SOURCE McKinsey & Company, 2015, www.McKinsey.com/industries/retail/our-insights/ready-to-where-getting-sharp-on-apparel-omnichannel-excellence journeys involve an omnichannel experience, whether it be online research leading to an in-store purchase, or in-store browsing and try-on leading to an online late-night shopping spree (Briedis et al, 2019). This is in combination with the fact that in some industries, like apparel for example, omnichannel consumers purchase up to 70 per cent more frequently than their offline-only counterparts (Kluge et al, 2021; Amed et al, 2022). Opening a new store has been shown to increase traffic to a brand's website by over one-third (ICSC, 2018). And brands like Macy's see 200–300 per cent higher online sales in areas where they also have a physical presence (Ali, 2021).

For the retailer with a wide range of SKUs and sizes, the in-store experience will be especially popular with its customers. A majority of consumers want the ability to compare specifics like colour, size, fit and texture, and see on-store as the channel that best satisfies their needs for this (McCormack, 2020).

Pop-up stores to dip your toes

For some companies like Warby Parker, an omnichannel strategy just makes sense. Their vertical integration involved bringing eye exams in-house to reduce costs and increase convenience for customers – this is something that has to happen in the physical world. Starting as an online-only success, Warby Parker now has over 150 brick-and-mortar stores at the time of writing in 2022 (many of them offering eye exams) (Melton, 2022). For other brands, the need for omnichannel isn't so obvious, so getting some D2C companies to switch – well, overcoming that online inertia is often no easy task for a brand and a team.

One way you can dip your toes into omnichannel e-commerce is through pop-up stores. Pop-up stores allow your brand to gain physical exposure, generate buzz around your product and leverage exposure by turning it into an event in the same way as Gymshark does with their worldwide pop-ups. As ThirdLove (a women's D2C lingerie label made by women for women) co-founder and CEO Heidi Zak says, physical stores are not just physical shopping spaces, but also powerful marketing tools (Milnes, 2019).

Opening pop-up stores also gives you the opportunity to gather extensive amounts of data from physical locations in many different regions, without signing 10-plus-year leases for retail properties that might not turn you a profit. Casper mattresses, as an example, gathered data from pop-up stores for two whole years before opening their permanent locations (Craparotta, 2019).

Having a physical location also lends your store greater credibility, which enables your customers (or importantly, potential customers) to see you as trustworthy. Approximately one-third of consumers just don't trust online-only stores, which is a blow to many direct-to-consumer brands. The brands they do trust, though? They have brick-and-mortar stores, too. Almost three-quarters of consumers say they trust omnichannel retailers (Itani et al, 2023).

Physical for brand values amplification

The fact is that most of your brand values are going to be rooted in the physical world. To make an impact with your customers, with your people, you need to engage in the physical, not only the digital. To do this as a D2C operator, you could be donating to charities that will put the boots on the ground to live out your values, like Who Gives a Crap building toilets in Africa, or Leesa providing beds to those without. A physical store gives your brand a unique way to live out its values, such as the value of minimalism, which Everlane conveys through its psychical store that is complete with wallet-less shopping enabled by its integrated ID system, which also facilitates the application of existing credits to your purchase and enables in-store returns. Or mattress brand Leesa, which fills its store with art created by homeless, formerly homeless and disabled artists (Leesa, 2016). It's one thing to tell your customers about your brand values, it's another thing to show them. Physical stores provide your brand not only with marketing opportunities, but with real brand equity-building values expression. While the metaverse is all the rage in the press, in-store locations and events are the original immersive experience delivery system that is tried and true, and penetrates across generations.

Why physical stores?

Brands like Warby Parker, Thirdlove and Leesa all built strong online brands, and then parlayed this huge brand equity, and brand affinity, into in-store success. The key here is to build a brand, not just a revenue engine. If your 'brand' is based on ever-increasing amounts of advertising, and you're not building brand equity and brand loyalty through your values and community, then consumers will pass you by on the street. 2PM (an industry-leading community and source of thought leadership in the commerce and media spaces) founder Web Smith adds that while CAC (customer acquisition costs) is lower in owned stores, for it to work, it's essential to have built a brand, and no Facebook ad can buy you a strong brand (Moore, 2021).

By far one of my favourite examples of a stellar omnichannel brand, which actually started out in stores – and not just any store and every store that would take them – started out with a clear channel strategy in alignment with their ideal customer profile and their brand values and voice. That brand is Tony's Chocolonely.

I'll explain why I am in such admiration of their strategy. First, as I mentioned, they started out distributing in-store. But they didn't just start out distributing in any store – they had a clear narrow target market they wanted to reach. Why? Because they had a very clear and unique brand positioning in their market as a value-driven chocolate brand. Tony's Chocolonely is an impact company that makes chocolate rather than a chocolate company that makes impact – selling 100 per cent slave-free chocolate, and the assurance that everyone gets their fair share (Sutherland, 2022). But that kind of messaging gets lost on the shelves of big-name stores, where the staff are focused on stocking shelves, not on selling products, let alone the values behind them. So how do you ensure that your brand gets the attention it needs in-store to let its values and voice shine? Sure, you can do it through advertising, or organic marketing, but Tony's Chocolonely started out with a no paid media policy, which led them to get creative with their distribution. But how do you use your distribution to communicate your values? You sell into smaller brick-and-mortar stores where your brand has a chance to shine, shoppers come to browse, not just to do their weekly groceries and dash, and the staff are more intimately aware of the products they have on offer, interact with shoppers throughout the purchase process, and often act as product recommendation agents. Tony's Chocolonely went into independent grassroots stores, coffee shops, delis and then premium retail to give their product the best chance to shine based on its differentiated values and brand story. Only after they had built their brand through their independent grassroots retailers and public relations stunts did they explore relationships with bigger partners to expand and scale their distribution strategy (Sutherland, 2022). Marketer extraordinaire Rory Sutherland drew parallels in his podcast between San Pellegrino, Rolling Rock and Peroni beer, and their distribution strategies which strictly controlled their initial distribution channels to those that were the best fit for brand values and persona. Sutherland, who has engineered campaigns for some of the world's leading brands, and is a fundamental and thought-provoking cog in the Ogilvy team (one that is just as likely to switch positions and change the structure of the system altogether with his sharp outside-the-box thinking as he is to spin up and accelerate campaigns forward), says that the first place you see a product has a profound effect on the associations you form with that brand (Sutherland, 2022).

What is so masterful about Tony's Chocolonely is that their values make their way right into the product design itself. No single piece of their chocolate bar is the same shape. Why? Because nothing is equal in the chocolate world – not like the regular equal-sized squares that other companies use. If you left Chapter 3, 'Brand core: the foundation for growth', still unsure of the utility and power of design, let this be evidence that you're only limited by your creativity as to the power of branding and design for building your brand.

Building a strong brand like this, through either founder values, or irreplicable founder presence, as 2X eCommerce podcast guest Josh Elizetxe and founder of Snow® Teeth Whitening says, is a great way to build a moat around your brand. Combine that with strong protection of intellectual property, and you have a brand that is so magnetic to consumers and insulated from competitive threats that it becomes easier and more desirable for brands to work with you than to work against you (2X eCommerce, 2018; Elizetxe, 2019). I'll give you a few examples. Let's start with Tony's Chocolonely. In 2021 Aldi launched a fairtrade-certified and 100 per cent responsibly sourced chocolate bar, complete with uniquely sized pieces, just like Tony's Chocolonely. But they didn't do it in direct competition with Tony's Chocolonely, they did it in collaboration with them. Granted, Tony's Chocolonely had to set up the infrastructure to facilitate such collaborations through Tony's Open Chain – an industry initiative enabling chocolate brands to transform their supply chains in alignment with the core principles of Tony's Chocolonely for a fairer cocoa industry, better-paid workers and traceable beans (Briggs, 2021; Tony's Open Chain, 2022). It shows that having a strong vision and values opens up powerful new ways of thinking that then open up new opportunities for a brand. I'll explain. Any other chocolate company that sees themselves in the business of making chocolate – that's all they do, they make chocolate. Industry-wide initiatives to transform the industry on a mass scale just aren't on their radar, and they're stuck tweaking operations and marketing campaigns. Whereas a brand like Tony's Chocolonely, with a big, hairy, audacious goal (transforming the cocoa industry), that mission and those values unlock powerful new ways of thinking for a brand, which led to initiatives like Tony's Open Chain, which led to collaboration rather than competition. Consider if the ailing railway industry had seen itself as being in the business of transforming transportation for the people, rather than simply being in the business of providing transportation via locomotive. A company with the vision to transform transportation for the people opens up a whole world of new and different ways of thinking to the company's entire cross-functional growth stack. They wouldn't be blindsided by an increase in air travel eating away at their profits; they would ride the wave to success. Now, the locomotive and aerospace industries are vastly different, some might say chalk and cheese. But the exercise shows you that vision and values connect you to higher-level thinking that opens up new opportunities for your brand. It doesn't mean you need to pursue them all, but it will pull you away from undifferentiated competition, and into innovation and collaboration. Ways of thinking, whether as a company or as an individual, drive all that we do.

A marketplace-first approach

What does it take to bring an idea formed in Korea to a US juggernaut skincare brand with over 30 retail partnerships and over $100 million in revenue? Sure, it can be done as a DTC brand – but in today's world where marketplaces own the product discovery phase, if you want strong growth then tapping into these magnetic watering holes is a great way to leverage your brand's reach and exposure. But that's only part of the equation – the other half is your in-store strategy.

Innovative new brands are recognizing the power and simplicity of marketplaces to launch and scale their brands in a way that is not only cost-effective, but also in line with all the data-driven insights we are seeing as to how shoppers are behaving online.

That is through a marketplace-first strategy, following a brick-and-mortar watering hole strategy that minimizes direct investment and takes advantage of huge amounts of existing IP and infrastructure, not to mention marketing budget and loyal customer bases. And then finally moving into substantial direct investment in owned platforms. In this example, our featured retailer followed the core lines of thought in this chapter almost to the tee. We know that marketplaces attract a majority of consumers for their product search and discovery. We also know that the percentage of online sales happening through marketplaces is only growing, especially when it comes to purchases made on Amazon.

Of course, this strategy does mean that consumers may miss out on the benefits of things like click and collect, and the smooth customer experiences that completely owned channels offer – as an example, the DTC retailer who owns their site and their in-store experience. But when you're scaling, if you want to reach, and you want eyeballs, and you don't have huge budgets – then rolling out across marketplaces and securing retail partnerships with existing big names is exactly how you do it. Even then, not having your own fully owned multichannel ecosystem doesn't actually mean that consumers miss out on things like click and collect – in all likelihood, once you get into brick-and-mortar retail stores, they will already have their own click-and-collect systems in place. Even marketplaces have a host of collection point options to suit consumers. Not to mention that in a channel-agnostic world, consumers are content to browse on one platform and make their purchases on another – for example, conducting their search on Amazon and buying on another retailer's platform or visiting a store.

What you do miss out on, however, is the owned customer data and remarketing ability – so you should be wary of this when negotiating agreements, and get a hold of as much of your data as possible. It's very easy for a database engineer to set up some rules to pipe customer data into your owned database – but then the legal structure needs to be in place to allow for that. The whole ecosystem needs to be aligned toward this goal, so you should be aware of that very early in negotiations. Ensure you're collecting as much future value for your owned platforms as you can.

The playbook? Take advantage of the huge footfall-hitting websites like Amazon, as well as the ease of setting up and even logistics done for you to grow recognition for your brand. Use your marketplace popularity to develop partnerships with brick-and-mortar retailers, again with existing systems and audiences, not to mention marketing budgets, and build your brand recognition. Then, invest in your own infrastructure like a website, CDP and full-scale omnichannel team, complete with your own distributed logistics to capture the groundswell of support that you've been building using other people's channels.

The brand as an example? Hero Cosmetics. Not only is Hero a case study in effective omnichannel strategy, but it's also a case study in everything that makes a great brand, from strategy to execution, across product, positioning, marketing, distribution and more. Hero's three co-founders launched the brand in 2017 after Ju Rhyu had dabbled with the idea on and off for several years. Finally finding the right timing and right group of co-founders, they launched with a single product – a gentle-on-the-skin hydrocolloid patch that differentiated itself through the absence of harsh acids common in acne treatment products at the time. Differentiated product, tick. But, what they did next wasn't what most direct-to-consumer brands would do. They didn't get set up with their own Shopify store and run acquisition marketing to fill their funnel. Instead, they started as an Amazon native brand, achieving the number one position for 'acne patches' and 'pimple patches' (talk about great on platform SEO) and expanded both their product offerings and channels from there. Ju and Hero's strategy? One SKU on Amazon, then a few more SKUs. One SKU on Target, then a few more SKUs (Kaziukenas, 2022a). As of 2022, Hero has scaled to five additional marketplaces outside of their native Amazon, including niche marketplaces like Ulta, a dedicated beauty marketplace and GoPuff, a consumer packaged goods-focused marketplace. Hero's founders exited their business for $600 million after just five years of operation and executing on their omnichannel strategy (Shacknai, 2022). Hero aren't alone in the arena, either. Anker, another Amazon-first brand, despite doing over $1 billion in sales on the platform, recognized the need for channel diversification. While in 2016 Anker's share of revenue from Amazon was approximately 80 per cent, five years later in 2021 it was only just over 50 per cent – a result of channel diversification by launching on other marketplaces, as well as their own direct-to-consumer storefront. But, like any savvy digital retailer, Steven Yang, founder of Anker, realized, as I mentioned earlier in this chapter, the power of in-store to tap into consumers' already-established habits and preferences, Now offline channels like Walmart, Best Buy and even Apple drive a significant share of Anker's revenue (Kaziukenas, 2022b).

Actually, while it might seem like a new strategy because there are new, very modern digital channels involved, it's actually much like the strategy of old. When we think of DTC brand journeys, there is the traditional brick and mortar to online, or online to brick and mortar. But the traditional organic evolution of a product-based commerce business has been from the market stall (today, the online equivalent being marketplaces such as Etsy, Amazon, Walmart and more), to an owned store (today this can be either a website or brick-and-mortar store). The discovery that a marketplace allows, for a relatively small investment, is ideal for any fledgling commerce business. But whereas in the past this gave you access to a neighbourhood, today it gives you access to a large portion of the entire world. Sure, the competition is higher, too – but if you've taken your time to intentionally craft a winning brand by diving deep into your cross-functional growth stack, building it from the ground up with your branding and culture, and layering on top of that an integrated set of nodes to offer superior customer journeys and experiences, combined with conversion and retention rate optimization, you have all the blocks you need to build a winning e-commerce growth stack in any configuration you choose, whether you're just starting out and leveraging marketplaces for exposure, or adding a new channel to your existing stack to move with changing consumer behaviour.

Challenges in an omnichannel world

Omnichannel retail is not without its challenges. Without a data strategy to enable the measurement of KPIs (and the vision and strategy of leadership to set the right KPIs) your brand will be flying blind (or perhaps more aptly put, with the wrong map). The best retailers are completely changing their ways of thinking to adjust to a world where omnichannel experiences are not only demanded by consumers, but also more profitable for e-commerce brands (Burns and Harris, 2022). Earlier in this chapter I mentioned that your ways of thinking needed to change in an omnichannel world. This is because you're not only driving results from one channel, and at times it may even seem as if you are going backwards if you don't have an understanding of how your omnichannel cross-functional growth stack drives growth for your brand. When it comes to measuring the success of your omnichannel venture, naturally you will turn to your data team and your key performance indicators.

If after implementing your omnichannel strategy you haven't designed performance metrics that reward your whole enterprise (which now includes external channels like marketplaces), and you are still operating on your individual channel KPIs, then it's time to sit down with your data team and see how you can do better. For example, an online retailer with in-store channels can underestimate the performance of their online channel by 100 per cent (or more) if they don't account for the influence their online channels have on their offline stores (Kluge et al, 2021). This is because consumers spend between an additional 50–100 per cent in-store than they do online. Not to mention that a majority of customers research online before buying in-store (PwC, 2011).

Wrapping up

To wrap things up, it's clear that omnichannel marketing is a key component for businesses looking to thrive in today's competitive market. By providing a seamless and integrated experience across all channels, you can create a strong brand presence and increase customer loyalty. If you want to learn more about how to implement an effective omnichannel marketing strategy, be sure to visit my website. There, you'll find useful guides and resources, including platform breakdowns and SEO tips specifically for omnichannel marketing: 2xecommerce.com/book/chapter12.

In the next chapter we will delve into the importance of product development and innovation for growth. Stay tuned to learn how to stay ahead of the competition and drive long-term success for your business.

References

2X eCommerce (2018) S03 EP60, How Josh Elizetxe is building an 8-figure world class beauty tech brand, https://2xecommerce.com/podcast/ep160/ (archived at https://perma.cc/37V3-XF76)

Ali, F (2021) Macy's ecommerce sales grow 20% in 2020, *Digital Commerce 360*, 1 Mar, www.digitalcommerce360.com/2021/03/01/macys-ecommerce-sales-grow-20-in-2020/#:~:text=That%20means%20digital%20represented%2053 (archived at https://perma.cc/5D35-FS5T)

Amed, I et al (2022) The State of Fashion 2023, *McKinsey & Company*, 29 Nov, www.McKinsey.com/industries/retail/our-insights/state-of-fashion (archived at https://perma.cc/VCA4-RM4U)

Anthropologie (2022) Curated by Anthropologie FAQs, www.anthropologie.com/help/cba-faqs (archived at https://perma.cc/5HXQ-QHXP)

Briedis, H, Harris, T, Pacchia, M and Ungerman, K (2019) Ready to 'where': getting sharp on apparel omnichannel excellence, *McKinsey & Company*, 9 Aug, www.McKinsey.com/industries/retail/our-insights/ready-to-where-getting-sharp-on-apparel-omnichannel-excellence (archived at https://perma.cc/Q5ME-8XB5)

Briggs, F (2021) Aldi launches new own-label chocolate bar with Tony's Chocolonely, Aldi Press Office, www.aldipresscentre.co.uk/business-news/aldi-launches-new-own-label-chocolate-bar-with-tonys-chocolonely/ (archived at https://perma.cc/4LXJ-JB23)

Burns, T and Harris, T (2022) Forecasting the future of stores, *McKinsey & Company*, 24 Mar, www.McKinsey.com/industries/retail/our-insights/forecasting-the-future-of-stores (archived at https://perma.cc/MV6C-2JAY)

Craparotta, J (2019) Top 5 reasons why DTC retailers love pop-up stores, *Cura Group*, 15 Oct, www.curagroup.com/blog/top-5-reasons-why-dtc-retailers-love-pop-up-stores-0 (archived at https://perma.cc/ET9M-4AMP)

eCommerce DB (2022) eCommerce revenue analytics, https://ecommercedb.com/en/store/newegg.com (archived at https://perma.cc/7BYR-ZJLW)

Elizetxe (2019) iStack Training. Josh Elizetxe takes aim at the moon (and Procter & Gamble)| RBM E51, *YouTube*, 11 Jan, www.youtube.com/watch?v=3TSRH0dRYlA (archived at https://perma.cc/F4VB-6ZVC)

Fresen, N (2021) Boots market share climbs to over 40%, *Retail Bulletin*, 14 Oct, www.theretailbulletin.com/health-and-beauty/boots-market-share-climbs-to-over-40-14-10-2021/ (archived at https://perma.cc/LAJ2-DYGP)

Howland, D (2022) Victoria's Secret launches online marketplace dominated by women-led brands, *Retail Dive*, 26 May, www.retaildive.com/news/victorias-secret-launches-online-marketplace-women-led-brands/624466/ (archived at https://perma.cc/NC3S-PGN2)

ICSC (2018) Physical stores key to retail success, study finds, International Council of Shopping Centers, 15 Oct, icsc.com (archived at https://perma.cc/47NR-QVM9)

Itani, O, Loureiro, S, Correia, SM and Ramadan, Z (2023) Engaging with omnichannel brands: the role of consumer empowerment, *International Journal of Retail & Distribution Management*, 51 (2), pp 238–61, www.emerald.com/insight/content/doi/10.1108/IJRDM-02-2022-0044/full/html (archived at https://perma.cc/W8H8-DSTV)

Jungle Scout (2021) Amazon Advertising Report 2022, www.junglescout.com/amazon-advertising-report/ (archived at https://perma.cc/QT48-DJLB)

Kaziukenas, J (2022a) Target is not scaling its marketplace, *Marketplace Pulse*, 1 Mar, www.marketplacepulse.com/articles/target-is-not-scaling-its-marketplace (archived at https://perma.cc/Y4VZ-9XXG)

Kaziukenas, J (2022b) Amazon-native brand's Anker sales hit $1B, *Marketplace Pulse*, 7 Jun, www.marketplacepulse.com/articles/amazon-native-brand-anker-reaches-1-billion-sales (archived at https://perma.cc/9ULQ-G7UV)

Kluge, P, Schmid, M, Silliman, E and Villepelet, C (2021) Omnichannel: it's time for the online tail to wag the retail dog, *McKinsey & Company*, 3 Dec, www.McKinsey.com/industries/retail/our-insights/omnichannel-its-time-for-the-online-tail-to-wag-the-retail-dog (archived at https://perma.cc/DQJ8-D6M5)

Leesa (2016) Leesa Sleep & ArtLifting open world's first 'Leesa Dream Gallery' in SoHo, NYC, www.leesa.com/article/leesa-dream-gallery (archived at https://perma.cc/9WF9-YPJD)

Maier, E and Wieringa, J (2020) Acquiring customers through online marketplaces? The effect of marketplace sales on sales in a retailer's own channels, *International Journal of Research in Marketing*, 38 (3), pp 311–28

McCormack, D (2020) From clicks to bricks: expanding brand loyalty through physical stores, *BHDP*, 22 Oct, www.bhdp.com/insights/clicks-bricks-expanding-brand-loyalty-through-physical-stores (archived at https://perma.cc/A9W5-AZX9)

Melton, J (2022) Warby Parker to expand store footprint and hold the line in prices, *Digital Commerce 360*, 31 Mar, www.digitalcommerce360.com/2022/03/31/warby-parker-to-expand-store-footprint-and-hold-the-line-in-prices/ (archived at https://perma.cc/29MM-HG2M)

Milnes, H (2019) ThirdLove's first physical store is about marketing as much as finding new customers, *Modern Retail*, 23 Jul, www.modernretail.co/startups/thirdloves-first-physical-store-is-about-marketing-as-much-as-finding-new-customers/?utm_campaign=mrdis&utm_medium=email&utm_source=mrdaily&utm_content=230719 (archived at https://perma.cc/F3G2-52AG)

Moore, A (2019) Want to be insanely successful? Put all your eggs in one basket, *Thrive Global*, https://thriveglobal.com/stories/want-to-be-insanely-successful-put-all-your-eggs-in-one-basket/ (archived at https://perma.cc/RQE5-7RKU)

Moore, K (2021) 11 DTC brands opening physical retail stores in 2021 (and why), *Shopify*, 13 May, www.shopify.com/retail/dtc-to-brick-and-mortar (archived at https://perma.cc/6PHU-JHTD)

Omnisend (2019) The complete guide to omnichannel marketing automation, www.omnisend.com/resources/library/landing-omnichannel-whitepaper/ (archived at https://perma.cc/RK9H-JDPY)

Osterloff, E (nd) Mutualism: eight examples of species that work together to get ahead, *Natural History Museum*, www.nhm.ac.uk/discover/mutualism-examples-of-species-that-work-together.html (archived at https://perma.cc/66G7-MJ3L)

PwC (2011) Customers take control, Multichannel Survey, www.pwc.com/ve/es/publicaciones/assets/global-rc-multi-channel-survey.pdf (archived at https://perma.cc/2TRV-EH8W)

Shacknai, G (2022) Hero cosmetics acquired by Church & Dwight for $630 million, *Forbes*, www.forbes.com/sites/gabbyshacknai/2022/09/06/hero-cosmetics-acquired-by-church--dwight-for-630-million/?sh=727c001deb8f (archived at https://perma.cc/LF4Y-VCCK)

Simpson, J, Ohri, L and Lobaugh, K (2016) The new digital divide, *Deloitte*, www2.deloitte.com/us/en/insights/industry/retail-distribution/digital-divide-changing-consumer-behavior.html?id=us:2el:3pr:dup3325:awa:dup:091416 (archived at https://perma.cc/9NPY-6VBH)

Smith, W, Milnes, H Remy, A and Williams, C (2022) Memo: a Hero's acquisition, *2PM, Inc.*, https://2pml.com/2022/09/07/hero/ (archived at https://perma.cc/U3R6-2EXY).

Sopadjieva, E, Dholakia, MU and Benjamin, B (2017) A study of 46,000 shoppers shows that omnichannel retailing works, *Harvard Business Review*, https://hbr.org/2017/01/a-study-of-46000-shoppers-shows-that-omnichannel-retailing-works (archived at https://perma.cc/A4TG-JJMN)

Sutherland, R (2022) S01 EP27, Rory gets a taste of Tony's Chocolonely with the Countess of Cocoa Nicola Matthews, https://shows.acast.com/on-brand-with-rory-sutherland/episodes/rory-gets-a-taste-of-tonys-chocolonely-with-nicola-matthews (archived at https://perma.cc/L5JA-XSJH)

Tony's Open Chain (2022) www.tonysopenchain.com/ (archived at https://perma.cc/7H3D-CCD9)

Urban Outfitters (2022) Our brands, www.urbn.com/our-brands (archived at https://perma.cc/B235-QWHQ)

Vermut, M (2018) Why omnichannel is the future of retail for millennials (and everyone else, too), *AdAge*, 27 Apr, https://adage.com/article/neustar/omnichannel-future-retail-millennials/315054 (archived at https://perma.cc/QL9W-YAA9)

Zimmerman, B (2020) Why Nike cut ties with Amazon and what it means for other retailers, *Forbes*, 22 Jan, www.forbes.com/sites/forbesbusinesscouncil/2020/01/22/why-nike-cut-ties-with-amazon-and-what-it-means-for-other-retailers/?sh=36876abd64ff (archived at https://perma.cc/HMN6-N78T)

Further reading

McKinsey & Company (2019*) The State of Fashion 2019*, London

McKinsey & Company (2022) Breakdown of shopping journeys in apparel, www.McKinsey.com/~/media/McKinsey/industries/retail/our%20insights/ready%20to%20where%20getting%20sharp%20on%20apparel%20omnichannel%20excellence/svgz-ready-to-where-ex1.svgz (archived at https://perma.cc/YFG2-FC4V)

McKinsey & Company (2022) Goods are distributed to end customers over a growing number of network nodes, www.McKinsey.com/~/media/McKinsey/industries/retail/our%20insights/better%20service%20with%20connected%20inventory/svgz-better-service-with-connected-inventory-ex1.svgz (archived at https://perma.cc/VPX4-MR45)

Nadel, D (2021) The 2021 Amazon Consumer Behavior Report, *Feedvisor*, https://s3.amazonaws.com/media.mediapost.com/uploads/2021_Consumer_Behavior_Report.pdf (archived at https://perma.cc/C2A4-QCLW)

Stern, LW, Sivadas, E, Ansary, AI and Palmatier, RW (2019) *Marketing Channel Strategy: An omni-channel approach*, Routledge, New York, NY

13

Product development cycles for growth

Your product decides whether you'll be praised or persecuted

To set the tone, and really drive the importance of this chapter home, I will begin with this insight: your customers will applaud your product, or complain about your product – nothing else. So which will it be for you?

In a hyper-connected social media-driven world you can't afford to be mediocre. Growth requires the participation of your entire growth stack, not least your product, which sets the tone for absolutely everything your brand does. A great product won't save bad marketing, neither would great marketing save a bad product.

When it comes to getting your product to market, you might be tempted to skimp on the product development stage and simply take what is available through manufacturers and wholesalers, and add your branding and marketing to make the product shine. A formal and optimized product development roadmap that goes deep into your product can feel like a waste of time and money, especially when you're just getting started, if you've already completed thorough market research, have a strong brand identity and marketing plan, and have a clear vision for what your final product will look like. Especially if your goal is to bring in revenue as soon as possible. But this approach is one that could have serious limiting effects on your upside potential.

No matter how well your product meets current demand, draws first purchases and converts, or aligns with current trends, it won't sell in the long term unless it's also a great product on its own merits, and often that means your product becomes a lot more than just a product, it becomes its own living organism with its own innovation and development cadence. It becomes an ecosystem with complementary products as you expand product lines strategically, be it through development or joint ventures (something that we will cover in Chapter 15). And importantly, your product becomes an offer as you bring your entire culture, messaging and product together into an authentic and aligned consumer brand juggernaut.

Product-led growth for e-commerce

Product-led growth is a popular term in the software as a service (SaaS) industry. It is the notion that acquisition, conversion and retention are all driven by your product, primarily. A business that aligns itself behind a product-led growth strategy believes that the product itself accounts for the largest share of sustainable long-term business growth and potential for scale.

However, it's something that is talked about much less in the e-commerce world. One reason is that the technical complexity and user flows of our product in e-commerce are often less complex than they are in SaaS, and we don't tend to have the extensive feature and integration needs that a business-to-business SaaS user does. A t-shirt is a vastly different product than Salesforce, even if your e-commerce store does still serve as a graphical user interface, much like a web or mobile app. But, while as e-commerce stores our user flows might not be as complex as Salesforce's, we do have an ecosystem of products that not only stand alone, but interact together in uniquely complex ways with nearly unlimited combinations of features and adjacent complimentary products – products that we may sell ourselves, or that are available through other suppliers and complement our own. Not to

FIGURE 13.1 Product-led growth strategy

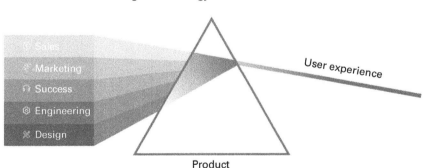

mention the varied lifestyles our customers live, and the myriad ways they integrate our products into their lives, and the reasons why.

Even if you're only a single-product seller, your users have entire lifestyles and rituals built around their use of your product, which may or may not involve other products, too. And the world, and consumers, are forever evolving. As they say, the only constant is change.

To develop real competitive advantage, your products' utility should evolve through innovation with a product-led mindset. The beauty of this approach is that in the SaaS world, as it should be in the e-commerce world, product-led, when you peel back the layers, means customer-centric.

This is because at the end of the day, it is customer needs through continuous feedback loops and customer research that drive the evolution of the product, beating away at it with bug reports, reviews, user data and more. To avoid confusion between product-led SaaS growth and what we are talking about here in this chapter, I will refer to it as product-first growth.

That is not because product is necessarily more important than branding – and you should spend 80 per cent of your time and resources on it – it simply highlights that at its core, as an e-commerce operator, you are in the business of selling physical products, and you cannot talk about growth without talking about product – in fact, without starting with a product. And since we are starting with a product, or at least the idea or proof of concept of a product, as is sometimes the case with crowdfunded product campaigns, your product is something that sets the foundation for your later growth.

The other reason is that many brands just don't have such a strong focus nor a dedicated team focused solely on product. More established brands do, but many small and mid-market brands don't integrate this until much later in their growth cycle. Without a strong product and product development lifecycle process, problems that you will typically experience later down the road will manifest as issues such as low customer lifetime value, high acquisition costs, low word of mouth, little interest in participating in your brand community and, in general, a stagnating brand that no amount of increased marketing spend can jolt back to life.

Snow® Teeth Whitening is one of the brightest examples of a brand that won through product and intelligent cross-functional growth stack optimization. First, much like Hero Cosmetics, whose product strategy I will introduce you to later, with product, through innovation. Second, through differentiated marketing. This combination took Snow® to over $100 million in sales in just four years. I'll start with the product. Founder Josh Elizetxe spent hours of his own time and thousands of dollars of his own money to develop, test and refine the first iterations of the Snow® Teeth Whitening Kit. Why? Because he'd realized there was a huge gap in the market for teeth whitening products that weren't horribly uncomfortable to use like whitening strips, or terribly branded like medical devices. Josh found himself wondering why products in the space looked so unattractive, and like they belonged in a medical office rather than someone's home as a direct-to-consumer product. His goal? To create a product that works better than the competition, looks better than the competition and is marketed in a way that his competition couldn't compete with. Through product development and refinement based on real customer feedback (Josh literally called his customers to get feedback on his product and improve it), he created the most advanced teeth whitening system on the market at the time, and possibly still to this day. Over half a million customers agree. His real genius, though, shows in his cross-functional approach. He knew that to compete with the big names like GlaxoSmithKline, he had to be not only better, but also different in a way that would be very hard for them to replicate. He didn't want their big budgets and huge research and development departments eating away at his competitive advantage. So, he set out to be the next Elon Musk or Steve Jobs. He created his own brand, a personal brand, intimately tied to that of his company. Something that faceless corporations like GSK cannot do. Now, people aren't just buying from an oral care company, they're buying from Josh.

When you innovate like Snow®, protect your innovation with patents where possible. Combine that with a differentiated marketing angle like Elizetxe did, with a huge founder personality presence that conglomerates just cannot replicate, and you protect your brand from even the likes of Amazon on multiple fronts (Singh, 2020). You become very difficult to compete with. When developing your e-commerce business, stack multiple competitive advantages on top of one another by winning on product, and then winning on things like customer service, turnaround and customer experience as well.

Building offers, not just products

To create a successful product and brand, you need to create products that not only satisfy customers, but also go above and beyond to delight them. Product development should be integrated into your entire brand strategy. Without it, your brand will rely solely on marketing, and will eventually be overtaken by a cross-functional growth stack brand with a more compelling offer.

Your offer is more than just your product. For example, Patagonia donates a portion of its proceeds to charity, which is intangible. However, it still affects consumers because they can see the impact of their purchase on the environment. An offer is what you build around your product to meet the needs and desires of your customers that the product itself cannot. But for it to be effective, it must be authentically aligned with your product.

For a brand, alignment means satisfying all customer needs in terms of functionality and psychology.

As Oren Schauble, product marketing and M&A roll-up expert (and 2X eCommerce podcast #358 guest), says, 'Trends and brands come and go; even if you get initial traction, know you've got to evolve quickly as things change' (Schauble, 2022; 2X eCommerce, 2022). Product development is a constant. Schauble has some practical advice that you can likely implement today for your own brand. One of the biggest opportunities he sees to offer innovation is in documentation and content enablement. Schauble adds that any brand can sell fitness equipment, but what he wants to see is that it comes with 100 videos of different exercises that you can do with the kettle-bell (2X eCommerce, 2022). You could go further and add nutrition plans. But don't stop there – think about who your target audience is. Is there something else you can do to further differentiate your offer? As an example, if I was selling fitness equipment to seniors (a large market at the time of writing in 2022 as baby boomers go into retirement), I would consider other angles like heart health, collaborations with a cardiovascular health-oriented application that tracks exercise and diet and more. Not to mention that a good understanding of your target market will help you narrow your content itself; exercises you would build content around for young 18–30-year-old males may not be the same as you would suggest for the 60+ age group.

So, while this chapter is about products, it's really about teaching you to build offers. Real offers with real competitive advantages, leveraging the entire growth stack, with your product strategy as an integral part of that. Companies like Shein and Amazon have come under fire for allegedly replicating the products of individual brands, often undercutting them on price for very similarly designed products. At least on the surface. You probably responded to the section in one of two ways. You were either inspired, seeing the potential in the me-too model employed by both large and small operators that utilize a wide range of SKUs to captivate the market. Or, and probably most likely, you as an independent DTC brand felt frustration towards me-too copycat brands that can throw their weight around and crush smaller independent retailers on a whim, often by replicating their surface-level innovations. The fact is that today, anybody can build something in China, put a label on it, and make it similar to your product – even Amazon itself. They have the data advantage, and they can and will compete with you. My advice – to win on product today you need to **win on real innovation, offer, brand and messaging.** All of it, together. If you are weak in one area, you will get eaten alive out there.

The product + marketing + customer experience loop

Consumers crave novelty and the nature of the world we live in today is that of continuous improvement – we expect new car models every five years, new phone models every year, new and improved recipes, eye-catching packaging and technology to generally improve our lives. Frequent product launches and novelty. It's how the Shein marketplace was able to overtake Amazon to become the number one shopping app in the United States, largely by adding thousands of items to their marketplace every single day. If you didn't know, Shein is a Chinese online fast-fashion retailer known for its affordably priced apparel, and at the time of writing in 2022, has achieved at least seven years of consistent 100 per cent sales growth. For an outsider, a newcomer, or anyone who hasn't worked with a Boohoo, Shein, or H&M, it's probably hard to imagine the sheer scale of retail operations today and how much product development is required to be competitive in the market. Shein is prolific in this area, much more so than even giants like H&M and Boohoo. It releases as many as 10,000 new items per day, and consistently around 6,000 new products each day on average (Williams, 2022; Vara, 2022; SHEIN, 2021). Yes, you read that right, thousands upon thousands… But, not all products remain, of course, with small batches being commissioned to start with, and items only remaining on the online storefront if they perform. Nevertheless, it's a sound product development strategy that integrates rapid testing and iteration while tapping into consumer psychology and desire for novelty. Not to mention that the potentially short product runs mean that if you don't check in on the app one day, you may well miss out on something you would really like. This FOMO keeps users coming back and scrolling – that and incentive systems that reward users with loyalty points simply for checking in on Shein each day (Oliver, 2021). This snippet from the *Daily Mail* sums it up well: 'Its popularity lies in the fact that its garments are astonishingly cheap, and reflect the latest trends. Between 700 and 1,000 new styles, many costing under £10, are uploaded every day' (Oliver, 2021).

'If a design sells out quickly, Shein places a large order of the product', according to a Coresight Research report. 'If it does not sell out quickly, Shein sells the remaining pieces and abandons the design' (Verhaeghe, nd).

Driving development with data

Take a moment to think about the huge amount of content out there on the internet, whether it's on Netflix, your favourite news aggregator app or TikTok. What makes the user experience on these platforms so good for consumers, and in some cases like TikTok borderline addictive as your attempts to pry your attention away from the constant stream of bite-sized content often prove fruitless, is a combination of novelty and superior recommendation engines. Having thousands or millions of potential novel experiences at your fingertips keeps you coming back, and recommendation engines expert in feeding you the exact content you want to see make the experience all the more delectable.

Frequent product releases and expanding product lines (they don't need to expand to infinity) form the typical growth roadmap for a direct-to-consumer brand. Many of the best brands have begun with one winning product to start with, and then expanding from there. This will be refreshing to hear for any bootstrapped founders reading this right now. Just look at the retail behemoth Nike today, with its line of thousands of products, and it is hard to imagine that it all began with one shoe. For an example of a data-driven strategy to keep up with fast-changing consumer preferences and trends, we turn to Shein. Shein uses AI to trawl its users' on-site search behaviour (hello first-party data) and their social media behaviour, to generate recommendations for their designers and product teams. You can even implement some of Shein's tactics yourself, without expensive AI systems. Part of Shein's strategy is to use Google's Trend Finder to discover what people are searching for in real time (Oliver, 2021).

Product development roadmap and product launch cadence

Developing products can be a challenging process, but with proper preparation and planning, it can be a powerful growth driver for your company. I strongly believe that every company should have a product development roadmap and at least one employee who is responsible for it. Don't leave it to chance – actively generate new ideas. A solid product development road-map and product launch cadence are key to scaling your brand long-term.

To get started, conduct a competitive analysis regularly. Once a month should be a good cadence for most businesses. Choose your top four or five competitors and evaluate everything about their brand – what else can customers do with their product, what other experiences can they offer? Remember, we're no longer talking about products, but offers. How does their marketing align with their product? How does it not? How does their marketing feed back into their product?

Setting up your cadence strategy requires that you first create a product roadmap. A product roadmap is a visual representation of your product development timeline, outlining the goals and objectives of your product. Next, create a product validation plan. A product validation plan outlines the steps you need to take to validate your product idea. You should have technical, legal, environmental, brand alignment and customer validation. Your validation plan should identify the target person or audience, and the best way to reach them and collect the data you need. For Shein, their approach is to validate ideas through existing alternatives on the market that are gaining traction online, and then further validate for their specific audiences by producing and testing small product runs. Finally, create a product marketing plan for your product launch. This will help you to outline the core goals and objectives of your product launch, as well as all the steps you need to take to build an offer around your product.

One great example of a well-implemented product cadence is Hero Cosmetics. Similar to how they strategically expanded from one sales channel to many, they followed the same approach with their product. Launching first with their hydrocolloid acne patches in 2017, Hero earned a name for themselves as a specialist in acne patches and acne patches alone. This allowed them to put all their focus into developing, improving and marketing one single product, and absolutely owning the niche. This allowed them to get into stores like Anthropologie and Target. It's hard to understate the significance of this – because focusing on one product alone allowed Hero to build a reputation for category leadership and innova-tion, something that would have been incredibly expensive for a bootstrapped company to do across 20+ inventory items. Hero stuck to their guns and held off on expanding into new products until they knew they were ready and had built their credibility in their original niche to levels that would rub off on anything else they did. That takes time, but patience is worth it. Fast-forward to today and they have 27 products at the time of writing in 2022, and added 15 of those in one year alone (Flora, 2022). That is the kind of cadence that keeps customers surprised and delighted and engaged with your brand. Yours might not be as fast paced as that, but the point is you need to use your product strategy as a way to keep your consumer involved with your brand, and repurchasing. Your product launch cadence is like the heartbeat of your company. If you're not innovating and developing, you're flatlining.

In summary, using product development cycles and new product releases as part of your brand-building strategy can be a powerful way to generate excitement and keep your customers interested and engaged. As we move on to our next chapter, we will discuss the critical role of company culture in supporting your brand-building efforts. Building a strong and positive culture, as well as facilitating experimentation within your organization, can improve employee satisfaction and productivity and also enhance your brand's reputation and appeal to customers and potential employees alike. This culture of experimentation will go a long way to facilitating your product innovation success.

References

2X eCommerce (2022) S07, EP16, 9-figure M&A roll-ups and product innovation, https://2xecommerce.com/podcast/ep358/ (archived at https://perma.cc/5SD9-JCHM)

Flora, M (2022) How Hero cosmetics started with 1 SKU and became the new face of acne care, *ShipBob*, 1 Oct, www.shipbob.com/blog/hero/ (archived at https://perma.cc/TB85-5SFB)

Oliver, A (2021) China's fast-fashion spy machine: how shadowy teen brand Shein uses algorithms to harvest data on its users and find out what they want to buy – before its mega-factory spits the clothes out at rock-bottom prices, *Mail Online*, 28 Aug, www.dailymail.co.uk/news/article-9936113/How-shadowy-teen-brand-Shein-uses-algorithms-harvest-data-users.html (archived at https://perma.cc/M3TN-FCTU)

Schauble, OJ (2022) Differentiating saturated product niches – product people, *LinkedIn*, 23 Jun, www.linkedin.com/pulse/differentiating-saturated-product-niches-people-oren-schauble/?trk=pulse-article_more-articles_related-content-card (archived at https://perma.cc/V4GH-R3J5)

SHEIN (2021) SHEIN Together Fest, *Cision PR Newswire*, 22 Apr, www.prnewswire.com/news-releases/shein-together-fest-301274374.html (archived at https://perma.cc/864S-5P4B)

Singh, TR (2020) How teeth whitening kit Snow became the apple of oral care, *Better Marketing*, 1 Sep, https://bettermarketing.pub/how-teeth-whitening-kit-snow-became-the-apple-of-oral-care-975e905817a9 (archived at https://perma.cc/4SVW-3QWH)

Vara, V (2022) Fast, cheap, and out of control: inside Shein's sudden rise, *Wired*, 4 May, www.wired.com/story/fast-cheap-out-of-control-inside-rise-of-shein/ (archived at https://perma.cc/3FJL-X6TY)

Verhaeghe, S (nd) How Shein is revolutionizing the fashion industry, *Duke & Grace*, 1 Jul, www.dukeandgrace.com/en/blog/how-shein-is-revolutionizing-the-fashion-industry (archived at https://perma.cc/BP6X-MKMD)

Williams, D (2022) Shein: the unacceptable face of throwaway fast fashion, *The Guardian*, 10 Apr, www.theguardian.com/fashion/2022/apr/10/shein-the-unacceptable-face-of-throwaway-fast-fashion (archived at https://perma.cc/WU4D-QHPT)

Further reading

2X eCommerce (2020) S04 EP22, Product creators' blueprint – step by step to turn ideas into products with Filip Valica, https://2xecommerce.com/podcast/ep189/ (archived at https://perma.cc/R2J9-E2DC)

NORNA (2020) How Shein revolutionised retail for the 21st century, https://norna.ai/news/?p=378 (archived at https://perma.cc/Z4ZV-RGW9)

PLG Collective (2022) What is product-led growth?, www.productled.org/foundations/what-is-product-led-growth (archived at https://perma.cc/AFR8-NE5Z)

14

How to cultivate a culture of experimentation

Failure is a prerequisite to invention/why you need a culture of experimentation

Failure is not an option, but it is the rule. Any entrepreneur knows the amount of experimentation, trying and failing that goes into building a brand. To grow anything requires risk, including the risk of failure and setback. Companies that create a culture of experimentation, where failure and success are both embraced, achieve better results than those that don't. The irony is that a culture where success is the only option generates more failures, but those failures are hidden instead of being learned from. Organizations that build competitive advantages create systems to minimize failure and learn from it when it happens. In a competitive environment, every brand needs to develop a culture of innovation and experimentation. Even if you're a market leader, you are a challenger brand because the world and consumer preferences are rapidly changing. Company culture can have a huge impact on innovation and can be changed. Steve Jobs did it at Apple, and companies like Amazon, Google and Microsoft all have cultures that support innovation and experimentation. You can do it too. Create a culture that supports experimentation, learns from failure and rewards success to foster innovation and growth.

Failure is all around you and is essential for innovation. Everyday products and innovations are the results of failures, such as bubble wrap and WD-40 (which, if you didn't know, gets its name for being the 40th iteration after 39 failures). The difference between WD-39 and WD-40 is about half a billion dollars per year in revenue (Companies Market Cap, 2022). And if

James Dyson, the inventor of the Dyson vacuum, had used the same naming convention, his first model would have been called the Dyson-5271 (Patel, 2015).

Nassim Taleb, leading expert in risk and author of the *Incerto* series, including *The Black Swan*, gives us the following: 'Learn to fail with pride – and do so fast and cleanly. Maximize trial and error – by mastering the error part' (Doctrow, 2009).

In this chapter you will learn how to set the conditions to do just that.

Building a culture of experimentation

A culture of experimentation is crucial for a thriving business. In today's constantly changing world, companies need strong cultures and processes around experimentation and failure to stay afloat. Building a culture of experimentation involves allowing employees to feel comfortable taking risks and trying out new ideas. This leads to greater collaboration and a stronger bottom line. Here's how to make it happen for your brand:

- It's not personal. Employees need to know that failure is not a personal rebuke. Encourage well-thought-out experimentation and show that success and failure are not mutually exclusive.

- Be deeply involved in the process. As a leader, you need to be collaboratively involved in the ideation and experimentation process. Thomas Edison's machinist and draftsman said that when he worked with Edison, he didn't feel like a workman, he felt as if he was making something together with Edison (Dodgson and Gann, 2010).

- Avoid the blame game to create truly collaborative environments. The blame game hinders collaboration and creativity and means employees will hide failures (Google, 2022; Friedman, 2019). Worse, the blame game is contagious – when people observe someone else doing it, they're more likely to do it themselves (Sutton, 2010; Fast, 2010).

- Hold back on the praise. Praise too can hinder motivation and lead to complacency. Instead, focus on progress and learning. This is because where there is praise there is also room for a lack of praise or even criticism.

- Make experimentation a part of your company's DNA. Experimentation should be ingrained in your company's culture and processes. This means providing resources, setting clear goals and tracking progress.

Tips for experimentation

Business experimentation is the process of testing new ideas or solutions in a controlled way. The keyword here is 'controlled'. To succeed at business experimentation, you need an experimental mindset and a plan. Start by creating an experimentation roadmap to organize and prioritize experiments based on business goals and impact. Approach experimentation like a scientist, with a clear hypothesis and business success metrics. Set up your team to create good experiments and provide resources and support.

Beyond that, build transparency and communication into the process, and involve leadership in experimentation. As an example, when Alan Mulally joined Ford as the CEO in 2006 (having come from Boeing) he implemented a new system to uncover failures within the company's operations. It was simple enough; reports were to be colour-coded green, yellow or red depending on the information within. Green for all good, red for problems, and you get the rest. The problem? For the first few meetings, all reports came back colour-coded green even though the company had lost several billion dollars the year prior. There were problems, but the team wasn't willing to highlight them. Eventually, with some culture building, that changed and reports started flowing in vibrant shades of red, yellow and green (Edmondson, 2011; Taylor, 2009).

Joint ventures are also great tools for experimentation to collaborate, utilize the intellectual capital of other companies and reduce risk. They are also powerful for creating new products and services that may not be possible on your own. This can be a great way to get things off the ground quickly and at a lower cost than if you were to go it alone. However, they can bring with them additional complexities – you and your joint venture partner should be on board with one another when it comes to all cultural, procedural and operational aspects for your joint venture experiments to be a success. If partners can't work together effectively it's setting you up for bad experiments.

Finally, make experimentation part of your company's DNA by providing resources, setting goals and tracking progress.

And if you fail, make the most of it. Most failures have multiple causes, which likely intersect and intercorrelate with one another, so extracting lessons from these requires dedicated and well-thought-out processes; not surprisingly, cross-functionality and cross-organizational learning are key (Brown, 2019; Ross and Fonstad, 2019). Charles F. Kettering, who was head of research at General Motors between 1920 and 1947, and who is considered one of the greatest innovators of all time, perhaps second only to Thomas Edison who we mentioned before, said that you must analyse each failure to find its cause, adding that failing is one of the greatest arts in the world – and that he himself had been wrong 99.9 per cent of the time. But it was those practice shots, as he called them, that allowed him to fail toward success.

Failure can occur for many reasons. I've summarized the top five here. The first two are reprimandable – the rest, they're on you as a leader:

- Deviance: when an individual or team violates your prescribed processes.

- Inattention: when a deviation is less intentional but indicates a lack of engagement.

- A lack of ability: as a manager or leader, assigning tasks is on you, and not giving your team the best chance at success by choosing the wrong people or not supplying the resources they need to be able to do their work falls on you.

- Inadequate processes: this is why I highlight the need to not only experiment more, but to experiment better. Look not only to improve the results of your experiments, but to improve the experimental processes themselves (Edmondson, 2011).

- Your processes are too complex: user experience isn't just for your customers. Every single process that your employees need to undertake is part of their own user experience at your company. Approach the creation and structure of your processes with the same care and attention to detail as you do user flows on your website and in your email automations.

The general process when it comes to learning from failure is to feed new lessons into your entire organizational documentation and learning system, and evaluate the success of your initiatives as a whole to find the bigger lessons at play and improve your business and experimentation processes in general (Prince, 2015). Opportunities for learning like this have been shown to increase productivity and innovation, creating positive feedback loops for your organization (Deloitte, 2015).

Wrapping up experimentation culture for e-commerce brands

E-commerce is a complex and ever-changing business, which makes it critical for companies to constantly adapt to new trends and technologies. In an environment where new players are emerging and trends are shifting at lightning speed, e-commerce leaders need to create cultures that encourage experimentation and risk-taking. As long as you experiment intelligently and systematically, learn from your failures and keep trying to succeed, you will find yourself progressing towards your goals. In fact, the most successful entrepreneurs are the ones who have failed the most. Those who have failed the most are also the ones who have learned the most, and they have learned the most because they have failed the most. Failure is just a part of business, and it's something everyone experiences. By learning from your failures and using them to improve your business, you're actually strengthening yourself and your organization. So, don't be afraid of failure – embrace it and use it to your advantage.

Where should you foster experimentation?

- **Supply chain** – experimenting with new suppliers, ingredients or materials, manufacturing processes, shipping routes or shipping providers. The idea here is to encourage your sourcing and supply chain team to test with low MOQs and gradually scale what is working.

- **Product innovation** – your product launch process should be iterative and experimental. Test new product launches as concepts or pre-launch to your core base of highly engaged customers. Run focus groups, carry out research – learn and iterate from quantitative and qualitative data.

- **On-site user experience** – this is a discipline in its own right; conversion rate optimization (CRO) which is heavily experimental and iterative-driven based on data and feedback loops. Your website is the virtual portal through which your potential and existing customers access your offering, so it is paramount to utilize an experimentation-driven approach to improve their experience. You will find the need to focus on CRO as your on-site traffic and order processing scale up. Although the net improvements from successful experiments tend to be low-percentage improvements on conversations, when CRO is ongoing these improvements do add up to meaningful transformations in both conversion and visitor satisfaction, because the primary aim of CRO is to remove impediments and unintended roadblocks in the on-site shopping experience your e-commerce business delivers.

- **Tech stack** – as your operations and business continue to evolve, your technology team should be constantly testing the capabilities of your existing technology stack to not only support your current needs but to sustain your operations as you scale up. It is paramount to negotiate contracts with vendors and lean towards flexible contractual terms to allow you to be nimble to rapid change without bearing significant financial costs. Also understanding your true switching cost from a time, resource and cost perspective should be factored in; as an example, understanding the switching costs of an e-commerce platform.

- **Marketing** – performance marketing is a unique blend of experimentation and creativity. What sets apart elite performance marketing teams from others is their ability to rapidly test, learn and iterate their marketing messages, copy and creatives to specific audiences. Your performance marketing team should be hugely immersed in taking an experimental approach to buying media.

- **Post-purchase experience** – although often neglected, this is a hugely important hub for experimentation and insight-driven learning. Testing free shipping thresholds, shipping carrier options, unboxing messaging and even the returns/exchange process can hugely improve customer satisfaction and net promoter scores and, more importantly, retention rates and customer lifetime value maximization.

Experimentation should be organization-wide, with all departments adequately educated and provided with the necessary reporting systems that enable them to share their learnings.

References

Brown, S (2019) Forget 'fail fast.' Here's how to truly master digital innovation, *MIT Management*, 9 Oct, https://mitsloan.mit.edu/ideas-made-to-matter/forget-fail-fast-heres-how-to-truly-master-digital-innovation (archived at https://perma.cc/N7SG-HQCY)

Companies Market Cap (2022) WD-40 Company (WDFC) – Revenue, https://companiesmarketcap.com/wd-40-company/revenue/ (archived at https://perma.cc/9CQN-36U6)

Deloitte (2015) Leading in Learning. Building capabilities to deliver on your business strategy, www2.deloitte.com/content/dam/Deloitte/global/Documents/HumanCapital/gx-cons-hc-learning-solutions-placemat.pdf (archived at https://perma.cc/H7BQ-MGTG)

Doctrow, C (2009) Black Swan author's rules for living, https://boingboing.net/2009/01/29/black-swan-authors-r.html (archived at https://perma.cc/L29V-57YA)

Dodgson, M and Gann, D (2010) 'Thomas Edison's Organizational Genius', in *Innovation: A very short introduction*, 1st edn, Oxford University Press, Oxford

Edmondson, AC (2011) Strategies for learning from failure, *Harvard Business Review*, Apr, https://hbr.org/2011/04/strategies-for-learning-from-failure (archived at https://perma.cc/2UUA-PD76)

Fast, NJ (2010) How to stop the blame game, *Harvard Business Review*, 13 May, https://hbr.org/2010/05/how-to-stop-the-blame-game (archived at https://perma.cc/2AL6-5SLM)

Friedman, Z (2019) Google says the best teams have these 5 things, *Forbes*, 28 Jan, www.forbes.com/sites/zackfriedman/2019/01/28/google-says-the-best-teams-have-these-5-things/?sh=188ef4795a30 (archived at https://perma.cc/8SNQ-MUGN)

Google (2022) Guide: Understand team effectiveness, re:Work Withgoogle, https://rework.withgoogle.com/print/guides/5721312655835136/ (archived at https://perma.cc/EG8R-MDKY)

Patel, S (2015) 8 successful products that only exist because of failure, *Forbes*, 16 Jan, www.forbes.com/sites/sujanpatel/2015/01/16/8-successful-products-that-only-exist-because-of-failure/?sh=4df62a161c8c (archived at https://perma.cc/5BKL-WWDH)

Prince, RA (2015) How to learn from your business mistakes, *Forbes*, 23 Jul, www.forbes.com/sites/russalanprince/2015/07/23/how-to-learn-from-your-business-mistakes/?sh=7a6753f51f66 (archived at https://perma.cc/3ES3-3W56)

Ross, JW and Fonstad, NO (2019) Learn from hypotheses, not failures, *MIT Center For Information System Research*, 16 May, https://cisr.mit.edu/publication/2019_0501_LearningFast_RossFonstad (archived at https://perma.cc/9387-ZGLX)

Sutton, RI (2010) Blame is contagious, except when people have high self-worth, *Psychology Today*, 27 Mar, www.psychologytoday.com/intl/blog/work-matters/201003/blame-is-contagious-except-when-people-have-high-self-worth (archived at https://perma.cc/3ZK7-B2NL)

Taylor, A (2009) Fixing up Ford: if business were politics, Detroit would be the Middle East. So how is an outsider like Alan Mulally finding solutions? And why does he seem to be enjoying himself?, *Archive Fortune*, 12 May

Further reading

Braze (2015) 3 marketing experiments that (actually) paid off, 16 Dec, www.braze.com/resources/articles/three-ingenious-marketing-experiments-paid-off (archived at https://perma.cc/ERZ8-AUTM)

Kahneman, D (2012) *Thinking, Fast and Slow*, Farrar, Straus and Giroux, New York, NY

Keller, S (2017) Attracting and retaining the right talent, *McKinsey & Company*, 24 Nov, www.McKinsey.com/capabilities/people-and-organizational-performance/our-insights/attracting-and-retaining-the-right-talent (archived at https://perma.cc/9QWX-YM75)

Kuratko, DF, Montagno, RV and Hornsby, JS (2009) Developing an intrapreneurial assessment instrument for an effective corporate entrepreneurial environment, *Strategic Management Journal*, 11, special issue, pp 49–58

New Republique (2020) How to build a culture of experimentation and be like Amazon, *Inside Retail*, 9 Dec, https://insideretail.com.au/business/how-to-build-a-culture-of-experimentation-and-be-like-amazon-202012 (archived at https://perma.cc/P296-GBTZ)

Toyota Motor Corporation (2019) Toyota production system, https://global.toyota/en/company/vision-and-philosophy/production-system/ (archived at https://perma.cc/RTJ3-AJ84)

Wingard, DJ (2020) Don't fail fast – fail smart, *Forbes*, 21 Feb, www.forbes.com/sites/jasonwingard/2020/02/21/dont-fail-fast--fail-smart/?sh=39ec69ce1b3a (archived at https://perma.cc/Y7W6-JRJN)

15

Alternative but effective routes to e-commerce growth

We've established throughout this book that the fundamental ways to grow a brand are through product, branding, audience building, acquisition, retention, community and gradually expanding into new selling channels.

This chapter aims to shed light on more overlooked yet effective ways of instigating sustained e-commerce growth. By this stage in the book, you're already an expert in building integrated acquisition and retention campaigns founded on evergreen consumer psychology tactics.

The next step in your e-commerce journey is to integrate business development, cultural design and finance to parlay all that you have learned into something much bigger. With the knowledge you will uncover in the following chapters, you will be able to not only 2X your results but 2X the speed at which you achieve them.

In this chapter, I will teach you methods to both supercharge the uptake of your marketing messaging and prepare your business for rapid growth from the ground up by putting the right systems and policies in place to set your brand up for M&A success and rapid growth that results from advanced finance and investment strategies. All in all, it will set the foundation for you to start building brand, culture and thriving profitable ecosystems that are attractive to investors – on top of building performance-enhanced revenue streams based on the essential first principles of e-commerce, as you have learned to do by this stage in the book.

Growth through inclusivity and sustainability

The retail industry is changing rapidly. Customers demand more transparency, better experiences and more ethical practices from the brands they support. E-commerce sales have been growing rapidly for several years now, largely aided by the rapid adoption of new technologies. But as digital commerce moves toward a level of maturity and technology becomes more readily adoptable by even small and mid-market retail businesses, the growth levers that brands need to pull to achieve best-in-market status move further into the intangible, the psychological and the experiential. Don't get me wrong; technology is necessary, operational efficiencies are necessary, and everything in the growth stack is necessary. But the future of commerce will be owned by those businesses that can lever intangible psychological attachments to their physical offering.

If you approach starting a company as just a way to sell products instead of seeing it as something much bigger than that, as something that can capture the hearts and minds of consumers, stand up for the things they believe in and be a beacon for their most dearly held ideas and strongest values – then you will not see your brand grow into something sustainable and scalable in the long run.

The bottom line is that when you start an e-commerce business, you have the opportunity to create a brand that:

- truly stands out from the crowd
- connects deeply with its customers
- is sustainable and scalable
- is inclusive and ethical
- makes a real and positive impact on the world
- surprises and delights your customers

Before you even think about starting your e-commerce business, you need to be mindful of your company's values and mission:

- What are the core values that drive your decision making?
- What are the company's core beliefs, and what do they stand for?
- What is your company's mission?
- Why are you in business?
- What problem are you solving through your company's products or services?
- What benefits will your customers receive from using your products or services?
- What psychological benefits will consumers take away from interacting with your brand experience?

Most importantly, why is your specific product needed, and why is your specific brand needed? Because anyone can sell a product and start a brand – why is your brand needed more than others?

Personally, I love Patagonia as a brand. Every time I buy from Patagonia, I don't only feel good about getting some clothing that is functional and makes me look great, I feel good about buying from Patagonia because it is Patagonia. And Patagonia is synonymous with the most environmentally friendly and sustainable choice in fashion.

It's an ethos that is close to my own heart and one that I have set out to spread to the world through my work with Octillion Capital Partners – where my partners and I grow an ecosystem of inclusive and sustainable brands in the health, beauty and food and beverage industries.

It's not just the right thing to do. When you deliver on sustainability and inclusivity and communicate to your employees and customers, you'll help your business to stand out in the rapidly growing and increasingly rowdy digital commerce industry. Or any industry, for that matter. You will build strong company culture and loyal advocate communities.

Inclusivity

Diversity and inclusion (D&I) are two words that sit on the tip of consumers' tongues, particularly younger-generation Millennial and Gen Z consumers who have typically had lifelong diverse cultural and social experiences. Diversity is not only recognizing that different people are interacting with your brand; it's also taking the time and effort to understand and cater to your valued audiences to create a better customer experience for all. Inclusion is the process of including previously overlooked groups to make everyone feel like they belong. It is removing the subtle barriers (so subtle that you as a brand may not notice them due to blind spots) that exist and overcoming them to delight and surprise customers of all stripes. When people feel like they belong, they're more likely to invest in your company, your tribe, their tribe – whether they are consumers or employees.

Inclusion for your audiences

Inclusivity in advertising means embracing your customers' cultural and social diversity in your brand's educative and creative content. Two-thirds of consumers don't see themselves represented in advertising, and the same amount would like to see brands do more to remove old-fashioned gender roles from their advertising (Lacey, 2018). And a full three-quarters of consumers say that the advertising they see doesn't reflect the world around them (Lacey, 2018). But, just like greenwashing can come back to bite you in the rear end, so can misguided but well-intentioned attempts at inclusivity – at the very least, focus group your planned campaigns with your intended audiences extensively. This is where social listening comes in as a key feedback mechanism to inform your future campaigns, and to cut them short where you can rather than throwing good money after bad.

One great example of inclusive marketing would be something like a campaign for a women's brand for which the advertising featured women athletes of different body types, abilities and ethnicities. Another key aspect of inclusive marketing is social listening, which involves monitoring and analysing online conversations about your brand and industry. Social listening can provide valuable insights into what your audience thinks and feels, allowing you to adjust your messaging and approach accordingly. By prioritizing inclusive marketing and social listening, brands can create campaigns that resonate with diverse audiences and stand out in a crowded marketplace.

Inclusion for your employees

Inclusivity doesn't only matter for your marketing and advertising results. It's also what leads to more profitable and more productive teams. The most inclusive companies for gender are 15 per cent more likely to have returns above their industry's average, and the most racially diverse companies are 35 per cent more likely to beat their industry's average (Hunt et al, 2015). And if your brand wants to innovate, as we covered in Chapter 13, 'Product development cycles for growth', then diversity should be at the forefront of your strategy. Research shows that diverse R&D teams are more likely to come up with radical new innovations (Diaz Garcia et al, 2014). The upside potential of greater diversity is almost unquantifiable, but some estimates suggest we could add $12 trillion to global growth by improving gender equality alone (Woetzel et al, 2015). Your task is simple: build a culture that embraces diversity and your company will not only be more profitable, it will also cut costs in hiring and training as your employee churn dips, and the quality of applicants to new positions improves (Deloitte, 2022).

Sustainability – please don't greenwash

I wanted to take a little extra time to really explain what sustainability means, or, more to the point, what it is not. Sustainable commerce is not just a buzzword you can throw around without responsibility in your marketing and public relations. Greenwashing is the practice of hyping up your brand's sustainability in a way that misleads consumers and gives them a false representation of your brand. It has become so prevalent that there are entire websites like Greenwash.com that track companies to see if their green marketing efforts are legitimate or not. As an example, Greenwash.com claims that as much as 40 per cent of the clothing consumers return to companies to be recycled actually gets shipped abroad to be landfilled or burnt (Greenwash, 2022). For the overwhelming majority of consumers, greenwashing is seen as a huge violation of trust.

Steps that best-in-class sustainable brands are taking to win on sustainability, that you can too, are:

- calculating and offsetting carbon emissions
- setting carbon-negative goals and timelines
- removing all plastic from their products
- recycling materials from pre-loved products
- donating to conservation charities
- funding renewable energy initiatives
- innovating with fully recyclable products
- operating as transparent B-corporations
- using renewable energy sources to power operations

Measuring performance on inclusivity and sustainability

Just as you meticulously track your performance data from campaigns, collect first-party customer data about product perceptions and brand experiences using things like surveys and questionnaires, and use social listening to uncover what people are saying about your products online, you need to do the same for your performance on inclusivity and sustainability for all stakeholders involved. In this case, that is not only your customers but your employees, too.

This data collection endeavour actually starts with your company culture. You must first create a safe environment for your employees to give feedback on how you can improve. Only then can you get the reliable insights you need to do better as a company.

Amplifying your company culture and values

Essentially, your company culture decides the strength of the magnetic pull your brand will have. It is the core foundation of everything you do. Sure, you can amplify that with marketing, but it is culture that sets the tone for what kind of magnitude your brand can operate at. If your company culture is strong, you will be able to scale by a factor of 100; if it's not, then by a factor of 2. Marketing is what sets the base number by which we scale. Let's say that we have two companies, both starting at a base score of 10, and a cultural factor of 2, that's 10^2. One company works hard on their marketing, and doubles their base, but does nothing to work on their culture. Now they're at 20^2, which is equal to 400. The second company still works on their marketing, and increases their base from 10 to 15, and their cultural factor to 3, now they're at 15^3 – do you know what that equals? No need to get out the calculator, because I will tell you: it's 3,375.

Working on company culture has the same effect for brands, because company culture permeates everything you do as a brand. It doesn't just help spread your message, it improves the message you're spreading. It doesn't just affect your team and their life satisfaction, it affects the products they produce, the operational efficiencies they achieve. It finds its way into every crevice of your company, even the ones you don't notice or may not even know exist – the private water cooler chats that lead to new and great product ideas – and it will improve absolutely everything that you do as a brand. Culture is intangible; you can't touch it, but it is felt deeply throughout your organization.

It also helps your brand attract top talent, the kind of talent you need to become a top brand (McQueen, 2018). It's estimated that talent at the top of the chain is approximately 400 per cent more productive than the average employee. But that doesn't tell the whole story for highly complex jobs, where they are a whopping 800 per cent more productive (Aguinis and O'Boyle, 2012; Hunter et al. 1990). And if you thought that you could unlock a huge upside like this without building a strong company culture, you're wrong. One in five high performers is likely to leave your company within the next six months, making them more likely to leave than the average employee. Not to mention less than half of high performers say they're satisfied with their jobs (Willyerd, 2014).

Joint ventures for growth

If you didn't know, a joint venture is when two (or more) commercial organizations come together, jointly deploy their resources and collaborate to develop a competitive advantage in the market. You've heard the saying, 'two heads are better than one', right?

Well, it's no different for businesses. Now, like any relationship, it doesn't always work out. But that never stopped you from dating, did it? When it comes to joint ventures, you still need to vet your deals and find the right match, just like you do when you're dating – but when you do find the right one, you create a powerful force to be reckoned with. Many will say that joint ventures are a great way to dilute the risk involved with launching a new venture, especially financial risk. But they do come with their own inherent risks, many of them to do with the intangibles we have been discussing in this chapter – and by the time tangible results begin to show, the damage has already well and truly been done.

I have been highlighting the importance of company culture in this chapter. Any mismatch between your culture and that of your joint venture partner can doom your relationship to failure – not to mention you run the risk of finding your company culture and brand in the equivalent of therapy for months or years trying to rebuild.

Joint ventures bring with them several advantages for your brand, not least:

- penetrate into new markets or deeper into existing ones
- new revenue streams
- shared intellectual property gains
- skillset synergies and symbiotic relationships
- create higher barriers to entry for competition
- greater economies of scale

Especially attractive for fledgling or bootstrapped DTC brands is the shared investment and expenses and being able to lean on the technical expertise and know-how of another company to fill a hole in your skills matrix. For an up-and-coming brand, a joint venture can do as influencer marketing does – it lends your brand credibility and authority.

In episode #324 of my 2X eCommerce podcast, I sat down with David Perry of Carro to discuss all things 'Collaborative Commerce', and why it could disrupt certain facets of the traditional wholesaling model (2X eCommerce, 2021). Thanks to technological advancements, clean API integrations between platforms and a need to transcend purely technological and inventory breadth and depth advantages, brands are becoming increasingly more collaborative in order to stand out. In Chapter 12, 'Channel marketing' and Chapter 13, 'Product development cycles for growth' collectively, I spoke both about brands shifting to marketplace models because consumers essentially demand the convenience of being able to buy products and their complements in the one place, and about the need for brands to consistently release new products to continue surprising and delighting their customers all the way to sustained attention for their brand. Another way to go about this, albeit as a supplementary route, is through joint venture opportunities that enable you to add products that are not necessarily in your vertical, but perfectly complement what they currently sell. Platforms like Carro and Disco (another co-op commerce network) enable brands to seamlessly add products from other stores into their cart for cross-sells and bundling.

Learnings from high-profile joint ventures

One of the highest profile and more interesting joint ventures on the brand side is the JV between The North Face and Gucci – two brands with very different target markets. And that's what joint ventures are all about: coming together to combine your unique competitive advantages and access new markets or revenue streams as a result. Not to let an opportunity go to waste, The North Face and Gucci also partnered with augmented reality company Niantic and even with Pokémon GO to have their digital collection available for avatars within the popular mobile game (Ferere, 2021). Their digital collection even featured a limited edition X Gucci The North Face tent available in the Pokémon GO app. Together the brands were able to amplify the real-world shopping experience through highly experiential and on-brand (for both The North Face and Gucci) shopping experiences, at a time when in-store retail had been decimated by the coronavirus pandemic.

Undoubtedly it also came with shared costs and expenses, which was no doubt attractive during an uncertain retail environment, where brands were experimenting with new tactics to engage consumers. Why outlay the entire cost yourself, when you can partner up and experiment together? The downside is reduced, and the upside is often multiplied as you get access to symbiotic relationships through cooperation. To truly understand the power that this move had for both brands, it's necessary to put yourself in the shoes of consumers at the time. Many were restricted to how far away they could go from home, and for how long. That meant The North Face products weren't making it out into the wilderness like they used to. They needed a new image to adapt to changing consumer demands and lifestyles. Gucci needed to revamp their brand image, something they have set out to do since at least 2017, to appeal to a more environmentally conscious and values-based Gen Z audience (Danziger, 2017). And both brands needed to enter the digital world.

But when implementing your own JV strategy like this, remember that there are two other levers that brand partnerships typically leverage. These are rarity and exclusivity. Products created through shorter-term joint ventures are typically rare, in that there are not many of them created, and they only run for a limited time. This creates fear of missing out (FOMO), and the time and quantity limits motivate consumers to act. Typically, these products are also exclusively available through select locations so as to maximize the benefit to the specific brands that have innovated together. In this case, the Gucci X The North Face collection was limited to Gucci X The North Face locations and Pokémon GO as a digital channel. Which ensured that the hype and footfall came directly to both brands, and not their retail distribution partners (Gurzki, 2022).

Growing through roll-up M&A

The goal of a merger is to bring together complementary companies to create a new, stronger entity. For example, M&A is often used to expand market share, reach, distribution channels and product lines, or to acquire intellectual property and synergistic innovations and achieve economies of scale. By rolling up the third-, fourth- and fifth-largest companies or brands in your vertical, you can easily boost your way to the number one spot with your new entity.

Hopefully, each brand will bring with it its own unique advantage, so that the value of the rolled-up entity is greater than the sum of its parts. In fact, not hopefully, this is exactly what you should be looking for in a roll-up opportunity. Take for example Oren Schauble, who I mentioned in Chapter 2, 'Collaborative cross-functional growth'. Through M&A roll-ups, as he mentions in episode #358 of the 2X eCommerce podcast, Oren was able to build himself a share in a consumer and retail empire. How? He achieved this through horizontal and vertical integrations, rolling up competitor brands with synergistic opportunities (2X eCommerce, 2022). The first stage of Oren's strategy involved a merger with two other existing brands. The second stage was to merge with a public shell, specifically set up to acquire more companies for their portfolio, and to facilitate their going public. The whole process, Oren says, took two years, so M&A rollups definitely aren't a quick-fix solution, or for the faint-hearted. Oren's initial horizontal integration was to merge a retail store and a brand together, both based out of California. He then added vertical integration into the mix, bringing in a distribution company from Oregon. The strategy paid off, and the group of companies that Oren and his co-founders built was valued at $80 million when it went public. In 2021 alone, that company did $60 million in revenue (2X eCommerce, 2022).

But economies of scale can only be achieved if you actually take steps to integrate the businesses together into one cohesive system. If you don't do this, you are essentially managing separate entities, even if they have the same ownership. Functions need to be streamlined and consolidated, and tech stacks merged and integrated together. However, by doing this, you open your business up to much faster growth, and even higher-value multiples. With every M&A comes essentially the acquisition of new customers that you can now up-sell and cross-sell to – which is the simplest way to ensure that your M&A roll-up strategy results in a revenue effect that is greater than the sum of its parts. Although I don't want to leave you thinking that M&A roll-ups are your free ticket to fast growth. A roll-up strategy will not generate revenue on its own. They require meticulous planning, thorough integration, project management and a clear plan for realizing synergies and growth opportunities. Otherwise all you are doing is acquiring new revenue streams (and spending a lot of money in the process) – that's additive growth. What you want is multiplicative growth.

Things to look out for when pursuing an M&A roll-up strategy are retail verticals with positive growth expectations based on reputable forecasts, returns to scale, a lack of industry consolidation and no clear industry leader. Ignore your due diligence on these five factors at your peril, because research shows that two-thirds of M&A roll-ups fail to deliver value for investors (Carrol and Mui, 2008). Sebastian Rymarz, Heyday CEO overseeing the company's aggressive acquisitions strategy, says that on average out of every 100 brands they review, they only consider buying one (Lunden, 2021). That's not 'buy', that's 'consider' – they may not even acquire it. So you can see the level of scrutiny a brand should undergo before even considering acquiring it. But when done right, M&A can be such a profitable strategy that companies specializing in rolling up consumer and retail brands (Hall, 2021).

Public relations for growth

Today's consumers have grown increasingly sceptical of brands, and rightfully so. In light of recent scandals like Tropicana accidentally making light of alcoholism, Volkswagen's famous emissions cheating or Abercrombie & Fitch stating that their brand is 'exclusionary' and only caters to 'cool kids' as opposed to being inclusive, and other high-profile PR nightmares, consumers are taking a much closer look at the companies they support (Velasco, 2013; Hakim, 2016; Honkus, 2020).

Today's consumers demand to know where their products come from, how they are made and what values really stand behind them. Delivering on customers' needs in these areas is not only the right thing to do, but also necessary to thrive in this new era of transparency and accountability. Just as company culture and values, and as an extension, a brand's story, have become some of the most important factors for today's consumers when it comes to buying from brands, they have also become the key ingredients for driving and capturing the news cycle. So, it naturally makes sense to talk about public relations in this chapter, which is why I have left it until now.

It is culture that sets the tone for the kind of press that you get organically, and the kind of press that you can get with a little public relations work on your end. Your company culture sets the tone for how the news cycle talks about your brand.

Without a strong, well-defined culture, a set of clear values for your target market, and compelling founder and brand stories, your brand will simply fall flat when it comes to public relations. It's different when it comes to paid ads – Meta and Google will take your money for any campaign you want to run, whether you have a compelling brand story or not.

Public relations, on the other hand, deals with limited publishing space and output capacity. Several journalists have incentive to write articles that attract and drive traffic on digital versions of publications and physical publications can only publish a limited number of stories before they run out of pages.

To kickstart your public relations strategy, and capitalize on your latent brand equity, you will need to have a PR specialist (or agency) that can network with journalists and editors at your target media outlets, build outreach lists and uncover PR opportunities for your brand.

They will look at your messaging from a public relations perspective rather than a marketing perspective, with an understanding of what messages drive newsworthiness in the current media climate – which may very well be different to the messaging that drives sales for your brand from your social media and paid advertising.

As you grow you will also need a spokesperson who is comfortable and adept at giving video interviews. If you're a founder, it's unavoidable that the press will want to speak with you directly – you should undergo at least some media training. You will be surprised at the nuances involved.

Guerilla marketing

When brand-building teams sit in dark rooms in undisclosed locations and prepare their public relations strategies, often the most enthusiastically discussed topic is guerilla marketing or PR stunts. These are the sexiest of all PR activities and can certainly get your brand huge reach. But it's also hit-and-miss. You simply can't hinge your entire PR strategy on getting consistent PR through public relations stunts. Nor should you, unless the Joker archetype is a significant part of your brand personality. Everything you do in your growth stack is a reflection of your brand, but not only that, it also reflects back upon your brand, altering perceptions and turning your brand into something else in the eyes of consumers. You can either reaffirm the brand you have set out for yourself or let your customers define it from their interpretation of your messaging.

PR stunts and guerilla marketing often bring a good dose of playfulness and the Joker archetype. So unless these are large parts of your brand personality, PR stunts aren't something you want to be doing too many of, even if you could reliably generate PR this way. In the cross-functional digital commerce world, you are only guaranteed that each node in the growth stack affects another, not that there will be a positive symbiotic relationship between them. It may be the case that something you do in PR has a negative effect on your brand, despite your best intentions. Keep it simple, and don't give consumers cause for confusion. Or put differently, don't let the PR tail wag the brand dog.

One great example of brand-driven PR stunts is Weight Watchers' 2018 healthy food drive through London's Borough market. The free drive-through, featuring delicious dishes like oat waffles, butternut squash falafels and carbonara – being healthy and tasty options of traditionally tasty but not-so-healthy foods – was a perfect extension of the Weight Watchers brand (Peterson, 2022). The PR stunt garnered attention for Weight Watchers, generating brand and product offering awareness and trial uptake of their new product. Not to mention, by giving something away for free, Weight Watchers triggered reciprocity, which, you will recall from Chapter 6, is a powerful tool of persuasion.

Or take WePay as an example, who communicated their values superbly using little more than a block of ice. Now, before you think this was a climate change play, it wasn't. You see, WePay's main competitor, PayPal, was copping some flak online for freezing users' accounts. So what did WePay do? They sent a giant block of ice full of cash to PayPal's annual developer conference. The stunt got them confronted by security, onto the first page of *TechCrunch*, a 300 per cent increase in traffic, and more than doubled their signups (Bodnar, 2020). Whenever you launch a campaign like this, it's rarely enough to simply launch it and let the press do the rest. Your entire messaging system needs to be aligned with the public relations stunt.

Wrapping up

In this chapter we have covered some important alternative routes to growth, including advanced M&A strategies specific to e-commerce brands, how to build a brand rather than just building revenue streams through ESG, and how diversity and inclusivity set your brand up to springboard to greater growth. But that's not the end of your alternative routes to growth, so we're not wrapping up just yet. In the next chapter we will cover the all-important pillar of finance and how you can use e-commerce-specific financing strategies to accelerate growth for your brand.

References

2X eCommerce (2021) S06 EP50, How collaborative commerce could potentially disrupt traditional wholesaling, https://2xecommerce.com/podcast/ep324/ (archived at https://perma.cc/LG3G-SNLX)

2X eCommerce (2022) S07 EP16, 9-figure M&A roll-ups and product innovation, https://2xecommerce.com/podcast/ep358/ (archived at https://perma.cc/ RU8X-ZNSJ)

Aguinis, H and O'Boyle Jr E (2012) The best and the rest: revisiting the norm of normality in individual performance, *Personal Psychology*, 65 (1), Spring 2012, pp 79–119

Bodnar, K (2020) How a block of ice increased one company's customers by 225%, *HubSpot*, 5 Sep, https://blog.hubspot.com/blog/tabid/6307/bid/7007/how-a-block-of-ice-increased-one-company-s-customers-by-225.aspx (archived at https://perma.cc/5UR9-CWRT)

Carroll, P and Mui, C (2008) Seven ways to fail big, *Harvard Business Review*, Sep, https://hbr.org/2008/09/seven-ways-to-fail-big (archived at https://perma.cc/ EK2N-V6CS)

Danziger, PN (2017) Gucci's cracked the luxury code with millennials, thanks to its dream team of Bizzarri and Michele, *Forbes*, 16 Nov, www.forbes.com/sites/ pamdanziger/2017/11/16/guccis-cracked-the-luxury-code-with-millennials-thanks-to-its-dream-team-of-bizzarri-and-michele/?sh=8e7f0715239b (archived at https://perma.cc/2P9L-LT7B)

Deloitte (2022) Inclusive mobility: how mobilizing a diverse workforce can drive business performance, www2.deloitte.com/content/dam/Deloitte/us/Documents/ Tax/us-tax-inclusive-mobility-mobilize-diverse-workforce-drive-business-performance.pdf (archived at https://perma.cc/JL44-VMPQ)

Diaz-Garcia, C, Gonzalez-Moreno, A and Saez-Martinez, FJ (2014) Gender diversity within R&D teams: its impact on radicalness of innovation, *Organization & Management*, 15 (2), pp 149–60

Ferere, C (2021) Gucci Pins: The North Face x Gucci Outerwear collection is taking back retail, *Forbes*, 8 Jan, www.forbes.com/sites/cassellferere/2021/01/08/ gucci-pins-the-north-face-x-gucci-outerwear-collection-is-taking-back-retail/?sh=7220849f2219 (archived at https://perma.cc/N2UJ-MQCM)

Greenwash (2022) H&M – Greenwash, https://greenwash.com/brands/h-and-m/ (archived at https://perma.cc/P86X-MU23)

Gurzki, H (2022) How luxury brands are manufacturing scarcity in the digital economy, *Harvard Business Review*, 28 Jan, https://hbr.org/2022/01/how-luxury-brands-are-manufacturing-scarcity-in-the-digital-economy (archived at https:// perma.cc/J67Y-Q9FT)

Hakim, D (2016) VW's crisis strategy: forward, reverse, u-turn, *The New York Times*, 26 Feb, www.nytimes.com/2016/02/28/business/international/vws-crisis-strategy-forward-reverse-u-turn.html (archived at https://perma.cc/6GVL-3NRG)

Hall, C (2021) E-commerce marketplace aggregators are hot on Thrasio's heels as companies raise $2.3B, *Crunchbase News*, 2 Mar, https://news.crunchbase.com/ fintech-ecommerce/e-commerce-marketplace-aggregators-are-hot-on-thrasios-heels-as-companies-raise-2-3b/ (archived at https://perma.cc/RV89-LANA)

Honkus, M (2020) Tropicana apologizes and removes ad campaign encouraging parents to drink mimosas, *PEOPLE*, 18 Dec, https://people.com/food/tropicana-apologizes-for-ad-campaign-encouraging-parents-to-drink-mimosas/ (archived at https://perma.cc/9DR4-3EUX)

Hunt, DV, Layton, D and Prince, S (2015) Why diversity matters, *McKinsey & Company*, 1 Jan, www.McKinsey.com/capabilities/people-and-organizational-performance/our-insights/why-diversity-matters (archived at https://perma.cc/SE8W-KTUU)

Hunter, JE, Judiesch, MK, and Schmidt, FL (1990) Individual differences in output variability as a function of job complexity, *Journal of Applied Psychology*, February 1990, 75 (1), pp 28–42

Lacey, N (2018) Advertising is out of Sync with world's consumers, Ipsos, 2 Oct, www.ipsos.com/en-us/news-polls/Advertising-out-of-sync-with-consumers# (archived at https://perma.cc/DK2J-GK3G)

Lunden, I (2021) Heyday raises $555M to buy up and scale more D2C brands in the Amazon marketplace universe, *TechCrunch*, 16 Nov, https://techcrunch.com/2021/11/16/heyday-raises-555m-to-buy-up-and-scale-more-d2c-brands-on-the-amazon-marketplace-universe/ (archived at https://perma.cc/8U7F-6B2S)

McQueen, N (2018) Workplace culture trends: the key to hiring (and keeping) top talent in 2018, *Linkedin*, 26 Jun, https://blog.linkedin.com/2018/june/26/workplace-culture-trends-the-key-to-hiring-and-keeping-top-talent (archived at https://perma.cc/E3TJ-E5EZ)

Peterson, K (2022) PR stunt – meaning & examples, *Mmarxcommunications*, 21 May, https://marxcommunications.com/pr-stunt-meaning/ (archived at https://perma.cc/A2XK-NY8H)

Velasco, S (2013) Mike Jeffries wants no fat customers at A&F. Bad business?, *Christian Science Monitor*, 9 May, www.csmonitor.com/Business/2013/0509/Mike-Jeffries-wants-no-fat-customers-at-A-F.-Bad-business (archived at https://perma.cc/A4FE-ELM7)

Willyerd, K (2014) What high performers want at work, *Harvard Business Review*, 18 Nov, https://hbr.org/2014/11/what-high-performers-want-at-work (archived at https://perma.cc/498H-MNVX)

Woetzel, J, Madgavkar, A, Ellingrud, K, Labaye, E, Devillard, S, Kutcher, E, Manyika, J, Dobbs, R and Krishnan, M (2015) How advancing women's equality can add $12 trillion to global growth, *McKinsey & Company*, 1 Sep, www.McKinsey.com/featured-insights/employment-and-growth/how-advancing-womens-equality-can-add-12-trillion-to-global-growth (archived at https://perma.cc/NCR9-QB6F)

Further reading

2X eCommerce (2021) Ori Goronovitch: Advanced performance marketing for Q4 and BFCM, *YouTube*, 25 Oct, www.youtube.com/watch?v=0w-T5RwLdyJE&t=1090s (archived at https://perma.cc/9CYV-7QHJ)

Capgemini (2020) Consumer products and retail: How sustainability is fundamentally changing consumer preferences, *Capgemini Research Institute*, www.capgemini.com/gb-en/wp-content/uploads/sites/5/2022/05/Final-Infographic-1.pdf (archived at https://perma.cc/D48J-M7NS)

Coffey, A (2019) *The Private Equity Playbook: Management's guide to working with private equity*, Lioncrest Publishing, Austin, TX

Deibel, W (2018) *Buy Then Build: How acquisition entrepreneurs outsmart the startup game*, Lioncrest Publishing, Austin, TX

Gara, A (2021) The $30 billion kitty: meet the investor who made a fortune on pet food, *Forbes*, 27 Sep, www.forbes.com/sites/antoinegara/2021/09/27/the-30-billion-kitty-meet-the-investor-who-made-a-fortune-on-pet-food/?sh=7d36c70735dc (archived at https://perma.cc/TN5H-ZZ55)

16

Finance: what you should know and an overview for growth

Engineering e-commerce growth through finance

Finance and capital are crucial for e-commerce businesses. Just like how a car needs fuel to run, e-commerce stores need capital to grow and succeed. Without adequate financing, an e-commerce store will struggle to expand, improve its product offering and compete with other businesses in the market. Access to capital enables e-commerce businesses to invest in inventory, marketing and technology, which are all essential for driving growth and staying competitive. In short, it allows brands to fund, innovate and integrate the key growth levers in their cross-functional growth stack. Estimates indicate that 90 per cent of e-commerce businesses fail within the first four months. This high rate of failure can be attributed to a variety of factors, including lack of capital and pricing and costing issues (Tariq, 2021). Even established brands like Diapers.com, which was later acquired by Amazon, have struggled to turn a profit. In fact, of the top 10 largest consumer and retail mergers facilitated by leveraged buyouts in the United States, at least 50 per cent have filed for bankruptcy or been on the brink of doing so (Unglesbee, 2022). As you continue to grow your e-commerce business, access to growth capital will become increasingly important. This capital serves as the foundation of your company and the fuel that drives accelerated growth. In this chapter I will provide you with the steps you need to take, when to take them, and how to navigate the unique financial landscape of the e-commerce industry.

The modern finance stack for e-commerce stores

Why do e-commerce businesses need financing?

According to Sean De Clerq on the 2X eCommerce Podcast, episode #295, buying directly from a factory often requires a deposit of 30–50 per cent for the production run (2X eCommerce, 2021). Then you must wait a month for the production slot, pay for the inventory in full and wait another month for it to arrive. If you sell through a channel like a big box retailer, you may be on payment terms of up to 90 days, meaning it could take up to six months to see a profit from the inventory you purchased. In these situations, capital, financing and better payment terms can help sustain growth. However, it's important to have a solid business plan before taking on debt.

Sometimes you just need capital, financing and the ability to negotiate better payment terms to grow sustainably. Otherwise, you're purchasing inventory in $10,000 spurts and waiting for that $10k to turn into $20k so you have another $10k of profit to fund more inventory, and that $10k only ever turns into another $20k, half of which is profit, so you're always playing with the same $10k orders. It's walking a fine line and can actually really hold back your growth. Every now and then you need some fuel to take you to the next level and get you playing with bigger sums to scale to meet demand. Not to mention that larger order sizes often mean bulk discounts, so you can even buy up several more months of inventory to lock in economies of scale on the supplier side.

Now I will outline the top financing and funding options used by e-commerce stores today. How will you know which one is right for you? Well, you should take some advice from the e-commerce finance specialists at our annual Commerce Accel event in 2022. Leonardo Felisberto, global head of business development at Seller Funding, says to explore as many options as possible to find the best vendor for your needs – options that I will outline for you in this chapter (Felisberto, personal communication, 22 September 2022). Juan Braschi of Boopos adds that sometimes you need to build a custom solution based on your needs from the offerings of several different providers. After reading this chapter you will have all the tools you need (Braschi, personal communication, 22 September 2022).

Short-duration financing

Picture this: business is booming and orders are increasing every day; you see the potential for exponential growth but you're also facing a cash flow crunch. You can't possibly fund all the expenses you need to scale, like paid media, inventory, freight and marketing. You need to place a bulk order, lead times on freight are long and you need to scale your marketing simultaneously in preparation. In situations like this, you want some kind of short-term capital injection. Commonly, because investors usually aren't too excited to fund your inventory purchases, e-commerce businesses need to turn to some kind of debt-based financing. But traditional bank loans get loaned out all at once, and you have to start making the repayments immediately. To fill the gap in short-term cash crunches in a way that is catered to the specific needs of e-commerce businesses, options like revenue-based financing and purchase order and inventory financing have gained popularity.

REVENUE-BASED FINANCING

Revenue-based financing provides funding for your business, but you only need to pay it back when there is a commensurate return on investment from the funding through sales. If sales slow down, your repayment amounts become smaller as well. There are many revenue-based financing options available to sellers today, but it's a relatively new option in the e-commerce industry. It can be a good way to get the funding you need without giving up too much equity (typically you don't give up any at all, nor do you need to put up assets as collateral), and the approval process is typically quick and algorithmic. However, there may be restrictions on how you can use the funding. It's worth evaluating multiple providers to find the best fit for your business. Rates on revenue-based financing can typically be as low as several per cent up to 35 per cent so it pays to evaluate many different providers to find the best fit.

PURCHASE ORDER AND INVENTORY FINANCING

Purchase order financing is similar to revenue-based financing, but it is only applicable to specific purchase orders or arrangements with your suppliers. If you have a good reputation and solid financials, you may be able to negotiate to have your inventory sent without payment. Alternatively, a third party will finance the purchase of your inventory, pay your suppliers, and you will pay them back in instalments. This type of financing can be expensive, with monthly interest rates ranging from 1–6 per cent and annual rates of 5–20 per cent or even 50 per cent in some cases (Treece and Tarver, 2022). Given that the average margin for an e-commerce store is around 45 per cent, that is really not leaving a lot of profit. While it can be useful for saving your supply chain, it is important to stick to a desired debt-to-equity ratio and work closely with your CFO to develop a strategy.

NON-EQUITY CROWDFUNDING

Non-equity crowdfunding is the crowdfunding that you are most likely familiar with already. It's platforms like Kickstarter and Indigogo that allow you to raise funds for your business with product pre-sales or donations. There are even platforms like Kickfurther that blend inventory financing and non-equity crowdfunding. Inventory crowdfunding enables anybody to invest in funding an e-commerce brand's product launch. As the brand, you get working capital, and the investor receives their return when your inventory sells. It's a great way to avoid stockouts, given that approximately 87 per cent of consumers buy from competitors if their primary brand was out of stock (2X eCommerce, 2021).

Medium-duration financing

CROWDFUNDED CREDIT

This is not like a Kickstarter campaign where you crowdfund your product idea in exchange for delivery of that product at a later date. Crowdfunded credit is mostly targeted at main street businesses, but there is a trend of them moving into e-commerce. Crowdfunded credit platforms allow members of the public to participate in funding small business loans for the expansion of businesses. Unlike RBFs, fundraising campaigns through crowdfunded credit platforms can finance fixed capital expenditure.

Loan repayments are typically on a monthly instalment basis and investors get payouts each quarter. Companies you might find helpful include Mainvest and Honeycomb Credit. I have added more providers relevant to online retailers at 2xecommerce.com/book/chapter16.

Long-duration funding

EQUITY CROWDFUNDING

Equity crowdfunding allows you to raise funds for your business by selling equity directly to investors, who receive a return on their investment once the business is profitable. This is different from selling a large number of shares to a single private equity investor or angel investor, as you sell a small number of shares to a group of several investors. However, it is highly regulated and you need to limit the amount you take from individual non-accredited investors or you could have your ability to offer shares revoked and even have to pay back any investments made (Black and Tarver, 2022). While you may receive more money in exchange for less of your equity, you do not get the dedicated support of a single private equity partner or angel investor. For investors, these equity shares are typically illiquid, and the risk of fraud is high due to asymmetries in information or businesses using loopholes in regulations to deceive less savvy investors (Corporate Finance Institute, 2022a).

I have an extensive and regularly updated list of equity crowdfunding platforms at 2xecommerce.com/book/chapter16.

ASSET-BASED LENDERS

Asset-based lending is a type of financing where assets act as collateral for the loan. This type of lending is typically used to satisfy a business's short- to long-term funding needs and is less risky for lenders, resulting in lower interest rates. However, it is riskier for the borrower as they could potentially lose their assets if they are unable to pay the balance of the loan. The loan-to-value ratio is typically higher if the assets used as collateral are liquid (easy to sell) (Corporate Finance Institute, 2022b). Examples of assets that can be used to secure a loan include inventory, property, plant and equipment and securities. The documentation required for asset-based lending is typically more extensive than for revenue-based funding, but having assets as collateral can help you take advantage of lower rates. It's important to carefully review any additional fees and charges when considering this type of financing. While revenue-based funding typically only allows you to pay for inventory and marketing, asset-based loans can be used to fund real-estate and machinery purchases among other things.

Summing up financing tools

Debt has a bad reputation in some circles, with some people saying never to take on debt, while others say that to make money, you need to spend money, and without debt they would never have been able to scale their businesses as far as they have. The truth is, there are pros and cons to taking on debt, just as there are with taking investment or not taking investment. Venture capitalists, for example, can provide the cash injection needed to propel a brand into a more powerful position, but at the cost of a chunk of equity. Debt finance is similar, but instead of losing equity, you retain it and pay a pound of flesh in the form of interest rates. Whether or not to take on debt depends on your business goals and whether you recognize a real opportunity. Growth often necessitates some kind of finance, especially if you want to avoid stockouts and maintain good customer experience.

As 2X eCommerce guest and CEO of Kickfurther, Sean De Clercq says in episode #295, if your business is growing, then you always need to be funding more inventory than your last batch of inventory, and the revenue for that doesn't come for another six months, and even before that, you're up for another even bigger batch of inventory (2X eCommerce, 2021). And customers aren't patient; if they can't buy from you, they'll find someone else to buy from, so you can't afford to be out of stock. And if you're looking to come from nothing and achieve market dominance, then you need extra rocket fuel for that. At the end of the day, there is always an overall cost of financing and an overall cost of not financing – which is slower growth.

Accounting and bookkeeping for e-commerce

Keeping accurate financial records is crucial for e-commerce businesses of all sizes. It's a foundational pillar for decision making and forecasting, and helps identify potential problems before they escalate. Some general tips:

- Invest in an automated finance system that is intuitive and easy to use, and offers mobile access.
- Integrate all your information systems, and consider building your own database for customized reports.
- Staying on top of your metrics enables you to answer key questions and make informed financial commitments.
- Consider using an accrual basis for accounting instead of a cash basis to get a more realistic picture of your business's financial health. If your accounting is run on a cash basis, buying inventory in bulk in January will show a huge loss for the month, and then you will show a huge profit for February to April when you sell that inventory.
- Clean books are essential for potential buyers, and can help you get a higher multiple when it comes to raising.

- When reporting, compare month to month.
- Each financial report should include not only key numbers but also key events and happenings in that week or month, like a boost in revenue due to a lucky bit of PR.
- Be cautious with your debt and maintain a healthy debt-to-equity ratio.

And as Nathan Hirsch, CEO at AccountsBalance and 2X eCommerce podcast #364 guest, said, no founder or entrepreneur should be doing their own books. His first reason is that it's just not a good use of your time when you can focus on growth and operations. His second reason is that you're probably just not that good at bookkeeping and will need to pay someone to fix up your books later down the road, which tends to be much more expensive than actually just doing them right in the first place (2X eCommerce, 2022).

Reporting essentials

Having data and then doing nothing with it is senseless. If you do that, then you've just created expensive systems and processes that aren't generating a return on investment. So here's what you need to report monthly, or every few weeks within your business to keep your finger on the pulse. You need to carve out time in your calendar to go over these results with your team and discuss what they might mean for your company, your products, operations and marketing.

Key reports to put together for your company include your profit and loss statement, cash flow statement and balance sheet.

In your reports, you want to include key metrics like:

- debt-to-equity ratio
- affiliate commissions
- cost of goods sold
- non-operating income
- cash conversion cycle (payback period)
- inventory turnover
- operating profit margin
- transaction volume
- net contribution margin

When it comes to your debt-to-equity ratio, most businesses will typically have a ratio of 2 or less, but fixed asset-heavy industries like mining may have a ratio higher than 2. As we are in the e-commerce industry here, dear readers, a debt-to-equity ratio of around 2–2.5 is a good benchmark for your ceiling. Any higher and it is a risk for your company and will make it hard to secure any additional financing or funding.

Building your finance team

There are three main roles that you will need to fill on the finance side to ensure you keep your head above water and can capitalize on opportunities to scale intelligently. The first is a tax expert. Your tax expert will cover your general tax strategies and end-of-year taxes.

They will also work closely with your second key finance hire, your bookkeeper. But before you go out and hire a full-time bookkeeper, you probably don't need one until you're at over $1 million in revenue; until then, an agency or freelancer will suffice.

Once you're clearing a few million a year, you're now getting into CFO territory. Now, that might be a full-time CFO, but chances are you will make use of a fractional CFO, who will be able to develop your long-term finance strategy. Of course, you might bring on a CFO earlier than that, and there's really no bad time to have that kind of support, with many revenue-based financing options for e-commerce stores taking on clients that are doing much less than $1 million per year.

Additionally, Nathan Hirsch recommends keeping your chartered private accountant (CPA) and your bookkeeper separate for a few reasons. The first is, well, economical. A CPA is typically more expensive than a bookkeeper, so by keeping the functions separate, you're saving costs.

The second reason is very much a practical one. Hirsch says that your CPA will be focused on bookkeeping so that they can do taxes with the result of their bookkeeping. A dedicated bookkeeper will focus on taxes and give you the information you need to make decisions every month (2X eCommerce, 2022).

Setting the right financial foundations starts with getting the right team and the right intellectual capital in place. It will serve you well all the way through to acquisition, private equity funding or IPO.

Pricing and margins

In any e-commerce business, your marketing and finance team must be aligned on pricing strategies for the company. Different pricing strategies will have vastly different effects on the company's short- and long-term balance sheets. No pricing decision should be made without collaboration between finance and marketing and modelling of the expected results. That's modelling with an upper and lower bound so that finance can see the likely best- and worst-case scenarios and accept or reject the proposal accordingly – or of course, shift things around to make room for the strategy.

For e-commerce stores, the average gross margin is about 45 per cent (eCommerce Fuel, 2022).

Wrapping up

This book is about cross-functional e-commerce growth – I cannot emphasize enough how critical financial engineering and education are to leading and growing an e-commerce business. By understanding the different financing options available and making smart financial decisions, you can fuel your business's growth and set yourself up for long-term success.

Now that you have a solid understanding of finance for e-commerce stores, it's time to focus on building your growth roadmap. In the next chapter, we will discuss how to create a growth roadmap that will guide your business through all stages of its e-commerce journey.

For more resources and the latest financial playbooks, including up-to-date lists of the e-commerce financing options and platforms, be sure to visit our website at 2xecommerce.com/book/chapter16.

References

2X eCommerce (2021) S06 EP21, Reducing cash conversion cycles with crowd-funded inventory finance, https://2xecommerce.com/podcast/ep295/ (archived at https://perma.cc/3YAP-52XE)

2X eCommerce (2022) S07 EP21, What you need to know about bookkeeping for ecommerce, https://2xecommerce.com/podcast/ep364/ (archived at https://perma.cc/U39U-LM3G)

Black, M and Tarver, J (2022) Equity crowdfunding: what is it & how does it work? *Forbes*, 31 Mar, www.forbes.com/advisor/business-loans/equity-crowdfunding/ (archived at https://perma.cc/W832-RYDJ)

Corporate Finance Institute (2022a) Equity Crowdfunding, 11 Nov, https://corporatefinanceinstitute.com/resources/valuation/equity-crowdfunding/ (archived at https://perma.cc/2E7G-C326)

Corporate Finance Institute (2022b) Asset-based Lending, 7 Nov, https://corporatefinanceinstitute.com/resources/commercial-lending/asset-based-lending/ (archived at https://perma.cc/7H94-W4XA)

eCommerceFuel (2022) eCommerce Trends Report 2022, 14 Jul, www.ecommercefuel.com/ecommerce-trends/ (archived at https://perma.cc/SU8B-TY4B)

Tariq, O (2021) We need to talk about e-commerce: too many digital brands are failing, and we need new tools to help keep founders on track, *Forbes*, 22 Jul, www.forbes.com/sites/forbestechcouncil/2021/07/22/we-need-to-talk-about-e-commerce-too-many-digital-brands-are-failing-and-we-need-new-tools-to-help-keep-founders-on-track/?sh=354047eb1c9c (archived at https://perma.cc/L65C-KMY6)

Treece, K and Tarver, J (2022) Purchase order financing: what it is and how it can help you, *Forbes*, 20 Oct, www.forbes.com/advisor/business-loans/purchase-order-financing/ (archived at https://perma.cc/4F7V-VLDL)

Unglesbee, B (2022) 18 retailers at risk of bankruptcy as consumers tighten wallets in 2022, *Retail Dive*, 3 Oct, www.retaildive.com/news/retailers-risk-bankruptcy-consumers-tighten-wallets-2022/632828/ (archived at https://perma.cc/QHB4-BR2K)

17

Tracking success: team makeup and key metrics

KPIs to drive your commerce success

KPIs (key performance indicators) are a set of key metrics that can help your business measure progress. Best-in-class brands pay meticulous attention to their analytics, focus on the right KPIs and use them to assess the performance of their business. KPIs help identify areas for improvement and inform decision making. Given that much of KPI capture can be automated, you should instate an organization-wide dashboard and dashboards for key functions in your business. There are several business performance metrics out there, but intelligence in 'business intelligence' is knowing what to track and how to build effective dashboards (not cluttered with geeky metrics) that help you make better decisions in your organization. In this chapter I will give you insights into which metrics you need to be measuring and show you how I structure some of my own dashboards for fast and effective decision making. We will cover operational and financial metrics that set the foundation for success, as well as marketing and customer success KPIs that will hone your brand's focus on the levers that will bring accelerated growth. You may already be familiar with some of the metrics we will uncover, but I'm sure there will be others that are new to you or serve as a friendly reminder to aid your decision making. The real insights this chapter will unfold are in reframing how you think of data, metrics and KPIs in the context of driving growth. However, there is a big difference between a metric and a KPI or an OKR. A metric is just data, and while it might help inform decision making, without KPIs your organization will lack a clear and strong sense of direction. Key performance indicators need to be specific to your business targets. That's why it is essential that you first benchmark your KPIs based on industry or past performance data and then report on your progress toward these KPIs regularly. Some metrics you will check weekly or bi-weekly, others monthly or quarterly. As a general rule, choose a time period that if you were to go without insights into that metric, you would likely make an error or miscalculation in your decision making. For inventory purchasing that might be monthly, for ad campaigns it might be weekly. Ensure that your reporting is more frequent than this level. With that in mind, let's dig deep into the metrics that you will use to track your progress towards the key results that matter for your organization.

Operations

Organizational KPIs form the lifeblood of your organization, because operations are critical at every stage in your value chain, from inventory and purchasing to your last-mile shipping. Let's kick off with the key metrics you need to track at the beginning of your supply chain (when you're purchasing), then move through to shipping and delivery. So, let's dive in.

Inventory and purchasing

Avoiding stock-outs and ensuring speedy last-mile logistics begins right at the start of the supply chain. That means your operations teams should have clear KPIs to keep lead times to a minimum (while maintaining quality, of course).

In order to deliver on your last-mile logistics promise, it is important to eliminate large outliers from your inventory lead times by ensuring 'average' computations are based on *median average* rather than *mean average*.

So when looking at average manufacturing times and freight lead times focus on the median in order to eliminate large outliers that could wreak havoc on your customer satisfaction.

Taking the median lead time will show you suppliers and manufacturers (or even freight routes) that are less reliable, while taking the median will obscure any outliers here.

If you utilize third-party suppliers and manufacturers, the key metrics for inventory and supply chain management are:

• supplier defect rate

- supplier lead time
- compliance rate
- purchase order accuracy
- vendor availability

Last-mile delivery

Total order fulfilment time

Total order fulfilment time is a key metric in your KPI growth stack. To optimize it, trial and experiment with different order fulfilment processes, such as Amazon FBA, a third-party logistics solution across multiple locations, or operational efficiencies within your own logistical structures. Customers have high standards when it comes to order fulfilment times. To narrow down inefficiencies in your chain and deliver a customer-centric last-mile experience, I suggest breaking your order fulfilment time down into source time, production time and delivery time. This will help you identify any inefficiencies and improve the overall customer experience.

Other last-mile metrics

- On-time delivery.
- Damage-free delivery.
- Order fill: the percentage of orders successfully delivered on the first shipment.
- In-full delivery: the percentage of deliveries delivered to the right customer in full.

Inventory-related KPIs

Inventory-related KPIs and the accurate measurement of associated metrics are essential for retailers. As Jason Wong, founder of Doe Lashes, said during one of our Commerce Accel Conferences, the average retailer has about 6 per cent accuracy on their inventory, and a study by the IHL group shows that retailers have lost over $1 trillion due to revenue distortion (Buzek, 2015). This leads to over-ordering and holding dead inventory that is sucking up all your profits, and on the other end of the stick, stock-outs that frustrate customers and tank your revenues. But going deeper than that, metrics related to your inventory and supply chain processes provide many more powerful insights into the health of your business and product offering.

Return rate

A high return rate is obviously not a good sign for your business, as it indicates that you're giving a large proportion of your revenues back as refunds.

To calculate your return rate divide the number of items that were sold and then returned by the total number of items sold during that period. Then multiply the result by 100 to get your return rate.

Inventory turnover ratio

This is how often you sell and replenish your stock during a certain time period, for example, in a year. A low ratio tells you that you're holding onto stock too long and it's not selling fast enough. You could solve this by bundling low-turnover goods with higher-turnover goods to move them out of your inventory backlog and reduce your purchase frequency of these items.

Basket size

Your basket size is the average number of items that are in each cart. That is, the average number of goods that your customers purchase in each bundle. This is a great metric to assess alongside your average order value. By comparing the two against your historical data, you will be able to tell if customers are buying more items or buying fewer more expensive items. You could also create a custom metric for the average value of products purchased to track this separately.

Average order value

Your average order might seem like something so simple that it's hardly worth taking the time to write a paragraph about. Calculating it seems easy enough, right? Take the total value of your orders, and then divide it by the total number of orders. But, to strip away the noise from the signal, and get sophisticated insights, ensure that you take out the shipping and handling charges and discounts from your average order value to avoid an inflated view of this metric. You could also calculate the average value returned for each order, that is the total value of all returned items divided by the number of orders, not the returned orders, but the total number of orders. That is the amount you can reasonably be expected to be returned as part of each order. By doing this, you really strip away your average order value to the amount that you can reasonably expect to keep from each order.

Cash conversion cycles

A cash conversion cycle (CCC) is the time it takes to turn inventory into cash. The clock starts ticking from the time you pay your supplier for your inventory, and finishes when you turn that inventory into cash through a sale. A low CCC is ideal as you don't suffer from opportunity costs due to lack of cash flow. If your CCC is rising, then your lead times are increasing somewhere in your growth stack, either on the supplier side or the marketing and conversion side. In either case, your other metrics will show you exactly where the problem is. To calculate your CCC, you also need to calculate three other important metrics: days inventory outstanding, days sales outstanding and days payable outstanding. I'll explain each of those now.

Days inventory outstanding: how much time it takes your store to sell the inventory that you have on hand. A high DIO may indicate targeting the wrong market, a lack of demand or pricing your inventory too high. A low DIO means that you're not ordering enough inventory and might be experiencing stock-outs. Days inventory outstanding is calculated as follows:

DIO = (average inventory/cost of goods sold) × 365

To calculate your average inventory:

Average inventory = (opening inventory + closing inventory) / 2

Days sales outstanding: how long it takes you to collect the cash from a sale. When you're selling through marketplaces or other retailers, you may have to wait weeks or even months for your pay-outs. Days sales outstanding is calculated as follows:

DSO = (accounts receivable/net credit sales) × 365

Days payable outstanding: how much money you owe your suppliers and when you will need to pay them back. A high DPO is good as it means you have a long time to keep money on hand, potentially earning interest and funding new investments. Days payable outstanding is calculated as follows:

DPO = (accounts payable/COGS) × 365

You will notice that I have used 365 as the multiple for these calculations – that would be if you wanted to calculate these metrics on a yearly timeframe. But you can choose whatever time period is of interest for you, be it three months or a year.

Other inventory-related metrics

- Inventory velocity: your opening stock divided by the sales forecast for your next period.
- Inventory days of supply: the amount of inventory you have on hand divided by the average daily usage of that inventory.

Finance

Sales dilution rate

Your sales dilution rate is the difference between your gross and net profit. It tells you exactly how much of your gross revenue was not actualized. That means what you didn't actually make, due to things like returns and discounts. This one is especially important if you are planning to implement on the strategies outlined in Chapter 16, 'Finance', because asset-based lenders or almost anybody offering you lines of credit will be paying close attention to your sales dilution rate to verify that you really can make your payments.

Lost profit

Lost profits can occur due to delayed deliveries, website downtime and more. The damaging event may have long-lasting effects for months or years. An experienced valuation analyst can help you integrate this into your reporting and decision-making stack. Don't just take it on the chin and move on – any lost profit event will significantly affect your brand's environment and may require adjustments to your forecasts and brand strategy.

While not a KPI per se, it is a metric that is worth calculating and reporting so that such information can be used to inform the rest of your KPIs and strategies to achieve them.

Other finance-related metrics

- Gross sales
- Net sales
- Gross margin by product type
- Revenue per visitor
- Cost per visitor
- Cost of returns
- Revenue by product line

Marketing

Marketing as a percentage of sales

This is a balancing act to find the optimal marketing spend that eliminates issues related to not reaching your audience because you're not spending enough on marketing and advertising, and reaching lots of customers but not turning a profit because you're spending too much on marketing. This will tell you whether your current marketing efforts are scalable or not, and if you can grow sustainably with your current revenues and marketing mix. Marketing is often one of the largest expenses associated with running an e-commerce business – as an example, the marketing and point-of-sale expenses for Adidas in 2019 made up almost 13 per cent of net sales (Statistia, 2023). Calculating this metric is as simple as dividing your marketing spend by your revenue and multiplying the result by 100 to get the percentage.

Marketing efficiency ratio (MER)

Your marketing efficiency ratio (MER) is calculated by dividing your revenue by your ad spend. This ratio shows you the leverage you're getting on each dollar of advertising. For example, if you spend $50,000 on ads and generate $150,000 in revenue, then your MER is 3X. Although MER sounds similar to return on ad spend (ROAS), the two metrics are not the same. ROAS measures campaign-level returns, while MER accounts for all revenue, whether it is directly linked to a campaign or not. Unlike ROAS, MER takes into account long lead times and repeat purchases. It is a useful KPI for tracking the long-term value of marketing collateral, such as SEO content. In a cookieless world, metrics like ROAS become less reliable, making MER a more consistent choice.

Conversion rate

Forty per cent of e-commerce marketers consider conversion rate to be their most important KPI (Greene, 2022). You might think that conversion rate is a simple enough metric to calculate. You simply take the number of purchases made, and then divide it by the number of customers who came to your site. That is, the number of unique users. But, if you calculated it this way you will run into problems when it comes to benchmarking this metric.

Conversion rate is the number of purchases divided by the number of sessions, not the number of unique users. So be sure to double-check this in your own calculations, that you haven't measured this KPI using the number of unique identified users. To go deeper, measure your conversion rate per channel and device to give each of the specific teams (like email and paid social) in your growth stack unique and relevant KPIs to strive for.

Other marketing metrics

Other marketing metrics that have been covered throughout the book, especially in our customer acquisition, search engine marketing and paid social chapters, include:

- Cost per click (CPC)
- Cost per thousand impressions (CPM)
- Customer acquisition cost (CAC)
- Click-through rate (CTR)
- First time versus returning customers
- Checkout conversion rate
- Add to cart conversion rate
- Average order value (AOV)
- Customer lifetime value (CLTV)

When setting your KPIs, you can choose to focus on the number of first-time and returning customers, or the revenue generated by each group. This is often shown as a percentage of returning customers. However, it's important to remember that there is no one-size-fits-all approach to KPIs. For example, if your business is rapidly acquiring new customers, it may not be realistic to expect a high percentage of returning customers during that time period. The key is to align your KPIs with your goals for the month or quarter. Customer acquisition cost should be checked regularly, particularly if you are running a lot of campaigns. The same is true for click-through rates, which will vary depending on the medium (e.g. paid ads, email, search ads, display ads). Setting detailed medium-level KPIs requires careful thought and research, but can provide valuable insights.

Search engine-specific metrics that we covered in Chapter 10 (plus a few new metrics) include:

- Organic sessions
- Total number of backlinks
- Total number of referring domains
- Number of links lost
- Number of links earned
- Bounce rate
- Dwell time
- Page speed
- Referral traffic
- Site visibility

Some tools that will help you when it comes to SEO-specific KPIs include webmaster tools and platforms like Semrush or Ahrefs.

Whatever metric you are measuring, go as granular as will be effective in your measurements. One common distinction is mobile versus desktop.

Customer success KPIs

Customer success is a vital function of all operational e-commerce teams. A set of customer-centric KPIs is sure to keep your brand aligned in the right direction to deliver on your customers' needs and scale sustainably. We've already discussed metrics like retention, churn, customer lifetime value and net promoter score in Chapter 7, so I won't go into too much detail on those, instead I'll take the opportunity to introduce you to some new metrics, leading indicators if you will, of what you can expect to show up in your retention and net promoter score metrics.

Customer effort score

Monetary costs are only part of the equation when it comes to the price your customers pay for your goods. There are also time costs for research, consideration and evaluation. All this takes not only time, but also cognitive resources and energy. So, customer effort score is a good metric to track the amount of resources your customers need to put into a customer journey with your brand. Customer effort score is derived from customer ratings on a 1–7 scale, indicating how much effort interacting with your brand required. A very good customer effort score might indicate that your customers are going straight to support for their queries instead of using self-serve options.

Ninety-six per cent of customers who give a high score to your brand become loyal; this is in comparison to only 9 per cent of those who give a low score, making CES an important KPI for your brand (Dixon, 2013).

First response time

How long does it take for your team to respond to customer service queries? If it's longer than four hours, you're likely disappointing at least half of your customers. Yet research shows that the average response time for customer service queries is approximately 12 hours (Macdonald, 2022). Twelve per cent of customers expect a response in less than 15 minutes. To calculate, simply take the total time it took for your team to respond to customer support requests for a time period and divide that by the total number of tickets responded to. Better yet, break it down by customer support channel to find ineffective touchpoints in your brand's customer experience.

First contact resolution

First contact resolution is the percentage of support tickets that your team is able to resolve on the very first interaction with the customer. A big part of this is giving your support agents enough knowledge and authority to actually solve these requests, so that things don't need to go all the way up the chain to get resolved. To calculate, simply divide your number of tickets resolved on the first touch by the total number of tickets issued and multiply the result by 100.

Self-service resolution rate

Over 80 per cent of consumers want more self-service options from brands (NICE, 2022). Enabling customers to resolve their queries themselves leads to a quicker task completion time as they don't need to wait for replies from customer support agents. It also reduces the load on your customer support team, and in turn your costs.

Other customer service metrics

- Task completion
- Customer retention
- Net promoter score
- Customer churn rate
- Repeat purchase rate

Just make sure that with things like churn, retention and repeat purchase rate that you set your time periods to realistic timeframes depending on the nature of the product that you're selling. Subscriptions, as I have already mentioned, can be tracked on the timeframe they renew at. Other products like mattresses will have much longer repurchase timeframes.

Other metrics

On-site

I wanted to take some time to go over on-site search logs, as it is such an important aspect of the experience you are delivering through your website. It sadly often gets overlooked and isn't talked about nearly enough. Search results from Google and other search engines are important for keywords and rankings, but the search activity on your website is where it really gets interesting. While you can't set KPIs for these things, you will do well to dig into your search refinements. Other metrics that you can track, rather than just investigate, include total site searches and searches per session.

Brand

We already covered many of the brand-related metrics in Chapter 3 but it's worth mentioning them again to give you a list of the key metrics you need to be tracking and developing KPIs from. Brand awareness, of course, comes first. If nobody knows about you, they're not buying from you. Brand awareness splits out into prompted awareness and unprompted awareness – unprompted signals a greater knowledge of your brand, and that your company has a greater share of the heart and mind of the consumer. Other brand metrics include:

- Brand name mentions, which you can track through social listening
- Share of voice, which is how much people are talking about your brand
- Share of impressions, which is how many people are looking at what is being said about your brand
- Earned media impressions
- Branded search

Reporting your key metrics

As a leader, you need to be aware of the KPIs that impact your company's growth strategy. These should be compiled into easy-to-understand reports and shared with relevant departments. Each department should have its own set of KPIs that it is responsible for achieving and reporting on. To effectively track and manage your KPIs, consider working with a business insights analyst to set up dashboards that automate data collection and visualization. Tools like Microsoft Power BI, Google Data Studio and Tableau are popular options for KPI dashboard reporting. Whatever platform you use, be sure to establish clear reporting standards and automate data collection as much as possible. Colour-coding can be a useful way to quickly assess your key metrics and determine how close you are to achieving your KPIs. For a more comprehensive list of dashboard reporting tools and KPIs, visit 2xecommerce.com/book/chapter17.

References

Buzek, G (2015) We lost Australia! Retail's $1.1 trillion inventory distortion problem, *IHL Group*, www.ihlservices.com/wp-content/uploads/2015/06/WeLostAustralia-Outline.pdf (archived at https://perma.cc/4Z6E-L7J2)

Dixon, M (2013) *The Effortless Experience: Conquering the new battleground for customer loyalty*, Portfolio

Greene, J (2022) 24 ecommerce KPIs for tracking & growing sales, *Databox*, 28 May, https://databox.com/ecommerce-kpis (archived at https://perma.cc/LK3Q-T99Q)

Macdonald, S (2022) 5 ways to reduce customer service response times, *Superoffice*, 15 Nov, www.superoffice.com/blog/response-times/# (archived at https://perma.cc/X5JC-XRRM)

NICE (2022) Customers demand more – is your business listening?, https://get.nice.com/Digital-CX-Research-Report.html (archived at https://perma.cc/E385-A6S8)

Statistia (2023) Marketing and point-of-sale (POS) expenses of the adidas Group from 2015 to 2022, www.statista.com/statistics/540836/adidas-marketing-spend/ (archived at https://perma.cc/2MZ7-AB9E)

18

Develop your growth roadmap

Introduction

The journey to building a great (or even a billion-dollar-plus unicorn) e-commerce-born brand is full of trials and tribulations. You have a vision of what you want to achieve, but putting all the pieces of the puzzle (or should I say all the pieces of the growth stack) together in the right order can be difficult, almost impossible, to get right the first time on your own. That's why I've created this growth roadmap for you to help you put everything you've learned in the previous chapters into action in a way that is optimal and in line with your brand's current growth phase. Pay attention to this chapter because it will save you a lot of headaches and unforced errors out there in the world of e-commerce. Scaling your revenue doesn't have to be painful if you're starting from the right first principles and working from a roadmap developed from proven best-in-class e-commerce growth strategies. In any case, even with the right map and the right tools, you are still going to need to persevere. The competition is tough out there, and they might just have this book in their hands too.

I fully suggest you make use of the full suite of additional resources that I have made available via 2xecommerce.com/book. Go and listen to the dozens of 2X eCommerce podcast episodes I have referenced throughout this book. Attend conferences like Commerce Accel. And join our group of like-minded e-commerce professionals dedicated to growing brands on 2xecommerce.com. Truly differentiating from the competition means you need to stay one step ahead, and that takes hard work and perseverance. But if you're one of the few who can put that in, then your brand's growth is on your horizon.

Growing from $0 to $1 million

If your e-commerce brand is starting out, one of the first major goals you'll want to set is reaching $1,000,000 in annual revenue – which, in perspective, means an average monthly revenue of $83,333 or daily revenue of about $2,750. Assuming your average order value (AOV) is in the range of $70–$100, then you'll be processing 30–40 orders a day and 900–1,200 orders a month.

The main thing here at this stage that you are coming up against is the fact that you may not have the budgets that bigger brands do. That makes competing with paid strategies difficult. The goal here is to grow organically and intelligently.

Make your mark by really nailing the first principles laid out in this book, especially the psychology-oriented ones, which can add huge leverage to all of your brand's marketing activities using the principles outlined in Chapter 4, 'Consumer behaviour'. Chapter 8, 'Audience and community building' combined with the 'Customer acquisition' principles outlined in Chapter 6 will help you set the foundation for building your base of your true 1,000 fans. Chapter 10, 'Search engine marketing', will help form your content and technical SEO foundation for organic growth. Circle back to Chapter 3, 'Brand core: the foundation for growth' to ensure that your branding is on lock because everything you do from here on out will either enhance or contradict that. You want a unified message to put out into the world. At the product and brand level, make sure you focus on a specific niche and that you know who this customer is. Marketing to everybody sells to nobody.

Automate one of your most effective marketing channels

Directly communicating with your customers or sign-ups (customers-to-be) is a critical layer in your growth stack, and in 2023, the two most established and accessible messaging channels for reaching out and communicating at scale are email and SMS.

Building out your email and SMS list should be your team's top priority; the bigger your list, the bigger your reach. After you have systems in place for email and SMS list building, segmentation and action-triggered messaging should all be set in place. Return to Chapter 9, 'Lifecycle marketing and personalized experiences', for a refresher.

Start building your influencer community

Influencer marketing, specifically micro-influencers, will be useful at this stage, especially if you're competing with established brands that might be drowning you out on the paid advertising side. Circle back to Chapter 6, 'Customer acquisition', to get the full suite of influencer marketing tactics you need to grow your brand. Micro-influencers, while they don't get the huge reach that the certified celebrities do, actually generate a higher return on investment, on average, than big guns do. This is ideal for a new up-and-coming brand looking for attention.

Organic is healthy for you

Organic content creation through platforms like YouTube, TikTok and Instagram is a powerful marketing tool that can help to grow your brand's organic reach, and scaling it is not dependent on continuously pumping money into ads. There's no cost per click, no cost per thousand impressions and no cost for conversions.

Setting up a real content engine at this stage should be one of your main priorities. Every blog post can be turned into several social media posts, podcasts and short video clips. But focus on owning and dominating one or two channels where you can dig deep into analytics and optimization without stretching your team to burnout. Later, the lessons you learn from building an audience on one platform can be parlayed into others.

When you're just starting out with your organic SEO content strategy, when it comes to your written content, focus on ranking at the top for keywords of low to medium difficulty. You just don't have the domain reputation and backlinks yet to compete on high-difficulty keywords with large established brands. That means you're typically targeting keywords with a difficulty of less than 30, and have at least 100 searches. With Semrush, Ahrefs and other keyword research tools you will be able to identify the ideal keywords for your brand at this stage.

Social proof is a key ingredient in brand growth sorcery

Being a new or lesser-known brand, you're suffering from a severe lack of social proof. Your word of mouth is low, as there is a lack of conversation about your brand online. Gathering customer feedback and reviews should be one of your main priorities. This will enable you to not only display some serious social proof online but to use the feedback gathered to improve your product and customer experience. Feature testimonials, verified product reviews and unboxings on your website and social media channels. Because you're lacking in social proof, you're also lacking in trust. That means the perceived risk of shopping with your brand is higher. You can counteract this with easy returns processes, great warranties and excellent customer service.

You've got this

As you can see, there is a LOT to do to get from $0 to $1 million. My key message here is that at this stage, strive to focus 80 per cent of your attention on organically growing your brand and reputation; this will include growing your customer data list, community building, influencer outreach, and your content and SEO strategy. If these activities get you to the $1m/year mark, then you have a strong chance at scaling this organic success with paid media towards other significant revenue milestones.

It's why many don't make it past the million-dollar mark. But tick all the boxes at this stage and you have the ideal foundation for scaling to $100 million and beyond. It might feel overwhelming now, and I guarantee you that you are not alone – every single brand owner has felt the very same way. Put in the work with this book as your guide, and you're already well on your way to achieving brand growth.

Bonus tips

- A Kickstarter campaign will enable you to generate revenue before you even have anything shipped. This is great for a new brand that needs to validate ideas and can't afford R&D costs that don't pay off.
- At the $10k+ per month in revenue level, cash flow-based financing will open up to you. As I mentioned in Chapter 16, 'Finance', if you're only relying on your profits generated from sales to fund your new inventory purchases, you are severely limiting your growth potential.
- Churn will send you into a cash flow crunch faster than anything else. Luckily for you, I have an entire chapter just for this, Chapter 7, 'Retention for long-term growth'.

- A marketplace-first strategy can help you get your product in front of customers without having to shoulder big website development costs. Consider selling on Amazon, Walmart, eBay or another marketplace before building out your own site.

Growing from $1 million to $10 million

Once your e-commerce brand reaches $1 million in sales, you'll want to set new goals and strategies for growing your company. The game has changed for your brand, as you can now afford services and resources that you just couldn't in the past. More software-as-a-service (SaaS) solutions and experienced professionals like fractional CFOs are more accessible to you. At this stage, if you have followed the principles that I outlined to get to $1 million in sales, you already have a good customer data list comprising email addresses, mobile numbers and first- and zero-party data. Now would be a great time to create lookalike audiences and scale up your organic marketing efforts through a coordinated paid marketing campaign.

Assuming your average order value (AOV) is in the range of $70–$100, at $5m annual revenue, you'll be processing 140–200 orders a day and 4,000–6,000 orders a month. And at $10m annual revenue, your numbers double up to 300–400 orders a day and 8,000–12,000 orders a month (assuming you are generating these orders direct-to-consumer as a single channel).

Build a content system

To get to $1 million you focused on owning one or two platforms for organic content rather than heavy cross-publishing. Now, though, it is time for marketing channel expansion and building a real content engine. Every blog post can be repurposed into several social media posts; every video can be repurposed into dozens of short clips across different platforms.

Many hands make light work

If you can at this stage, also set up your affiliate programme. This will set your brand up to grow relatively independent of effort on your end. Each affiliate will be out there promoting your product through videos and blog posts that your team does not have to put any effort into creating. You'll benefit from other websites linking to yours, otherwise known as backlinks, which will boost your search ranking, too. You will also benefit from an increase in user-generated content.

Increase your AOV

If you've added new products to your line during your growth journey, focus on generating up-sells and cross-sells on those items. You may need to promote them to your existing customers by adding free samples to orders, to induce trial. You should also definitely be promoting your best sellers in your email automation and social channels.

Focus on retention

Your entire team should understand and align on first principle number one for e-commerce growth (recall from Chapter 1) that *the customer is front and centre*. With this focus in mind, your goal would be to maintain not just a transactional relationship with your customers but also a long-term emotional connection. The tools in your arsenal are your messaging and communication channels, such as email, SMS, direct mail and social media, as well as your product offering. Ensure you track and optimize key retention metrics like *repeat purchase ratio, CLV, CLV to CAC ratio and even your churn rate*. You should have either a dedicated member of your team or a small team managing all of your retention marketing efforts. Remember, the goal is to create a habit-forming experience for customers – make it effortless from an emotional and cognitive standpoint for them to make repeat purchases as well as from a product utility perspective.

Growing from $10 million to $50 million

Customer date-centricity: test, iterate and optimize

Getting from $10 million to $50 million is your biggest leap yet. Scaling this much means that any inefficiencies will absolutely be magnified in proportion to the scale at which you are trying to grow. Focus on improving the data that you are gathering about your customers in a bid to serve your customer better – customer-centricity is critical at this stage, and so investing in a customer data platform should be on your list of priorities. Chapter 5,

'Customer data', covers all of the intricacies with zero-, first-, second- and third-party data collection.

A focus on operations and a team expansion would also be on the agenda. The theme for this season in your journey is going to be experimentation and testing. Test and iterate absolutely everything to build the kind of intellectual capital and compounding effects that will enable your brand to scale not only to $100 million but beyond.

You will at this stage start selling through multiple channels – this would mean investing in specialized talent to manage each selling channel with the view to consolidating a single customer view. Read Chapter 12, 'Channel marketing', for guidance managing multiple channels at scale and then Chapter 5, 'Customer data', for methodologies for consolidating a single customer view.

Finance

When your company reaches $10 million in sales, it's time you will probably need to start thinking about finding the right investors or the right finance stack to give you the serious growth capital that you need. Huel, a company you will hear more about a little later in this chapter, took on a £20 million investment just two years after their inception, an investment that enabled them to escape running on fumes and stressing about budgets, and instead focus on growth (Hearn, 2022). This extra investment allowed them to grow their team and their product line, two other key growth levers, and scale from $10 to $50 million.

Customer service at scale is a real pain point

Scalable customer service is essential at this stage, too. At this point in your business growth, it's crucial that you make sure your customer service is on point and that each customer is receiving the best experience possible. Doing this before now was manageable with a small team. But scaling rapidly like you are at this stage requires serious attention to detail. The best way to do this is to create a customer service strategy that includes a variety of integrated customer service channels. This will allow you to reach customers in multiple ways, including phone calls, emails, self-service options and conversational chatbots. Automation of responding to repetitive customer service queries as well as instating self-service processes will help ease the strain of responding to every single customer.

Growing from $50 million to $100 million

Scale up your paid strategy with creative iteration

It's from $100 million and beyond that we look at implementing new structures to layer into your growth stack. But from $50 million to $100 million, focus on doing what you know so far, doing it well and leveraging that as much as you can without changing your growth stack in any major ways.

At this stage you have the war chest to really compete with paid advertising, so ramping up your ad spend across the full funnel will be a great way to draw in new customers and convert existing ones. As you add more spend, you need to also dedicate more resources to experimentation with creative so that you can iterate and scale your winning ads. With a higher ad spend, the ROI from a 0.5 per cent improvement only gets larger and larger.

Product release cycles for growth

At this stage, plenty of customers are familiar with your brand and flagship product, so spice things up a bit with your product release cadence. You'll want to pay special attention to product development and making sure that you're diversifying your product line. You already have many customers who have become loyal to your brand so you have a pre-built customer base for new product launches.

The age of expansion

Now is also the time to circle back to Chapter 12, 'Channel marketing'. Why? Because there are very few single-channel brands at the $100 million level. Distribution is king when it comes to scaling to this level. If you went with the Hero Cosmetics-style approach from the beginning and started out as a marketplace-first brand, later expanding into your own store, then chances are you are well on your way to an omnichannel strategy. If you have not done that, then you will need to explore online marketplaces, retail partnerships and even unique distribution methods like those Huel pursued with their airport vending machines, making their healthy, nutritionally complete on-the-go products available to jet-setters and travellers in the United Kingdom's largest airport (not to mention rolling out to 500 supermarkets in the UK) (Hancocks, 2021).

Going international

Outside of the United States and China, very few companies reach $100 million in annual revenues without going international. Huel, a UK-based company, reached $100 million in just six years. In their second year, they had already expanded to the US, a move that the company admits felt premature at the time but one that has been key to their success.

Simply having your website available via the internet from anywhere in the world does not make for an international brand, especially not in the hearts and minds of consumers. Today's consumers are increasingly demanding more local offerings and experiences. At the very least, you need to offer localized opportunities for engagement for your consumers in both the digital and physical realms.

Growing $100m+

By the time you reach this level, you are likely operating across multiple channels, and internationally no less. But now, you're going to expand that strategy into new regions, and across new channels. It might mean finding a marketplace in South-East Asia and developing a strategic partnership with local third-party logistics partners. The complexity of scaling both the regions in which you operate and also the channels across which you sell requires a much more mature and strategic commerce organization. Mature teams that can deal with the complexities in your supply chain, operations and distribution. Not to mention the international marketing mix you're now working with, nuances in cultural semiotics as mentioned in Chapter 3, 'Brand core' and more. Your main focus at this stage of growth is to expand your team, and develop your strategic and knowledge capital to the enterprise level.

Develop enterprise-level expertise

Company culture is where the game is won and lost for a team of any size, but when you become large, and you become international, culture is more important than ever. The bigger you get, and the more press you get, the more eyes you will have on you. These eyes want to see you are using the influence you have been granted as a brand for good. Environmental, social and corporate governance (ESG) becomes critical. If you can show that you are acting with the best interests of the broader consumer (and employee) community at heart, you will then be trusted to take it to the next level and grow toward being a unicorn brand. It's that trust you earn that manifests as purchases from consumers, which is essentially permission for your brand to scale further. Fail to establish enough trust to secure this permission, and your brand's growth will stagnate.

Growing to $1 billion and beyond

At this stage, everything is about your tribe, joint ventures, mergers and acquisitions, growth hacking with data, and, most importantly, customer experience at scale.

Community is what will sustain you

A brand doesn't get to this size without a real tribe, a loyal tribe and an engaged tribe. If you recall from Chapter 8, 'Audience and community building', building a tribe is founded on having something to fight for, or someone to fight against. When you were growing and scaling, everything came with a hint of authenticity almost out of necessity, because you were doing things yourself. As a founder or founding team you were engaged in the growth process and you had to resort to things like clips filmed on your iPhone without any real flare or fanfare. You probably wrote blogs yourself and talked about what mattered to you online. People were able to see not only a company, but a personality, even if that personality wasn't perfectly formulated as a brand yet. But as you got larger, some of your founder voice got replaced by your brand voice, your influencers got bigger as you could afford larger contracts and your content team got large enough to create stunning brand creatives. Along the way, your brand lost a little bit of the authenticity it had on day one of your e-commerce journey. But it doesn't have to be this way. As a billion- or near-billion-dollar brand you now have the power to make your wildest company mission values come true, and most importantly, to communicate them authentically.

Sophisticated data to facilitate growth and experimentation at scale

This means in-house tech, data engineers, data scientists and analysts. You will be digging deep into what is now a verifiable ocean of data to make informed decisions about your brand's growth strategies, product development and more. Just like health and beauty unicorn Glossier did to reach a $1.8 billion valuation at the time of writing in 2022 (Ramaswamy, 2022). For one, they built their own point-of-sale system and commerce APIs, all done by their in-house technology team to enable their obsession with improving the customer experience based on feedback and data (Tom, 2018).

Big money requires large investments

To give you an idea of the kind of finance landscape you are dealing with at this scale, brands like Hero Cosmetics, Glossier, Allbirds and Gymshark, that I have mentioned throughout this book, have all raised investment or been acquired. Hero Cosmetics was acquired by Church & Dwight for $630 million to enable the company to benefit from Church & Dwight's expensive experience in manufacturing personal care products, expand their distribution worldwide and start building what Hero Cosmetics co-founder Ju Rhyu calls 'Hero 2.0', their much larger team that will tackle new growth challenges (Nesvig, 2022). To date in 2022, personal care and beauty company Glossier has raised over $250 million from 19 different investors including Sequoia Capital and IVP, and while they haven't been acquired themselves, they have made strategic acquisitions of their own to bolster their digital strategy (Crunchbase, 2022). Gymshark raised £200 million from General Atlantic for a 21 percent stake in the business to add fuel to their global expansion strategy (General Atlantic, 2022). And Allbirds has raised over $200 million from 25 investors, made five of its own investments in companies like Natural Fiber Welding and Yaguara, and had its IPO in 2021 (Crunchbase, 2022).

Your next steps

I'm Kunle Campbell. I am a co-founder at Octillion, an e-commerce acquisition platform company that exists to fight the epidemic of unhealthy foods and toxic skincare products. We were founded on the premise that the foods we put into our bodies and the products we apply to our bodies should be clean. We acquire, operate and grow digital-native ethical, clean food and clean beauty consumer brands to make them more accessible.

For over a decade, I've had numerous roles as a 'Fractional e-commerce CMO' and adviser to middle-market direct-to-consumer e-commerce businesses, coaching ambitious retail teams focused on unlocking growth throughout the entire operational value chain and commerce growth stack. I have published hundreds of podcast episodes with best-in-class brands and leading e-commerce experts, available through my 2X eCommerce podcast, dedicated to helping brands achieve rapid growth and scale in online retail. I'm also the host of the annual Commerce Accel conference which brings together commerce leaders and unicorn brand builders for action-packed, live, expert panel sessions and keynote speeches. I suggest that to further develop your brand strategy you:

- Make use of all the additional free resources I have provided for you over at 2xecommerce.com
- Download the specific expert insights you need for each stage of your growth journey by listening to my 2X eCommerce podcast
- Sign up for the Commerce Accel conference to get alerts when our hit annual event comes around

References

Crunchbase (2022) Glossier, www.crunchbase.com/organization/glossier/company_financials (archived at https://perma.cc/R8TY-8R3N)

General Atalantic (2020) Gymshark secures investment from General Atlantic valuing company at over £1 billion, www.generalatlantic.com/media-article/gymshark-secures-investment-from-general-atlantic-valuing-company-at-over-1-billion/ (archived at https://perma.cc/PW9M-BBKF)

Hancocks, N (2021) Huel sales set to take off with airport vending machines and supermarket expansion, *NUTRAingredients*, 22 Jul, www.nutraingredients.com/Article/2021/07/22/huel-sales-set-to-take-off-with-airport-vending-machines-and-supermarket-expansion# (archived at https://perma.cc/6U8X-XS8W)

Hearn, J (2022) Eight reasons why Huel hit £100M in six years, *FEBE*, www.febe.com/story/eight-reasons-why-huel-hit-100m-in-six-years/ (archived at https://perma.cc/S3XL-QCBA)

Nesvig, K (2022) Hero Cosmetics, parent company of Mighty Patch, was acquired for $630 million, *Allure*, 8 Sep, www.allure.com/story/the-mighty-patch-hero-cosmetics-acquired (archived at https://perma.cc/V69Z-J4ZS)

Ramaswamy, A (2022) Glossier just laid off one-third of its corporate employees, mostly in tech, *TechCrunch*, 26 Jan, https://techcrunch.com/2022/01/26/glossier-just-laid-off-one-third-of-its-corporate-employees-mostly-in-tech/ (archived at https://perma.cc/N6LS-JPSV)

Tom, M (2018) How Glossier leveraged tech to build a next-gen cosmetics company, *AWS Startups*, 27 Sep, https://aws.amazon.com/blogs/startups/how-glossier-leveraged-tech-to-build-a-next-generation-cosmetics-company/ (archived at https://perma.cc/6768-8VU7)

INDEX

NB: page numbers in *italic* indicate figures or tables

Printed in the USA
CPSIA information can be obtained
at www.ICGtesting.com
JSHW072046070324
58805JS00010B/34